ARTHUR MILLER

Arthur Miller

American Witness

JOHN LAHR

Yale

UNIVERSITY

PRESS

New Haven and London

Yale University Press books may be purchased in quantity for educational, business, or promotional use. For information, please e-mail sales.press@yale.edu (U.S. office) or sales@yaleup.co.uk (U.K. office).

Set in Janson Oldstyle type by Integrated Publishing Solutions. Printed in the United States of America.

Library of Congress Control Number: 2021953084
ISBN 978-0-300-23492-3 (hardcover : alk. paper)

A catalogue record for this book is available from the British Library.

This paper meets the requirements of ANSI/NISO Z39.48-1992 (Permanence of Paper).

10 9 8 7 6 5 4 3 2 1

Frontispiece: Arthur Miller returns to London to support Marilyn Monroe on the unhappy set of *The Prince and the Showgirl*, 1956. (Photo: © Keystone Press Agency/Keystone USA/ZumaPress.com.)

To
Georges Borchardt
Without whom . . .

CONTENTS

ARTHUR MILLER

1

◆▸◆◂◆

Meeting Miller

Go out and fight so life doesn't have
to be printed on dollar bills.

—Clifford Odets, *Awake and Sing*

ON A CRISP APRIL WEEKEND in 1948, Arthur Miller, who was thirty-three and enjoying his first flush of fame after the Broadway success the previous year of his play *All My Sons*, waved good-bye to his wife, Mary, and their two young children in Brooklyn, and set off for Roxbury, Connecticut, where he had recently purchased a Colonial house, which stood at the aptly named intersection of Tophet (another word for Hell) and Gold Mine. He intended to build a cabin on a hillock just behind the house to use as a writing studio where he could "shut the door and let things happen." "It was a purely instinctive act," Miller, who later traded up from that 44-acre property to a 110-acre spread on Painter Hill a few miles down the road, told me in 1998. "I had never built a building in my life."

Miller had a play in mind, too. All he knew so far was that it would be centered on a traveling salesman, who would die at the end, and that two of the lines were "Willy?" "It's all right. I came back"—words that to Miller contained "the whole disaster in a nutshell."

"I mean, imagine a salesman who can't get past Yonkers," he said. "It's the end of the world. It's like an actor saying, 'It's all right. I can't speak.'" As he worked on the cabin, he repeated those two lines like a kind of mantra. "I kept saying, 'As soon as I get the roof on and the windows in, I'm gonna start this thing,'" he recalled. "And, indeed, I started on a morning in spring. Everything was starting to bud."

Miller had fashioned a desk out of an old door. As he sat down to write, his tools were still stashed in a corner of the studio, which was as yet unpainted and smelled of raw wood. "I started in the morning, went through the day, then had dinner, and then I went back there and worked till—I don't know— one or two o'clock in the morning. It sort of unveiled itself. I was the stenographer. I could hear them. I could hear them, literally." When Miller finally lay down to sleep that first night, he realized that he'd been crying. "My eyes still burned and my throat was sore from talking it all out and shouting and laughing," he wrote in his 1987 autobiography, *Timebends*. In one day, he had produced, almost as it exists today, the first act of *Death of a Salesman*, a play that has since sold about eleven million copies, making it perhaps the most successful American play ever published. The show is staged somewhere in the world nearly every day of the year.

"He didn't write *Death of a Salesman*; he *released* it," the play's first director, Elia Kazan, said in his autobiography *Kazan: A Life*. "It was there inside him, stored up waiting to be turned loose." To Miller, there was a "dream's quality" to his memory of that day of writing and the day or two that followed. In his notebook for *Death of a Salesman*—a sixty-six-page document chronicling the play's creation that is kept with his papers at the University of Texas at Austin—he wrote, "He who understands everything about his subject cannot write it. I write as much to discover as to explain."

Bewildered, exhausted, and at the end of his tether, Willy has been driven crazy by his dream of winning and his fear of losing. He preaches a gospel of pluck and positivity, which hides his humiliated soul from the world and from himself. He is unmoored and full of furious disappointment. "I have such thoughts, I have such strange thoughts," he confesses to Linda, his loving but beleaguered wife. His children—Biff and Hap—whom he force fed dreams of glory in childhood, have become in adulthood enemies of promise, undermined by the very lessons of competition they learned at their father's knee.

After that first day of inspiration, it took Miller six weeks to conjure up the second act and make Willy remember enough "so he would kill himself." The form of the play—in which past and present coalesce in a lyrical dramatic arc—was one that Miller felt he'd been "searching for since the beginning of my writing life." *Death of a Salesman* seems to spill not from the playwright's omniscient viewpoint but directly from Willy's panic-stricken imagination. "The play is written from the sidewalk instead of from a skyscraper," Miller said. Ironically, he had considered beginning his drama, with a kind of Shakespearean foreshadowing of Willy's suicidal delirium, on the deck of a skyscraper. The notebook's first entry reads, "Scene 1—Atop Empire State. 2 guards. 'Who will die today? It's that kind of day . . . fog, and poor visibility. They like to jump into cloud. Who will it be today?'" As Miller navigated his way through the rush of characters and plot ideas, the notebook acted as ballast. "In every scene remember his size, ugliness," he reminds himself about Loman on the second page. "Remember his own attitude. Remember *pity*." He analyzes his characters' motives. "Willy wants his sons to destroy his failure" and "Willy resents Linda's unbroken, patient forgiveness (knowing there must be great hidden hatred for him in her heart)." In Miller's notebook, the characters are already fully formed. Of Willy's idealized elder son, Biff, who is a lost soul, fallen from his high school glory and full of anger at his father, he writes, "Biff is travelled, oppressed by guilt of failure, of not making money although a kind of indolence pleases him: an easy-going way of life. . . . Truthfully, Biff is not really bright enough to make a businessman. *Wants everything too fast.*" Miller also counsels himself on the emotional stakes of the play and the trajectory of its scenes: "Have it happen that Willy's life is in Biff's hands—aside from Biff succeeding. There is Willy's guilt to Biff re: The Woman. But is that retrievable? There is Biff's disdain for Willy's character, his false aims, his pretence and these Biff cannot finally give up or alter. Discover the link between Biff's work views and his anti-work feelings."

Although the notebook begins with a series of choppy asides and outlines, it soon becomes an expansive and precise handwritten log of Miller's contact with his inner voices. For instance, it reveals the development of Charley, Loman's laconic, evenhanded next-door neighbor, who was, for Miller, partly a projection of his own father and who speaks poignantly to Biff at Willy's graveside; what appears in the last scene of the play as a taut and memorable nine-line speech, a kind of eulogy, was mined from a much longer improvisation in the notebook (the words used in the play are indicated here in italics):

> A salesman doesn't build anything, *he don't put a bolt to a nut*, or a seed in the ground. A man who doesn't build anything must be liked. He must be cheerful on bad days. Even calamities mustn't break through. Cause one thing, he has got to be liked. *He don't tell you the law or give you medicine.* So there's no rock bottom to your life. All you know is that on good days or bad, you gotta come in cheerful. No calamity must be permitted to break through, Cause one thing always, you're a man who's gotta be believed. You're way out there *riding on a smile and a shoeshine. And when they start not*

smilin' back, the sky falls in. *And then you get a couple of spots on your hat and you're finished. Cause there's no rock bottom to your life.*

Here, as in all his notes for the play, the surprising absence of cross-outs reveals Miller's passionate urgency; the pages exude a startling alertness. He is listening not just to the voices of his characters but to the charmed country sounds around him, which seem to define his creative state of grace: "Roxbury—At night the insects softly thumping the screens like a blind man pushing with his fingers in the dark. . . . The crickets, frogs, whippoorwills all together, a scream from the breast of the earth when everyone is gone. The evening sky, faded grey, like the sea pressing up against the windows, or an opaque grey screen. (Through which someone is looking in at me?)"

On a bright-blue December afternoon in 1998, fifty years after he first set off to build the cabin, Miller, then eighty-three, returned to it with me and his third wife, the photographer Inge Morath. Although she had lived with Miller for more than three decades only a mile away from the *Salesman* studio, she had never seen the place. "The main house was occupied by people I didn't know. They were sort of engineer people. Very antipathetic," Miller said, as he swung his red Volkswagen into the driveway of the new, friendlier owners, who were writers. In a tan windbreaker and a baseball cap, he looked as rough-hewn and handy as any local farmer. (The dining-room tables and chairs in the cluttered 1770 farmhouse that was Miller's current home were his own handiwork, produced in his carpentry workshop.) After a cursory inspection of his former house, Miller, who stooped a little at six foot three, set off toward the cabin, up a steep hump that sat a few hundred paces behind the house. "In those days, I didn't think this hill was quite as steep," he said.

The cabin, a white clapboard construction in need of a new coat of paint, stood just over the top of the rise, facing west toward a thicket of birch trees and a field. "It will last as long as it's painted," Miller said, inspecting what he had wrought. "See, if a building has a sound roof, that's it, you'll keep it."

"I didn't know it was so tiny," Morath said. She snapped a few photos, then waved her husband into the foreground for a picture before we all crowded into what proved to be a single, high-ceilinged room. Except for a newly installed fluorescent light and some red linoleum that had been fitted over the floorboards, what Miller saw was what he'd built. He stepped outside to see if the cabin had been wired for electricity. (It had.) He inspected the three cinder blocks on which it was securely perched. "I did the concrete," he recalled. Leaving, he turned to take a last look. "I learned a lot doing it," he said. "The big problem was getting the rafters of the roof up there alone. I finally built it on the ground and then swung them up." He added, "It's a bit like playwriting, you know. You get to a certain point, you gotta squeeze your way out of it."

Where does the alchemy of a great play begin? The seeds of *Death of a Salesman* were planted decades before Miller stepped into his Connecticut cabin. "Selling was in the air through my boyhood," said Miller, whose father, Isidore, was a salesman turned owner of the lucrative Miltex Coat and Suit Company. Just as Miller was entering his teens, however, his father's business was wiped out by the Depression. Isidore's response was silence and sleep ("My father had trouble staying awake"); his son, who had to postpone going to college for two years because "nobody was in possession of the fare," responded with anger. "I had never raised my voice against my father, nor did he against me, then or ever," Miller wrote. "As I knew perfectly well, it was not he who angered me, only his failure to cope with his fortune's collapse. Thus I had two fathers, the real one and the metaphoric, and the latter I resented because he did not know how to win out over the general collapse." *Death of a Salesman* captures both a father's bewilderment ("What's the secret?" Willy asks various characters) and a son's fury at his father's powerlessness ("You fake! You phony little fake!" Biff says to Willy when they finally square off in act 2).

Soon after the play opened in New York, in 1949, Miller's mother, Augusta, found an early manuscript called "In Memoriam," a forgotten autobiographical fragment that Miller had written when he was about seventeen. The piece, which was published in the *New Yorker* in 1995, is about a Miltex salesman named Schoenzeit, who asked the young Miller for subway fare when Miller was helping him carry samples to an uptown buyer. (The real Schoenzeit killed himself the next day by throwing himself in front of the El train.) That character's "dejected soul" was the first sighting of what would become Willy Loman. "His emotions were displayed at the wrong times always, and he never quite knew when to laugh," Miller wrote.

In 1952, Miller, rummaging through his papers, found a forgotten 1937 notebook in which, in twenty pages of dialogue, he had made embryonic sketches of Willy, Biff, and Willy's second son, Happy. "It was the same family," he said. "But I was unable in that straightforward, realistic form to contain what I thought of as the man's poetry—that is, the zigzag shots of his mind." He added, "I just blotted it out."

Every masterpiece is a story of both accident and accomplishment. Of all the historical and personal forces that fed the making of *Death of a Salesman*, none was more important than a moment in 1947 when Miller's uncle Manny Newman accosted him in the lobby of the Colonial Theatre in Boston, after a matinee of Miller's play *All My Sons*. "People regarded him as a kind of strange, completely untruthful personality," Miller said of Newman, a salesman and a notorious fabulist, who would commit suicide within a year of their encounter. "I thought of him as a kind of wonderful inventor. There was something in him which was terribly moving, because his suffering was right on his skin, you see. He was the ultimate climber up the ladder, who was constantly being stepped on by those climbing past him. My sympathy for him was immense. I mean, how could he possibly have succeeded? There was no way." According to Miller, Newman was "cute and ugly, a Pan risen out of the earth, a bantam with a lisp." He and his family, including two sons, Abby and Buddy, lived modestly in Brooklyn. "It was a house without irony, trembling with resolutions and shouts of victories that had not yet taken place but surely would tomorrow," Miller recalled in *Timebends*. Newman was fiercely, wackily competitive; even when Miller was a child, in the few hours he spent in his presence his uncle drew him into a kind of imaginary contest "that never stopped in his mind." Miller, who was somewhat ungainly as a boy, was often compared unfavorably with his cousins, and whenever he visited them, he remembered, "I always had to expect some kind of insinuation of my entire life's probable failure."

When Newman approached Miller after that matinee, he had not seen his nephew for more than a decade. He had tears in his eyes, but instead of complimenting Miller, he told him, "Buddy is doing very well." Miller said, "He had simply picked up the conversation from fifteen years before. That element of competitiveness—his son competing with me—was so alive in his head that there was no gate to keep it from his mouth. He was living in two places at the same time." Miller continued, "So everything is in the present. For him to say 'Buddy is doing very well'—there are no boundaries. It's all now. It's all now. And that to me was wonderful."

At the time Miller was absorbed in the tryout of *All My Sons* and had "not the slightest interest in writing about a salesman." Before *All My Sons*, Miller's plays had not been naturalistic in style; this time, he had "resolved to write a play that could be put on," and had "put two years into *All My Sons* to be sure I believed every page of it." But Miller found naturalism, with its chronological exposition, "not sensuous enough" as a style; he began to imagine a kind of play in which, as in Greek drama, issues were confronted head-on, and the transitions between scenes were pointed, rather than disguised. The success of *All My Sons* emboldened him. "I could now move into unknown territory," he said. "And that unknown territory was basically that we're thinking on several planes at the same time. I wanted to find a way to try to make everything happen at once." In his introduction to the fiftieth-anniversary edition of *Death of a Salesman*, he wrote, "The play had to move forward not by following a narrow discrete line, but as a phalanx. . . . There was no model I could adapt for this play, no past history for the kind of work I felt it could become."

The notebook for the play shows Miller formulating a philosophy for the kind of cubist stage pictures that would become his new style: "Life is formless—its interconnections are cancelled by lapses of time, by events occurring in separate places, by the hiatus of memory. We live in the world made by man and the past. Form is the tension of these interconnections: man with man, man with the past and present environment. The drama at its best is a mass experience of this tension."

The play's structure is embedded in Loman's turbulent mind, which destroys the boundaries between then and now. As a result, Miller said, "There are no flashbacks, strictly speaking, in *Death of a Salesman*. It's always moving forward." In this way, he jettisoned what he called "the daylight continuity" of naturalism for the more fluid dark logic of dreams. "In a dream you don't have transitional material. The drama starts where it starts to mean something." He continued, "I wanted to start every scene at the last possible instant, no matter where that instant happened to be." He read me the first lines of the play: "'Willy?' 'It's all right. I came back.' 'Why? What's happened? Did something happen, Willy?' 'No, nothing happened.'" His new approach jump started both the scenes and the stage language, whose intensity Miller referred to as "emergency speech"—an "unashamedly open" idiom that replaced "the crabbed dramatic hints and pretexts of 'the natural.'" Willy dies without a secret; the play's structure, which crosscuts between heightened moments, encourages the idea of revelation. What Miller wanted the audience to say was not, he said, "What happens next and why?" but "Oh, God, of course."

When early in 1948 Miller visited his cousin Abby Newman to talk about the blighted life of Abby's late father, Miller himself had just such an epiphany. Abby told Miller, "He wanted a business for us. So we could all work together. A business for the boys." Miller, who used those words in the play, wrote in his autobiography, "This conventional, mundane wish was a shot of electricity that switched all the random iron filings in my mind in one direction. A hopelessly distracted Manny was transformed into a man with purpose: he had been trying to make a gift that would crown all those striving years; all those lies he told, all his imaginings and crazy exaggerations, even the almost military discipline he had laid on his boys, were in this instant given form and point. I suddenly understood him with my very blood."

Willy Loman is a salesman, but we are never told what product he lugs around in his two large sample cases. Once, a theatergoer buttonholed Miller and put the question to him: "What's he selling?" "Well, himself," Miller quipped. "That's who's in the valise." Willy's house echoes with his exhortations to his two floundering sons about the presentation and the imperialism of the self: "The man who creates personal interest is the man who gets ahead. Be liked and you will never want"; "Lick the world. You guys together could absolutely lick the civilized world." In his notebook, Miller wrote, "Willy longs to take off, be great" and "Willy wants his boys prepared for any life. 'Nobody will laugh at them—take advantage. They'll be big men.' It's the big men who command respect." In Willy's frenzied and exhausted attempt to claim himself and a future for his sons, Miller had stumbled on to a metaphor for postwar society's eagerness to pursue its self-interest after years of postponed life. In Willy's desperate appetite for success and in the brutal dicta offered by his rich brother, Ben ("Never fight fair with a stranger, boy. You'll never get out of the jungle that way"), *Death of a Salesman* caught the spirit of self-aggrandizement that was being fed by what Miller called "the biggest boom in the history of the world."

Americans had struggled through the Depression, then fought a world war to keep the nation's democratic dream alive; that dream was, broadly speaking, a dream of self-realization. America, with its ideal of freedom, challenged its citizens "to end up big," as Willy says. (In the play, Ben, to whom Willy looks for answers—the notebook points to him as "the visible evidence of what the boys can do and be. Superior family"—is literally a predatory imperialist who walked into the African jungle at seventeen and emerged four years later as a millionaire.) Miller was not the first to dramatize the barbarity of American individualism, but he was the first to stage this spiritual attrition as a journey to the interior of the American psyche. "In a certain sense, Willy is all the voices," Miller said. (His first title for the play was "The Inside of His Head," and he briefly toyed with the idea of having the proscenium designed in the shape of a head, with the action taking place inside it.)

The economic upheavals of the thirties were reflected in the social realism of the time; the plays held up a mirror to the external world, not to an internal one. But in the postwar boom, Tennessee Williams's *The Glass Menagerie* (1945) and *A Streetcar Named Desire* (1947), written in what Williams called his "personal lyricism," struck a new chord with American audiences. The plays were subjective, poetic, symbolic; they made a myth of the self, not of social remedies. The same was true of *Death of a Salesman*. Indeed, Miller did not intend the name Willy Loman to be a sort of socioeconomic indicator ("low man"). He took it from a chilling moment in Fritz Lang's film *The Testament of Dr. Mabuse* (1933), when, after a long and terrifying stakeout, a disgraced detective who thinks he can redeem himself by exposing a gang of forgers is pursued and duped by them. The chase ends with the detective on the phone to his former boss ("Lohmann? Help me, for God's sake! Lohmann!"); when we see him next, he is in an asylum, gowned and frightened and shouting into an invisible phone ("Lohmann? Lohmann? Lohmann?"). "What the name really meant to me was a terrified man calling into the void for help that will never come," Miller said.

Willy Loman's particular terror goes to the core of American individualism, in which the value of the self is hopelessly tangled with the question of wealth. "A man can't go out the way he came in," Willy says to Ben. "A man has got to add up to something." Willy, who at sixty has no job, no money, and no loyalty from his sons, is sensationally lacking in assets and in their social corollary—a sense of blessing. "He envies those who are blessed; he feels unblessed, but he's striving for it," Miller said. Although Willy's wife, Linda, famously says of him that "attention must be paid," he feels invisible to the world: "I'm not noticed." Later, Linda confides to the boys, "For five weeks he's been on straight commission, like a beginner, an unknown!" As Miller told me, "The whole idea of people failing is that they can no longer be loved. You haven't created a persona which people will pay for, see, experience, or come close to. It's almost like death. You have a deathly touch. People who succeed are loved because they exude some magical formula for fending off destruction, fending off death." He continued, "It's the most brutal way of looking at life that one can imagine, because it discards anyone who does not measure up. It wants to destroy them. It's been going on since Puritan times. You are beyond the blessing of God. You're beyond the reach of God. God rewards those who deserve it. It's a moral condemnation that goes on. You don't want to be near this failure."

Death of a Salesman was the first stage work to fully dramatize this punishing—and particularly American—interplay of panic and achievement. Eugene O'Neill raised the issue in *The Iceman Cometh* (1946) in the eerie calm of Harry Hope's bar, whose sodden habitués have retreated from competition into a perverse, stupefied contentment; as one character says, "No one here has to worry about where they're going next, because there is no farther they can go." But in Willy Loman, Miller was able to unite the aspiration and the desperation of American life in one character.

Willy is obsessed with the notion of winning—what Bertolt Brecht called "that black addiction of the brain." He cheats at cards; he encourages his feckless sons to seek every advantage. Elusive victory haunts him. When Biff and Happy tell Willy of their plan to go into business, he says, "Step on it, boys, there ain't a minute to lose," but their souls have been stifled by their father's heroic dreams, which smother them like a sort of spiritual kudzu. In another notebook entry, Biff rounds on Willy, saying, "I don't care if you live or die. You think I'm mad at you because of the Woman, don't you? I am, but I'm madder because you botched up my life, because I can't tear you out of my heart, because I keep trying to make good, be something for you, to succeed for you."

Miller's play was also the first to dissect cultural envy in action—that process of invidious comparison that drives society forward but also drives it crazy. "You lose your life to it!" Miller said of the envy that feeds Willy's restlessness. "It's the ultimate outer-directional emotion. In other words, I am doing this not because it's flowing from me but because it's flowing against him." He went on, "You're living in a mirror. It's a life of reflections. Emptiness. Emptiness. Emptiness." Willy is competing with his brother Ben; with Dave Singleman, a successful old salesman who could make a living "without ever leaving his room" and whose life ended with a placid, accomplished death on a train to Boston; with Charley's successful lawyer son Bernard. "Where's Willy in all this?" Miller asked. "He's competed himself to death." For all his fierce arguments with the past and fervent dreams of the future, Willy never occupies his present. Even as he fights, fumes, and flounders, he is sensationally absent from his life, a kind of living ghost. What really eludes him is not success but existence. He inhabits a vast, agitated, and awful isolation, which is both his folly and his tragedy.

In his notebook Miller wrote, "It is the combination of guilt (of failure), hate, and love—all in conflict that he resolves by 'accomplishing' a $20,000 death." In death, Willy is worth more than in life. He has confused wealth with love; his suicide is the ultimate expression of his belief in winning at all costs. As a father he overlooked Biff's small acts of larceny—taking sand from a building site, stealing basketballs, getting test answers from the nerdy, studious Bernard—and Biff has continued the habit into adulthood out of a desire for revenge. A notebook citation reads, "It is necessary to (1) reveal to Willy that Biff stole to queer himself, and did it to hurt Willy. (2) And that he did it because of the Woman and all the disillusionment it implied." In the final version of the play, Biff, who admits in passing that he spent three months in a Kansas City jail for stealing a suit, tells Willy, "I stole myself out of every good job since high school!" At first, Miller saw the twenty thousand dollars of insurance money as cash to put Biff on the straight and narrow. "My boy's a thief—with 20,000 he'd stop it," he wrote in the notebook. But in the end, he pitched Willy's suicide on a more grandiose and perverse note. In an early draft of the terrific penultimate scene, in which Biff exposes Willy and calls it quits with him and his dream, there is this exchange:

> BIFF, *to him:* What the hell do you want from me? What do you want from me?
> WILLY: —Greatness—
> BIFF: No—

In Miller's final draft, Willy, who will not accept his son's confession that he's a thief, takes Biff's greatness as a given when he visualizes his own suicide. "Can you imagine that magnificence with twenty thousand dollars in his pocket?" he says to Ben. He adds, "Imagine? When the mail comes he'll be ahead of Bernard again." As he goes to his death, Willy in his mind is on a football field with Biff and full of vindictive triumph: "When you hit, hit low and hit hard, because it's important, boy." "He dies sending his son through the goalposts," Miller told me. "He dies moving." He paused. "I think now that Kazan had it right from the beginning. He said, 'It's a love story.'"

On the last page of his notebook, Miller scribbled a short speech to deliver to the original cast (which included Lee J. Cobb as Willy, and Mildred Dunnock, Arthur Kennedy, and Cameron Mitchell) after they had read in galleys the soon to be published play. "I want you all to know now that the cannons are quiet that this production has been the most gratifying I have known. I believe you are the finest actors ever gathered for any play and I am exceedingly proud and gratified not only for myself but for the American theater." In its passage to greatness, *Death of a Salesman* was enhanced by the poetic set design of Jo Mielziner, who created a series of platforms, with Willy's house as a haunting omnipresent background. However, as Kazan pointed out in his autobiography, "The stage direction in the original manuscript that Art gave me to read directly after he'd finished it does not mention a home as a scenic element. It reads, 'A pinpoint travelling spot lights a small area of stage left. The Salesman is revealed. He takes out his keys and opens an invisible door.'" Kazan added, "It was a play waiting for a directorial solution." It got one.

Death of a Salesman also got its share of bad suggestions. Kazan's then wife, Molly Day Thatcher, who was a play reader for the Group Theatre and had some influence over Kazan, tried to get Miller, as he remembered it, "to cut out Uncle Ben, all the memory scenes, and simply make it a realistic little narrative." The co-producer, Kermit Bloomgarden, nervous about a play with the word *death* in its title, took a poll of theatergoers containing the question "Would you go to see a play called *Death of a Salesman*?" Nobody said yes. "They had a list of about fifteen titles," Miller recalled. "One was 'Free and Clear.' I'll never forget that."

In the more than seventy years since then, the surface of American life has changed, but its mad competitiveness has not. "I'm not aware of any change in the way people look at this play," Miller said in 1999, but he admitted that Willy's complaints about loyalty from the head office could sound strange to contemporary ears. "Workers now—not just workers but management—know that nobody will have much pity for them." He noted the erosion of the "unified audience" that followed the rise of the avant-garde in the early sixties. "The only theater available to a playwright in the late Forties was Broadway," he wrote in the fiftieth-anniversary edition of *Salesman*. "That theater had one single audience, not two or three. . . . That unified audience was the same for musicals, farces, O'Neill's tragedies, or some imported British, French, or Middle European lament. . . . The writer had to keep in mind that his proofs, so to speak, had to be accessible both to the lawyers in the audience and to the plumbers, to the doctors and the housewives, to the college students and the kids at the Saturday matinee. One result of this mix was the ideal, if not the frequent fulfilment, of a kind of play that would be complete rather than fragmentary, an emotional rather than an intellectual experience, a play basically of heart with its ulterior moral gesture integrated with action rather than rhetoric. In fact, it was a Shakespearean ideal, a theater for anyone with an understanding of English and perhaps some common sense."

But there was nothing Shakespearean in the response to "that damned disturbing play," as Kazan called it, on the night of its debut in Philadelphia, February 10, 1949. "The curtain came down and nothing happened," Miller said. "People sat there a good two or three minutes, then somebody stood up with his coat. Several men—I didn't see women doing this—were helpless. They were sitting there with handkerchiefs over their faces. It was like a funeral." He continued, "I didn't know whether the show was dead or alive. The cast was back there wondering what had happened. Nobody's pulled the curtain up. Finally, someone thought to applaud, and then the house came apart."

2

—◆◆◆◆—

Beginnings

We either die of the past, or we become an artist.

—Louise Bourgeois

DEATH OF A SALESMAN bore witness to the envy and the exhaustion of the mid-century American sweepstakes, but when Miller was born, in Harlem on October 17, 1915, the engine of American capitalism was still gathering its formidable momentum—and nowhere was that dynamism more apparent than in New York City. "Power seemed to have outgrown its servitude and to have asserted its freedom," Henry Adams wrote of New York a few years earlier. "The cylinder had exploded and thrown great masses of stone and steam against the sky. . . . Prosperity never before imagined, power never yet wielded by man, speed never reached by anything but a meteor, had made the world irritable, nervous, querulous, unreasonable and afraid."

Miller was the second child of Augusta and Isidore Miller. (His older brother, Kermit, was born in 1912; his sister, Joan, in 1922.) Both of his parents' families were first-generation émigrés from Poland for whom the American Experiment had almost immediately paid off. In the year Miller was born, when the average yearly U.S. wage was $687, Isidore had been approached by William Fox, a former wool "sponger," for a loan of $50,000 (about $1.2 million in today's money) to start a movie company on the West Coast. Distrusting the "sharp practices" of wool spongers, Isidore refused him the loan, and lost the chance to be a movie mogul at what would become 20th Century–Fox. The road not taken subsequently became part of the family saga. "Had he taken the risk, I would have been raised in Los Angeles, never learned what I did in Central Park and the streets of Harlem and Brooklyn, been spared the coming Depression, and arrived no doubt at a different personality," Miller wrote in *Timebends*.

Both sides of Miller's family had been engaged in the manufacture of clothing since they had come ashore at Ellis Island in the 1880s, with sewing machines under their arms. Prosperity had liberated them from the oppression of Old World penury; they had embraced the New World's "bright idea of property" and the values of ownership. They were unrepentant conservatives. They lived by the cruel logic of the bottom line and practiced the imperialism of privilege. According to Miller, his maternal grandfather, Louis Barnett, would invite union organizers to confer with him at the top of a stairway, "and while talking to them reasonably, would suddenly knock their heads together and throw the stunned men down the stairs."

By the twenties, Isidore's Miltex Coat and Suit Company had become, according to Miller, "one of the largest such businesses in the United States"; at its height, it employed about eight hundred people. His family had maids, oriental rugs, mahogany furniture, and a Knabe baby grand piano; they spent summers in a holiday cottage at a prime location in Far Rockaway, overlooking a pristine stretch of beach. Every working day, a chauffeured seven-seat National Highway Twelve sped Isidore back and forth between his home on 110th Street near

Fifth Avenue and the Garment District on West 32nd Street; on weekends, the limousine motored the family downtown to a Broadway show. "Our prosperity helped seal us inside our magical apartness," Miller recalled, adding, "If ever any Jew should have melted into the proverbial pot, it was our family in the twenties." Nonetheless, when his mother, known as Gussie, dropped a cup or cut herself, she'd mumble in Yiddish, "A shwartz yu'r on alle goyim!" (A black year on all gentiles).

From the Millers' catbird seat in their high-ceilinged sixth-floor apartment with its view of Central Park, the city's agitation seemed far away. They looked south over somnolent greenswards and glistening ponds, beyond the low-slung Manhattan skyline to New York Harbor in the distance. At the time, the city held 14 percent of all immigrant Jews in the country, and Harlem housed a Jewish population of around two hundred thousand. (By the end of the twenties, the number had dwindled to about five thousand.) "Our family knew almost no gentiles," Miller noted. Although the Millers were not pious—"they were too busy trying to assimilate into the United States"—they regularly attended a synagogue on 114th Street and observed the high holy days. (Miller was bar mitzvahed in 1925.) "In my most private reveries I was no sallow Talmud reader but Frank Merriwell or Tom Swift, heroic models of athletic verve and military courage," he recalled. Nonetheless, Miller's moral talent—as the director Harold Clurman, a founder of Group Theatre, called it—was rooted in the intellectual fervor and moral intensity of the Jewish community. In maturity, he came to understand the connection. Of *The Crucible*, his reimagining of the Salem witch trials, for instance, Miller wrote, "I felt strangely at home with these New Englanders, moved in the darkest part of my mind by some instinct that they were putative ur-Hebrews, with the same fierce idealism, devotion to God, tendency to legalistic reductiveness, the same longings for the pure and intellectually elegant argument. And God was driving them crazy as

He did the Jews trying to maintain their uniquely stainless vessel of faith in Him."

Miller's moral doggedness had as a model Isidore's fierce single-minded survival in the New World. When Isidore's parents had immigrated to America with his three brothers and three sisters, he had been left behind in Poland with an uncle, who soon died. (The pragmatic Millers had judged Isidore "slow" and feared that if he was refused entry to the United States the entire family would be sent back.) Isidore was more or less orphaned, passed from family to family, until he was sent for at the age of six. With a cardboard sign around his neck asking that he be delivered to the S.S. *Clearwater,* Isidore was put on a train to the German port of Hamburg. He made the three-week passage to New York alone in steerage, crammed beside the chains of the steering device. Twice a day a barrel of salt herring was shared out among the passengers; in the feeding frenzy, Isidore could only get his hands on scraps. He arrived at Ellis Island with loose teeth and "a scab on his head the size they used to say of a silver dollar," Miller wrote. Isidore was immediately shoehorned, with the rest of his large family, into a two-room cold-water walk-up on Stanton Street on the Lower East Side.

After a few months of school, Isidore took his place at the sewing machine doing piecework; he was "never to see the inside of a school again," according to Miller. By the age of twelve, Isidore had two boys working under him; by fifteen, already tall and with a genial personality, he had become a traveling salesman for his father's company, S. Miller and Sons, incorporated in 1909. (Isidore would rise to chief salesman there before starting his own business.) Abandonment had shaped him and contributed to the special connection he made with people. "There is a 'Do you like me?' in an orphan's eyes, an appeal out of bottomless loneliness that no parented person can really know," Miller wrote.

Over time, with the confidence that came with his spectacular success, Isidore exuded what Miller called "a baronial attitude." He seemed to have a natural way with waiters, cab drivers, even policemen, "who were inclined to salute," Miller recalled, adding, "Some undefinable authority emanated, perhaps because his great height, fair skin, blue eyes, square head, and reddish hair cast him as an important Irish detective. He even had a way of listening that without any show of skepticism would cause the speaker to stop exaggerating. His open, relaxed stare, blue-eyed and innocent, brought blushes to the faces of people unsure of themselves. It would have astonished him to be credited as some kind of moral force—if indeed he could have understood such an idea. Life was just too hard to allow most people most of the time to act unselfishly, least of all himself."

Even when, at the age of thirty-two, now chief salesman at S. Miller and Sons, Isidore decided to take a bride—the lively, handsome, seventeen-year-old Augusta Barnett—the event was as much a merger as a marriage. (Their wedding, held in 1911, was a formal affair with 250 guests.) Before the engagement, the fathers of the bride and the groom compared account books. Gussie frequently retold the story to her children. "'They were in there for hours,'" Miller recalled his mother saying. "'And finally they came out and'—how she laughed!—'said I was getting married!'" Miller went on, "Then suddenly her look would blacken, as she clenched her jaws in anger. 'Like a cow!' she would mutter, with my father often sitting there listening along with my brother and me, even nodding his head to confirm the story, so accepting was he of the unchanging tradition. Even so, my heart went out to him in his humiliation, however imperturbably he seemed to bear it; somehow it had become my job to distract them from their conflict, already a kind of artful acting."

Gussie, who was born in America, had graduated *cum laude*

from high school. She had cultural interests and intellectual ambitions: she could sing, play the piano, paint, and, with her extensive word hoard, tell a good story. An avid reader ("She could read a novel in an afternoon—the fastest reader I ever saw," Miller said), she paid graduate students from Columbia University to keep up with the latest literature. "She was pretentious, my mother," Joan Miller Copeland recalled much later. "But she had a right to be a snob. She had exquisite taste in everything." (Gussie would never let Joan near the kitchen. "You are not to learn how to do this," she would tell her. "Because you are going to marry a rich man and you will have maids.") Gussie took pride in her children but not in herself. The collapse of the family fortunes during the Depression put paid to her highbrow expectations and made a mockery of a life that had been bartered for wealth. "She was a woman haunted by a world she could not reach out to, by books she would not get to read, concerts she would not get to attend, and above all, interesting people she'd never get to meet," Miller recalled.

Isidore, by contrast, understood numbers but not letters: he could neither read nor write. To Miller, in some ways Isidore's ignorance "was merciful, keeping him from worrying about what was in or out, stylish or old fashioned." Nonetheless Augusta's chagrin at her husband's illiteracy found its way both into the family dynamic and into Miller's plays. "Two weeks after we were married," Miller has the mother say in his 1964 play *After the Fall*, "[we] sit down to dinner and Papa hands me a menu and asks me to read it to him. . . . Couldn't *read!* I got so frightened I nearly ran away." Except for movies and theater, Isidore and Augusta had little common currency for intellectual exchange. Isidore's lack of information and curiosity about a world beyond his business limited their social circle to relatives and to the "cloakies" Augusta so disdained.

The indulgent surface of the Miller household made it hard to recognize the undertow of contempt and humiliation, which would only intensify through the decades. "I couldn't help blushing for him when she made him her target since I admired his warm and gentle nature as much as I despaired of his illiterate mind," Miller said of his father, adding, "For the love of me and all of us she divided us against ourselves, unknowingly, innocently, because she believed—and I was beginning to believe myself—that with sufficient intelligence a person could outwit the situation. Why couldn't he do that?"

As a child, Miller hero-worshipped Isidore; as an adult, he clung to a mental picture of his "vastly tall and competent father" in his prime: his shirtsleeves rolled up, commanding his Miltex domain and its rows of workers hunched over their machines. "The gazes of the help upon us were filled with respect and a kind of congratulation for being who we were, the sons of the boss and our clever and pretty mother," Miller wrote in *Timebends*. "Here was the concord, the happiness I seem always to have been trying to press my parents toward—my father in his full power and she content with a mixture of glories, her admiration making him proud and strong, his strength keeping her safe."

Miller was profoundly affected by his father's illiteracy. His own lackluster performance at P.S. 170, where both his mother and his elder brother had distinguished themselves, was bewildering to him and to his parents. "What was the matter with me? Why was I like this? Dear God, please let me be good like my mother and father and brother," he thought. Once, after being called to P.S. 170 by the principal to discuss her underperforming and unruly son, Augusta violently grabbed Miller's wrist and clobbered him over the head with her purse, screaming, "What are you doing to me!"

By his own admission, Miller "was passed over by education": "I learned nothing really till possibly the last year in high school. I began to realize that those books were supposed to be telling me something." In his formative years he was, he told the TV journalist Mike Wallace, "unencumbered by thought" and "too busy, in the street, playing games and kidding around." He wrote in *Timebends*, "When I first heard—probably not until I left home for college—Jews referred to as 'the people of the Book,' I mistook it to mean books in general rather than the Bible, and the description, complimentary as it was, was news to me. Brought up among Jews until the age of twenty, I could recall none but my mother who ever read anything."

The source of Miller's passion for ignorance was close to home. "My father's illiteracy set me in conflict with learning for many years since I so wished to be like him," he recalled. "To become a reader meant to surpass him, and to claim the status of a writer was a bloody triumph; it was also a dangerously close identification with my mother and her secret resentment, if not contempt, for his stubborn incapacity with words." But there was also Gussie's persistent mantra about education and attainment, which implicitly indicted Isidore's intellectual inadequacy.

Gussie's children were vessels into which she poured her disappointments and desires. "Aren't there mothers who keep their dissatisfaction hidden to the grave?" Miller wrote in a line cut from the final draft of *After the Fall*. Gussie's love contaminated as it contained, which was why Miller could never completely mourn her. "Our relationship was unfinished," he wrote of her death in 1961, adding, "I was so much the incarnation of her own thwarted ambitions."

When Miller came to write his first play, *No Villain* (1935)— "probably the most autobiographical thing I ever wrote"—he channeled both his mother's adoration of him and her ambition for him ("I *feel* that way about you. . . . Someday you'll be a big man"). As the play makes clear, Miller already understood that he had won the oedipal battle, supplanting his depleted father in his mother's eyes. "Where's Arny gonna sleep?" the father asks about his son, who has returned briefly from college. "You wanna give him your bed," the mother, Esther, says hastily. Gussie's suffocating ardor is not verbalized in the play, but it is expressed in the stage directions. At her son's entrance, Esther "jumps up from her seat, screams 'Thank God' and rushes to hug Arnold, savagely. He kisses her but she holds him, sobbing to his chest, too long." Even in 1935, at age nineteen, Miller understood that his persona as a writer was a kind of co-production. In *No Villain*, when Esther imagines a glorious future for her son—"You study hard . . . make yourself respected . . . you'll have everything . . . you can do it"—Arny answers, with his tongue only partially in his cheek, "Whatever you say I'll be."

The young Miller may rarely have cracked a book; in order to survive the indigestible confusions of his family's dynamic, however, he developed a fictionalizing habit of mind, a kind of double vision that allowed him both to preserve the idea of Gussie and Isidore as loving parents and to vent his unacceptable aggression at them. "I had, it seemed, always moved on two planes at the same time, the actual reality and a metaphoric one in which, for example, my father appeared as a de-animated and forbidding avenger who I knew was and was-not my actual father. My mother was and was-not the woman who was tempting me sensually to capture her from my father, and was both culpable of disloyalty to him and, as herself, perfectly innocent. Until I began to write plays my frustration with this doubleness of reality was terrible, but once I could impersonate all conflicts on a third plane, the plane of art, I was able to enjoy my power—even if a twinge of shame continued to accompany the plays into the world."

In *The Price* (1968), Miller mined his ambivalent memories of his parents and the absence that echoed through his youth. "Was there ever any love here?" Walter, the "successful" brother, asks Victor, the "failed" brother, who sacrificed his life to support his parents, when they meet to sell off the family furniture. He goes on, "What was unbearable is not that it all fell apart, it was that there was never anything here. . . . There was nothing here but a straight financial arrangement."

In his short story "I Don't Need You Any More" (1959), which recounts the bewilderment of a five-year-old who feels overlooked and trapped in an incomprehensible parental drama, Miller mapped the forces that were pushing him into his own independent internal world: a cosseting, unhappy mother, an uneducated father, the masquerade of family unity, and an admired and resented older brother.

Although Gussie was more emotionally connected to "Arty"—they shared "an unspoken conspiracy against the restraints and prohibitions of reality"—"Kermie" claimed the family spotlight. Handsome, dutiful, and an outstanding athlete and student, Kermit was also the family's aspiring writer. "He loved Keats," Miller recalled. "It was all British romantic poets. He had this flowery writing, nineteenth-century stuff." He added, "I could make nothing of it but in those days I knew nothing about anything."

"Kermit was the man they relied on to carry on," whereas Miller "always felt to one side of the family": "I had my own space psychologically." His sense of separation began when he was six, around the time that his younger sister Joan was born. "I was caught between Joan, who had clearly taken my place as chief baby, and my brother, whose stature I could not begin to match," he wrote. Miller began to act out. He sleepwalked, and "about three times a month" he contemplated running away from home: what he called "a form of suicide designed to punish everybody." Even his frequent bike rides around Harlem were a symptom of his hankering for escape. "My sallies into Harlem began a pattern of retreating into myself when the competition overwhelmed me," he wrote. "As I coasted through Harlem on my bike, everything between 110th Street and 145th seemed under my control, for when I turned a corner into a new block the one behind me was wiped out of mind."

Miller's journey toward self-definition began in earnest in French class during his last year in high school. His French teacher "had large breasts and was a wonderful motherly woman. She loved me. Somehow, I connected with her. I couldn't call it intellectually. It was almost sensual," he said. Language and expression suddenly opened up to him. "Through French I learned a little bit about the structure of English, that it wasn't something that grew between the cracks in the sidewalk." Around this time, he also began to read. Thinking it was a detective novel, he picked up Dostoyevsky's *Crime and Punishment* and spent two transfixed months reading it. "I hadn't realized that words were like that—a kind of tidal drag on your spirit," he said.

Miller claimed to have "a very aural imagination": "What I hear means probably more to me than what I see," he said. Not surprising, then, that his first stab at expressing himself was as a singer of the popular hits of the day. When he was fifteen, for a few weeks Miller had his own radio show in Brooklyn. "Once I listened to what I was singing I got embarrassed," he said. "I realized that some damn good singers were walking around without work." Miller may have had big ears—"Pull in your ears we're coming into a tunnel," one of his uncles used to joke—but he also had good ears. "I write with my ears more than my brains. I never write until I can hear it. I think I've always thought of writing being an aural art, related to music. If I hear somebody talking, I can start," he told an interviewer.

It was radio comedians—whom Miller loved to imitate—who got him writing. "Nothing was more enjoyable than mimicry," he said. By his own admission, Miller, a tummler of sorts, "could always tell jokes." He doted on Jack Benny, Fred Allen, and Joe Penner, among many other radio Merry Andrews. One right-wing radio commentator in particular—Boake Carter, who mocked the New Deal and President Roosevelt with a memorable bow-wow delivery and a whiff of British Received Pronunciation—caught Miller's imagination. In the hope of making a few bucks, he wrote a take-off of Carter for *Major Bowes' Original Amateur Hour* and auditioned his material for the producers while he was still in high school, about fifteen years old. "There was a mob of tap dancers, bird callers, piano players—they were, of course, all out-of-work professionals," Miller recalled. "I was practically the only amateur in the building." Miller read his piece, and to his amazement the whole crowd started laughing. "When it was over, out of the sound booth came this little man with a curvature of the spine, a severe limp, and a cigar. He came up to me and said, 'Who wrote this?' I said 'I did.' He said, 'Can I see it?'" Miller handed over the script; the man, in turn, gave Miller his card: he worked at a Philadelphia advertising agency called Lord and Thomas. "I flew home on the subway," Miller recalled. "I waited and nothing happened." A few weeks later, listening to another radio comedian, Phil Baker, Miller heard his material. "Not done as well as I could do it," he said, adding, "The first thing I had ever written was stolen. I never got a nickel. I wrote them a letter. Nothing happened. But I saw that I could write stuff that could be spoken."

Miller graduated from Abraham Lincoln High School in Brooklyn in 1932; his parents did not attend the ceremony. In the yearbook he listed Stanford as his chosen college, which was either a face-saving pipe dream or a joke. Miller's grades were so bad ("miserable" was his adjective) that no college would accept him. His woeful situation only added to the seismic shock that had hit the Miller household in 1929 when the stock market crashed. Although 97.5 percent of the American population owned no stocks, Isidore Miller was among the 2.5 percent who did. "It was one of the most traumatic experiences of my life," Miller remembered, adding, "I changed social position, so to speak, in a minute. It was that quick. . . . At a very early age it became clear to me that you couldn't build anything on the usual foundations that people either believe in or pretend to believe in. There was no pattern anymore."

In fact, it took a couple of years for the Millers' wealth to entirely evaporate. "My father was the link to the outside world, and his news was bad every night," Miller said. Isidore had been part of "the orgy of mad speculation"—Herbert Hoover's 1927 term for the country's giddy buying spree that had no discernible relation to value. (In the frenzy, the market grew not by steady steps but by "great vaulting leaps," as John Kenneth Galbraith put it.) Having made, as Miller put it, "the world-shaking discovery that they could make more money in the stock market than they could make in their business," Isidore and his brothers had taken advantage of the extravagantly available credit in 1928. When the market collapsed, Miller explained, "it carried away the working capital of hundreds of perfectly good businesses, among which was his."

The avalanche of liquidation began on October 23, 1929, wiping out four billion dollars; by mid-November, twenty-six billion, roughly a third of the value of all stocks, had evaporated. By 1930, more than twenty-six thousand businesses had failed; in December of that year the New York City Bank of America—nicknamed "The Pants Pressers' Bank" because a large portion of its four hundred thousand depositors were from the garment trade—closed its doors. Of that year's 1,352 bank closures, New York City Bank's was the most ominous and the most symbolic. The day before the bank collapsed, as he recounted in *Timebends*, Miller joined a five-block-long line of depositors along Avenue J and succeeded in withdrawing his $14 of savings. Isidore was not so lucky. His money was part of the $286 million in savings nationwide that was wiped out.

The Crash was a moral catastrophe as well as a fiscal one. The loss of confidence and expectation—the vigorish to the dream of abundance for which both Gussie's and Isidore's families had traveled halfway around the world—left people like the Millers dazed, discombobulated, and unmoored. "People didn't know how to live without," Miller said. "The day the money stopped, their identity was gone. They did not know who the hell they were." The trauma was defining. "The value system collapsed. I was turning 12, 13, 14, and there I was without leaders anywhere in or out of the house." As a child growing up around conservative adults, Miller had "inherited the views of those around me. Overnight, almost literally, the specter of real want entered our house." The scar never left him. Throughout his writing life, in plays such as *After the Fall*, *The Price*, and *American Clock*, Miller would pick at the sore. "There was no mercy. Anywhere," he observes in *The Price*. "One day you're head of the family, at the head of the table, and suddenly you're shit. Overnight."

As a youth, Miller "never could bear the idea" of his parents struggling. The trauma of having observed their furious bewilderment reticulates through his plays. "You mean you saw everything going down and you throw good money after bad? Are you some kind of moron?" the mother asks in *After the Fall*. The stolid father answers, "You don't walk away from a business." In *The Price*, Miller depicts Gussie's first reaction to the news of Isidore's bankruptcy: "He made us sit down; and he told us it was all gone. And she vomited." The scene continues: "All over his arms. His hands. Just kept vomiting, like thirty-five years coming up. And he sat there. Stinking like a sewer. And a look came over his face. I'd never seen a man look like that. He was sitting there, letting it dry on his hands."

In retreat, the Millers left Manhattan to be near relatives at the end of the subway line in Midwood, Brooklyn—"a move into the wilderness," Miller, who was fifteen at the time, called it. "You might as well have been in Minnesota from their point of view." To Miller, however, Brooklyn was "the Wild West." "I couldn't have been happier," he said. "I loved the outdoors and in those days Brooklyn was wide open. We went around under the trees and bushes, hunted stuff. I was playing football. I was busy going to Coney Island fishing. I was doing absolutely anything except study."

As the Depression deepened, the Miller family's situation grew more precarious. "Even a fifty-dollar-a-month mortgage payment was becoming a strain," recalled Miller, who rose at 4:30 in the morning to deliver rolls before school. Kermit withdrew from New York University to help his father in one of his soon-to-fail coat businesses. They moved again, to smaller Brooklyn quarters, where Miller had to share a room with his maternal grandfather, and where space itself seemed to be as diminished as the hope of a return to wealth. "Some people don't bounce," a character says in *The Price*. Isidore was one of these; he seemed to deflate before his sons' eyes. An uncomplaining and increasingly absent presence, according to Miller, Isidore "grew more silent . . . his naps grew longer, his mouth seemed to dry up. He couldn't figure out how to live." Miller went on, "There was an aching absence in the house of any ruling idea or leadership. . . . He just managed to sort of pump along on a very low level but he never returned to his former glories. A man in business is no better off than last week's balance, and it keeps hanging there. He can't give it up, he can't make it happen anymore. So there was that—I'd call it despair— just a recognition that the great days are in the past."

Sometime in 1931, when Miller was sixteen, Isidore, walking toward school with his son, asked him for a quarter to take the subway. In that moment, at once heartbreaking and shocking, Miller felt the power shift from his father to him. The incident, later memorialized in Miller's 1980 play *The American Clock*, was a kind of watershed; a distance opened up between them. In 1932, when twelve million Americans were unemployed and the national income was half what it had been, Miller, while waiting his turn to play handball against the wall of the local drugstore, talked to another student, who told him about Marxism. Miller had stumbled on to ballast, a historical explanation for the chaos he saw everywhere around him. They continued the conversation on the beach at Coney Island, by which time Miller had been introduced to the notions of "historical materialism," "alienation of labor," "the class struggle," and "the proletarian revolution." The Marxian lens revolutionized how Miller saw society and his father. Isidore was now not just a businessman but the owner of the means of production: an unwitting exploiter of the labor force who added surplus value to the garments that made him profits—profits which were not shared fairly with the alienated workers. "Deep down in the comradely world of the Marxist promise is parricide," Miller later put it.

Marxist principles helped to separate Miller even farther from his father, who wanted him to join his brother in the business. "Pipe down on the red flag raising," Gussie wrote in one letter. Miller's first play, *No Villain*, centered around a strike at a clothing company, and the refusal of the owner's younger son to cross the picket line to join his father and his brother. "In my day when a father needed help, he got it like that!" Abe, the owner-father, says. "Nowadays you send 'em to college . . . and they find all kinds of brainwork . . . to . . . to . . . to get outa going to work." He goes on, "Oh no they ain't lazy, nononono. This is something brand new . . . all new stuff. Now they call it . . . principles. Those bums downstairs got 'em . . . The elevator boys got 'em. Yep, everybody now-a-days got principles, only I ain't got 'em. But who can tell? Maybe if I get 'em . . . even I won't have to work."

As Isidore grew more resigned and more flummoxed, Gussie grew more angry, "shuffling about in her carpet slippers, sighing, cursing with a sneer on her lips, weeping suddenly and then catching herself," Miller recalled. "Forget that you were rich," the older son tells his mother in *No Villain*, trying to stop her drizzle of complaint. "Forget," she replies. "Forget. Sure it's easy for you to say forget. You've got nothing to remember." Gussie made occasional sensational displays of her desperation. "She would put her head in the oven," Joan Copeland recalled. "I guess she didn't do it because she had a family to take care of."

To manufacture hope for herself, over time Gussie drifted into mysticism. She consulted Ouija boards and kept an eye on astrological charts. Every few weeks she took the Culver Line to Manhattan to have her fortune read. (In addition to her stringent household economies, Gussie contributed to the family treasury by playing in high-stakes bridge games that were sometimes raided by the police.) But it was in her almost messianic belief in the lanky, jug-eared Arty and his special destiny—she came to see him as "God chosen"—that she found the most solace for her disappointment. "My failures she simply swept aside as the fault of my teachers or a temporary fogging of my mind," he wrote.

According to Miller, the fog began to lift in earnest within three months of his high school graduation. His social desolation and his failure to be accepted at any college roused him from his intellectual torpor and focused his mind. He became serious. "It came over me suddenly," he said. "I had a severe change of personality, literally. I could almost feel it happening." At home, Miller's future was hotly debated. Isidore pushed for his son to work with him; Gussie and Kermit lobbied for him to educate himself instead of hitching his wagon to an ignorant man and a moribund business. When Miller wrote *No Villain*, the fracas about his future was still raw in his mind:

BEN: He wants to write. Writing and cloaks don't mix. Ask me. He's going to try till he drops to make good in the field he likes. It's the only way. We don't want him downtown. . . .

ABE: Alright, alright. . . . Only if he needs a job we can let him pack, that's all.

BEN: No, that's not all. That's the way I started, "letting me pack" and it's four years since I've seen the inside of a classroom. Never, he'll never get in the business if I can help it.

The Millers had no money to send Arty to college; if Miller wanted a higher education, it would be on his dime. From 1933 to 1934, he traveled by subway an hour into Manhattan, where he had a full-time, fifteen-dollar-a-week job as a stock clerk at Chadick-Delamater, the largest automobile-parts warehouse east of the Mississippi. Despite the family's struggle to meet the mortgage payments, Miller was allowed to save thirteen dollars of his weekly pay packet for tuition. His first stab at higher education was City College of New York (CCNY) night school, where he registered for courses in history and chemistry. "I got there about seven o'clock to start studying, but you couldn't sit down in the library because there were so many students," Miller recalled. "We were studying on our feet. They were brilliant guys and fanatics; they intended to be doctors, lawyers, Indian chiefs regardless of what. I had no such ambition. I just fell asleep." Miller lasted two weeks. "I decided I'd have to go to a school in the daytime, when I could sit down."

Miller latched on to the idea of going to the University of Michigan for three reasons: no math requirement, an out-of-state tuition fee of $65 a semester, and the news that they awarded literary prizes that ranged from $250 to $1,000. The idea of getting cold cash just for putting words on paper captured his imagination. "I was so discouraged and under the pall of New York City, I just thought, That's the place for me." He applied twice and was rejected twice. "They were right. I couldn't argue with them," he said. To pass the time at his tedious warehouse job, Miller began writing letters to himself. He decided to appeal to the university a third time, promising to be a good student. "I suppose my first literary creation was a letter to the dean," Miller, who "always believed in my luck," said. Miller's chutzpah paid off. The university accepted him on the condition that he kept up his grades and could show at least $500 in his bankbook. Saving the money took Miller about two years; looking back on the Depression in *The American Clock*, Miller, like his stand-in in the play, "waited with that kind of crazy expectation that comes when there is no hope, waiting for the dream to come back from wherever it had gone to hide."

At almost nineteen, in mid-September 1934, Miller arrived on campus in Ann Arbor. "Remember the Goal," Gussie wrote him a fortnight after he arrived. But what *was* the goal? The struggle to stay afloat in the midst of catastrophe had made Miller feel old beyond his years, lending him a gravity that would linger through his twenties. "It was not so much death I feared as insignificance," he wrote. For Miller, going to college was his way of claiming not just knowledge but his life. Once he was in the Midwest, he recalled with typical detachment, "My home ceased to interest me."

3

◆◄◆►◆

Stirrings

When they tie the can to a union man
Sit down! Sit down! . . .
When the boss won't talk, don't take a walk
Sit down! Sit down!

—Maurice Sugar, "Sit Down," UAW protest song

"College was, in one sense, very relaxed, because nobody expected to be able to practice anything he was studying," Miller explained. "There was a kind of 'time-out' between relief checks." Miller arrived at the University of Michigan with the sure knowledge that "the pattern of society was destroyed." All bets on the American dream were off. "I was thrown back on myself in a way that I don't think was reproduced in this country since possibly pioneer times when there was in effect no society." Miller was free to wager his life on his own imagination.

When he started his freshman year, he was almost nineteen, a little older and—having knocked around the streets of New York and worked various jobs—a little more experienced than most of his classmates. "I had more to say and that intrigued the professors, who also had no experience in life except from going to school. So I was news from outside," he said. "Make the most of your present opportunities," Gussie urged him in the first weeks of his first semester. Miller did just that. He threw himself into campus politics and into his writing. "I was involved in the idea of how to become a writer, how to succeed, how to get published," he recalled. "I remember reading that Sidney Kingsley, I think, had gone nine or ten years writing without recognition. When I read that, I thought it was incredible."

On January 6, 1935, while Miller was struggling to keep up his patchy first-semester grades and save money—he fed mice in a science lab for fifteen dollars a month, washed dishes at the university cafeteria for free meals—back in New York, in a dingy theater on Fourteenth Street, Elia Kazan, the young stage manager of the Group Theatre now turned actor, was living up to his hype as the "Proletariat Thunderbolt" in the premiere of Clifford Odets's one-act play *Waiting for Lefty*. "Strike! Strike! Strike!" he shouted with a fist raised in the play's last beat. The fiery words brought the audience to its feet. There were twenty-eight curtain calls. A public note of resistance had been sounded from the stage and a nerve struck. The dazed audience refused to leave the theater. The actors were as stunned as the paying customers. "None of us was ever to be the same again and I suppose we all knew it," Kazan recalled. "But we had no idea how far and how fast this change would go."

Within two months, *Lefty* was on Broadway, joining Odets's first full-length play, *Awake and Sing!*, which had opened the previous month and depicted a Jewish family's struggle to survive the Depression. In Odets, the theater had found its radical voice, "The Revolution's No. 1 Boy," as the *New Yorker* called him. Before long, Odets's success, a result of the public's hunger both for new theatrical forms and for a robust response to the failures of capitalism, would capture Miller's imagination. To Miller, Odets was "the great creative engine of the moment." Miller came to understand him as "a new phenomenon, a leftist challenge to the system, but even more, the poet suddenly leaping onto the stage and disposing of middle-class gentility, screaming and yelling and cursing like somebody off the Manhattan streets." Miller's brain, he said later, "was branded by the beauty of the Group Theatre productions," which "were of a different nature than anything to be seen on Broadway": "I got a sense of the street and the junkyard and the unemployment line—the smell of New York—which I didn't get in any other kind of production. People seemed to be talking to one another; in other productions, they seemed to be talking to the audience." Odets also gave license for the social outrage that Miller was beginning to define for himself. He served as a new kind of model: an exemplar of the playwright as a social and moral force. "After all, there *was* no politics in the American theatre until Odets," Miller, to whom Odets would pass the baton of political discourse when he decamped to Hollywood in the early forties, said.

As a freshman, Miller had not yet heard Odets's lyrical exhortations, but he was no stranger to the din of protest. "Michigan had one of the most politically active student bodies in the United States," he recalled. "The place was full of speeches, meetings, and leaflets. It was jumping with Issues." In addition to studying English and history, he was learning "the political facts of life." The month he started college, four hundred thousand textile workers, buoyed by FDR's National Industrial Recovery Act of 1933, which guaranteed labor's right to collective bargaining, went on strike. During the year, other major strikes broke out in San Francisco, Toledo, and Minneapolis. The Ann Arbor campus was about fifty miles from both Flint and Detroit, whose auto industries were the focus of much union agitation. Miller, who by the second semester of his freshman year had joined the staff of the *Michigan Daily*—he would eventually become the night editor—was getting his political education in public. He covered the struggles of labor and management, which brought him into contact with a gallery of working-class Americans. "I identified with the workers in no abstract way," he said. He wrote about the New Deal and the infiltration of the Communist Party on campus; he interviewed Walter Reuther, the charismatic leader of the fledgling United Auto Workers union; he investigated company spies; and in 1937 he reported on the famous sit-down strike at the General Motors Fisher Body Flint Plant No. 1. "It was nearly incredible to me," he noted, "that hundreds of ordinary factory workers, a large number of them recruited in the Southern states, where hostility to unions was endemic, had one day simply stopped the machines, locked the factory doors from within, and refused to leave until their union was recognized as their bargaining agent." The experience was defining. "The fact that I came from bosses helped to alienate me," he said.

The *Michigan Daily* articles that Miller sent home bore witness to his radicalization and to the Marxism he'd begun to soak up. (Kermit, while working to make his father "big again," as he said, had joined the Communist Party, which was a step too far for his militant younger brother.) "I notice in the Student News something about expulsion of undesirable students for the full term. I hope that your activities (which are subsiding in red circles, I hope) are not known in your school work," Gussie wrote. "It would be awful to get a setback just when you're starting to go somewhere. You never can tell who of your friends will snitch so be careful." (She addressed one of her letters to "Artovsky Millensky.") Even as it deepened his understanding of the American social fabric, Miller's college journalism sharpened his vocabulary and its deployment. "We all see a great improvement in your English so far as letters count," Gussie wrote. She floated the notion, suggested by a family friend, that Miller transfer to the Columbia School of Journalism. "Their Journalism School has so much money that scholarships are given freely but not to Communists."

However, although Miller wanted to write—"I was lusting to put something down on a piece of paper"—he didn't want to be a journalist. "I had to tell my father something 'cause he'd say, 'What are you going to do?' and you couldn't say you were going to be a writer," he said. "Who pays a writer? Journalists, he figured, are on somebody's pay roll when they are lucky. So I invented that."

By Easter of his sophomore year, Miller had gone through most of his $500 in savings. His hard-won probationary place at the university was in jeopardy. The straw he grasped at was the university's Hopwood Awards, which offered eye-watering prizes from $250 to $1,000 for distinguished writing in drama, fiction, poetry, and the essay. (The namesake of the award, Avery Hopwood, had made his fortune writing such commercial Broadway folderol as *Getting Gertie's Garter* and *Up in Mabel's Room*.) Miller had already been writing stories and essays; he had even started a novel. Despite the fact that he had seen only three plays in his life, he opted to stay in Ann Arbor over the Easter break in 1935 to write a play. "Why it had to be a play, rather than a story or a novel, I have never been sure, but it was like the difference, for an artist, between a sculpture and a drawing—it seemed more tangible," he said. "But it may mainly have been my love of mimicry, of imitating voices and sounds."

Channeling the voices and sounds of his family—a sort of blueprint of his internal world—Miller knocked out the first act of *No Villain* in three days. Here was the idealistic university student returning from the Midwest, the big-hearted older brother working in the floundering family garment business, the uneducated father perpetually assailed by the drizzle of his wife's contempt, the possessive self-pitying, neurotically anxious mother, the prospect of an arranged marriage, and a workers' strike, de rigueur in the politics of the day. "I knew when I started that I could write a play," Miller said. "I suppose that I've always believed that the form is somehow born in people or it isn't. I don't think it can be learned. My own experience is the best example." His jejune play—"I had spilled out into that first play everything I knew or could imagine about life"—set the creative pattern of a lifetime. "Art was not a writer who made up stories," Kazan, who directed the debut productions of *All My Sons*, *Death of a Salesman*, and *After the Fall*, said. "His material had to be experienced; he reported on his inner condition." The recalling and reshaping of his recent past was liberating and transformative. "I had never known such exhilaration—it was as though I had levitated and left the world below," Miller explained.

Miller, who had no working knowledge of theater, went across the hall in his rooming house to ask Jim Doll, who designed costumes for university theater productions, how long an act should be. (Doll was older than Miller, and half his teeth were missing, Miller recalled. "It was very common in the Depression. People didn't have money to go to the dentist.") Doll told him that an act of a three-act play should be about thirty minutes. "I had my alarm clock," Miller said. "I turned on the clock and read it. Just as the curtain was falling it went off. So I got the sense of timing from that." He added, "I finished the play and nearly collapsed from want of sleep." The act of reading it aloud was also an epiphany. "A playwright writes to hear it. It's a different phenomenon. The eye, the print mean nothing to me. When I read, I hear. If I can't hear it, I can't stay interested." Miller gave Doll the finished work, "close to despair that he might think nothing of it." Miller recalled the moment when Doll knocked on his door with his verdict. "It's a play, all right. It really is!" Doll told him. "I think it's the best student play I've ever read." Miller was so elated at Doll's reaction that he sprinted into the night—"uphill to the center of town, across the Law Quadrangle and down North University."

Throughout his adolescence, the shy Miller had been flirting unconsciously with the desire to cast a spell over an audience. He'd made a stab at being a crooner; prior to writing *No Villain*, he had even studied books on hypnosis and practiced on friends. When he submitted *No Villain* in his sophomore essay course, the professor, Erich Walter, took the unprecedented step of reading it aloud to the class as an example of the "condensation of language." Walter read poorly—it was "a horrible rendition," Miller said—but what mattered to the young writer was seeing the play meet an audience. "When I saw the students laughing, growing tense, absorbed . . . the last doubt disappeared," he recalled. "All that remained was perhaps a few months and I would be on Broadway." The artifice of theater allowed Miller to speak his heart directly to people and to be taken in; it gave him the license, he said, "to say the unspeakable." "Once I got the inkling that others were reached by what I wrote, an assumption arose that some kind of public business was happening inside me, that what perplexed or moved me must move others," he said, adding, "It was a sort of blessing I invented for myself." He changed his major from journalism to English.

In June 1936, *No Villain* won the Hopwood Award and a prize of $250. (Technically speaking, Miller came second. Two of the three judges voted *No Villain* second; one voted it first. The judges gave both of the top plays the $250 prize.) "I have never sweated an opening night the way I did at Hopwood time," Miller recalled. "The crowds would form to hear the featured speaker—some literary light from the book world—after which the presentation was made. How I hated those speakers holding up the awards! Those prizes meant more than recognition. In my case, at least, they meant the end of mouse-feeding and room-sharing and the beginning of a serious plan to become a playwright."

When Miller called home to announce his Hopwood victory, Gussie screamed, dropped the phone, and, according to Miller, "rushed outside to arouse relatives and neighbors to the new day dawning." To Miller the prize was a sweet moment of vindication, "an artillery shell fired through the ranks of my opposing army—down went all my old algebra teachers." By the time he returned to Michigan for his junior year, his "psychic sun was on the rise" and he was brimming with new confidence. Over the summer break, he'd become a denizen of Broadway. (Odets's *Golden Boy* and Ibsen's *A Doll's House* made deep impressions.)

Not long before the class in which he read *No Villain* aloud, Professor Walter had asked Miller to take a stroll on campus. In his essays, the instructor had told him, he exhibited a gift for criticism; if he studied for ten years, he might become a critic. As Miller recalled in *Timebends*, he nodded in feigned seriousness at Walter's suggestion, while thinking, "Ten years! I would be thirty before I could begin being a critic!" After reading *No Villain*, Walter made a different suggestion: he advised Miller to sign up for a seminar on playwriting that was taught by a professor named Kenneth Rowe. Rowe was on sabbatical in New York that year, working as a consultant with the Theatre Guild—then the dominant producer of quality theater on Broadway—to develop a program to give college-age aspiring playwrights practical knowledge of the commercial stage. In 1937, at the beginning of his junior year, Miller enrolled in Rowe's class.

Rowe, a small, tweedy man, was "hopeless" in the classroom. He didn't lead; he accompanied. But he soon became Miller's mentor and confidant. "He was a great audience. He loved whatever was good and what was bad he minimized," Miller said. Most important, he offered "a quiet refusal to encourage dreams of sudden glory and at the same time . . . sympathy with those dreams. His example . . . helped lay up standards and goals of a very private sort for a very public art. The theatre was not a carousel one jumped onto but an instrument one had to learn how to play." In learning to play the game of theater, one Rowe rule became cardinal for Miller: "The last thing a dramatist should do is try to conform to some notion as to what subject or treatment the audience wants."

In later years, Miller was reluctant to give Rowe full credit for his emergence. "It's hard to define what I took from Professor Rowe's classes," he said disingenuously. However, Rowe laid the foundations on which Miller's craft would eventually flourish. First and foremost was Rowe's passionate belief in the social importance of theater. He introduced Miller to the work of Henrik Ibsen, whose *Enemy of the People* Miller would successfully adapt for Broadway in 1950. "Ibsen was the one modern playwright who seemed to be able to create the density of experience, as I knew it to be, in a play," Miller said. A year after Miller graduated, Rowe published *Write That Play!* (1939), in which he set down the ideas that were central to the seminar that Miller had taken. A large section of the book was devoted to Ibsen and an analysis of *A Doll's House* as a model of play construction. "The basic structure of a play is the beginning of a conflict, the movement by complications to a crisis or turning point, and the movement to the resolution of the conflict," Rowe taught. The book continues: "Construction is so important in drama and so complicated in a long play, that the only way to get it right is to strip it bare and look at it. Deformities can be seen then and corrected before they affect the vital functioning of the play. The hard disciplined thinking required in the perfecting of a scenario may check the fine glow of inspiration for a time, but . . . the conception matures during the period of concentration on the scenario."

Nearly fifty years later, Rowe's primary image of Miller was of the young man bursting into his university office. "Professor Rowe, I've made a discovery," Miller said. He was then on the third draft of his senior project, *The Great Disobedience*, a prison play. Rowe wrote:

> Sitting straight, as usual, in the big Morris chair across from the desk, he explained that the discovery was a new method of revision. The end of the second act worried him, and he couldn't put his finger on the trouble, except that the right rhythm of intensity, the wave movement to a crest, wasn't there. He felt sure he had the material for a climax, and the climax didn't come off. He marked off the last section of the act into, as he put it, its "indivisible dramatic units." Then he numbered a card for each unit and wrote on the card what happened, the function, and the emotional effect. He laid the cards out on a table in order as in the play and studied them, concentrating especially on the emotional effects. He had been counting for his climax on the third card, I think it was, from the last, but he found the material on the fifth card had potentially more intensity. The effect of card five killed that of three but was itself not adequately led up to. He found he could switch five and three, with three becoming part of the build up to five as the climax. The procedure had worked so well that he was eager for me to tell my other students about it so they could use it too.

In addition to Ibsen's problem-crisis formula for dramatic construction, Rowe took as a template for good playwriting Ibsen's emphasis of character over thesis. "The general social problem is always the problem of a living individual, and developed accordingly," Rowe argued; it was a strategy that Miller would master. In *No Villain*, which was written before he took Rowe's class, Miller's characters and his plot are vivid but notional. (For instance, in the argy-bargy over where the returning son is to sleep, Miller alludes to but does not develop Arny's oedipal victory over his diminished father.) There are rumblings of proletarian revolt from the mouths of the young ("We had the party for the last three hundred years, now it's their turn," Ben says of the striking workers); laissez-faire exhortations from Esther ("Arnold, you got to realize you're the son of the owner . . . not the working people. It ain't your place with them"); and some Darwinian hectoring from Abe ("I'm in business. This ain't no college. This is business. Cut or get cut"). But as the play's title suggests, the author takes no side in the family's story.

By his second play, now under Rowe's tutelage, Miller's internal change from passive to active, from tentative to assertive was reflected in his title choice: *They Too Arise*. "My plays were revolving around the question of waking up an individual to what ultimately became a moral obligation to change the world," he said. "This wasn't something I learned from a book. It was something I had to solve for myself; it was a problem given to me by what happened in 1929–30."

While Miller was dismissing writers like Eugene O'Neill for "his fossilized individualism, his dirge-like longing for private salvation redolent of the alcoholic twenties," his sense of his own individuality was growing, along with his understanding of class struggle. In his life and in his plays he was imagining a radical self. The division in Miller between the claims of American success and the claims of socialist principle was acted out in the conflict between the two brothers, the pragmatic Harry and the idealistic Max, in *Honors at Dawn*, Miller's schematic entry for the 1937 Hopwood Award. Full of rousing Odets-inspired speeches and violent action, Max, a mechanic turned activist, denounces his spendthrift brother for informing on campus radicals to get a university loan and emerges as a kind of working-class hero. At the automobile plant where he is employed, Max urges the striking workers to seize the means of production. "It's gonna be ours," he tells them before being wounded by a gunshot, the badge of honor to which the title refers.

The melodrama won Miller his second Hopwood Award. In the same year, *They Too Arise* won first prize in the Theatre

Guild's Bureau of New Plays competition, which, in addition to its rich purse, offered the bonus of a guaranteed second year under Rowe's tutelage. (The other prize winner was Tennessee Williams.) Theresa Helburn, the artistic director of the Theatre Guild, found Miller "a brooding young man burning with all the injustice in the world." But on campus, Miller was a happy guy, liberated from economic necessity by his literary winnings. "I was one of the elite in the last two years: I didn't have to work anymore," he said. Miller bought himself his first typewriter, a secondhand Smith-Corona. His tuition was now assured; locally, at least, his name was made. When *They Too Arise* was staged for three performances at the university theater and then briefly remounted in Detroit, "I became known in that little pond as a playwright."

Emboldened by the success of his autobiographical family plays, in his senior year Miller decided to spread his narrative wings. "I wanted to get out of myself and use the world as my subject," he said. He visited Jackson Penitentiary, where a friend was the psychologist for eight thousand inmates. From that experience, Miller spun *The Great Disobedience*—the first play he had ever researched—which found no favor with the Hopwood judges, one of whom called it "turgid." Miller himself called it a "monster." "I laugh at the title," he wrote to Rowe, only months after his graduation in June 1938. "It was a great disobedience. It dragged me around a whole year with a ring in my nose."

On his return to New York, Miller began his assault on the legitimate theater by turning *They Too Arise* into a Broadway comedy he titled "The Grass Still Grows." This third skip of the family stone played to Miller's avowed strength: his talent for mimicry. "The scenario took me most of the time and the writing only two weeks," he reported. "After pushing that prison play, working with family stuff and comedy was like a holiday." Without Rowe to consult, Miller was apprehensive at first, but as he reported to his mentor, "After awhile I was glad you were away." Miller was in some real sense claiming his talent as his own. "By the time I was writing the third act I felt so imperious that I laughed out loud in this basement! For the first time in my life I felt bigger than the play I was writing!" he confided to Rowe. He continued, "Heretofore, by the time the last act came around I was either partly or completely submerged in it and struggling blindly for my life. But not then. No. Then I put my arms around the typewriter and was larger than it. I straddled it for the first time."

Miller finished "The Grass Still Grows" in August. "I had the best time I ever had while writing," he told Rowe. "The play moves fast, there's a hell of a lot of fun in it and there's body to it." Within days, he had found someone at the prestigious Leland Hayward Agency to represent his comedy. Miller seemed to be pushing at an open door. "I thought I was there at last," he said. He was meeting producers and having script conferences. The director Lee Strasberg, one of the founding panjandrums of the Group Theatre, recommended him to the Federal Theatre Project, a New Deal program set up to promote theater and live performance around the country. ("The red tape is so engulfing, so completely exasperating that I feel Republican at the mention of it," Miller complained.) Strasberg, Miller boasted, even mentioned him in a lecture to students of playwriting. The lofty Group Theatre was considering staging "The Grass Still Grows." "Finally they decided they didn't want to do another Jewish play this year," Miller explained to Rowe. "That was the point—Jewish. It was utterly inconceivable to me that a Broadway producer would refuse to put on a play which he thought would make money just because he had a suspicion that in these times it was better not to show Jews on the stage, especially when some of them are not always laudable in motive." Miller continued, "I also realized that the rich Jew has learned nothing whatsoever from

Germany. The play in my honest opinion would excite anti-Semitism only in Bund members who don't need a play to get excited. . . . As matters stand now [my agent] tells me . . . that he has found an Aryan on Broadway who is much interested. God bless that man whoever he is. I hope he makes a million on it and it gets the commendation of the *Jewish Daily Forward* in the bargain."

Through this initiation into the realities of show business, Miller was learning one of the Rialto's hardest lessons: the caprice of public taste. On November 9, while "The Grass Still Grows" was getting nowhere in New York, in Germany, Kristallnacht, the first explosion of Nazi violence against Jews, shocked the world. In just twenty-four hours, ninety-one Jews were murdered, thirty-six severely injured, and three hundred thousand sent to concentration camps. According to Miller's agent, producers were suddenly fishing for his work again. "Apparently the intense persecutions abroad have aroused some kind of pity for Jews generally after all the mass meetings and radio speeches, the Jews being hoisted toward the heroic or at least the oppressed martyr class," Miller wrote to Rowe two weeks after the rampage. He added, "The whole thing will be pretty disgusting if the same producers who turned the play down for 'altruistic' reasons now pick it up on an equally spurious pretext, and then later get credit for presenting a Jewish play in fearless defiance of a dangerous racial situation! Ach, as the ballet instructor in that low piece, 'Can't take it, etc.,' said, quote. It stinks. Unquote." But the enthusiasm of the moment soon faded, and prospects for the play dissipated.

Miller rewrote "The Grass Still Grows" yet again in 1939, replacing the filigree of political ideology with the filigree of romance; the commercialization made no difference. The play would never be performed or published. Nonetheless, he was undaunted. He was trying his hand at poetry, collaborating on a revue for the Workers Alliance with Norman Rosten, another veteran of Rowe's playwriting seminar, writing a radio play, and rewriting *The Great Disobedience*. "Will I always have to write my plays over once I have finished them?" he asked Rowe, striking a rare plaintive note.

For the most part, Miller's spirits were high; he had, as he said, "great confidence in my ability compared to other people, earlier than most people get it." Miller claimed that he always felt someone secretly watching over him. "It was, of course, the mother, the first audience. Actually the concept of her in a most primordial sense that perhaps only the boy-child, half lover and half rebel against her dominion, really knows in his mystifying blood." His letters to Rowe in 1938 and 1939 swagger with optimism. "I have little money and many debts but somehow I can't get myself to worry over it," he confided. Sitting in the basement of his parents' Brooklyn house, where he was temporarily holed up, Miller often flashed back to his days as big man on campus. "I can see every square foot of Ann Arbor in my head, and it's prettier than this city," he wrote. "But I'm glad I'm not back there." He went on, "Here one knows the maximum opposition and a man can confront it and learn more precisely what his place is in this world. . . . There are no make-up examinations . . . happily."

4

The Greasy Pole

How far behind all the other arts is the theater in this
country! How childish. It will be many years before
they accept any but the most literal realism.

—Clifford Odets, journal entry, 1940

BY THE TIME Miller set out his stall as playwright, in 1938—
"I was what you'd call a playwright without a theatre and, strictly
speaking, without a typewriter," he said—Broadway was the
place where serious new American drama went to die. As early
as 1933, Eugene O'Neill had declared Broadway a "show shop"
and abdicated his reign on the Rialto as America's great playwright. Rusticating in the backwaters of Georgia and Califor-
nia, he focused, over the decades, on a cycle of nine plays, of
which he managed to complete only two. O'Neill was an aesthetic rebel; his socialist political beliefs did not carry into his
plays, where his argument was with Man and God, not with
capitalism. "He had no relevancy at that time for what we were
worried about," Miller said of O'Neill, something that could
as easily have applied to most of the other marquee names of

the day: S. N. Behrman, Maxwell Anderson, Robert Sherwood, Philip Barry.

By 1940, Odets, who had inherited O'Neill's mantle as the heavyweight dramatic champion and to whom Miller "paid great attention," was singing the same sour tune. "The American theatre, excuse me, is vile and a stench hangs over it," he said. At the time there was no other arena for new plays; "American theatre," as Miller later ruefully observed, was "five blocks long, by about one and a half blocks wide." When Miller described Odets's theatrical ambition as "to burst the bounds of Broadway while remaining inside its embrace, there being no other place to go," he was also defining his own. However, whereas Odets had experience as an actor with the Group Theatre, Miller was a theatrical tyro. He had seen only a handful of Broadway plays and knew nothing about the Method or about actors. "I had no use for almost anything I could see," he said. "The reason was, first of all, it wasn't my stuff; and it seemed to me terribly old-fashioned. . . . I had no sense of theatricality, that is, the life of the actor, his microscopic view of the play."

With talking pictures not even a decade old, Broadway still incarnated show *business*. ("If it wasn't business," Woody Allen quipped decades later, "they'd have called it show show.") Broadway, which Miller came to see as a "surreal Coney Island," "a big calliope making a lot of noise," was capitalism at play— a high-risk, high-reward game in which the gap between the "haves" and the "have-nots" was widened by the phenomenon of stardom. Like all businesses, Broadway was run on the principle of the bottom line: find a product, capitalize it, market it, and if it makes a profit, repeat it. Form followed money. Market forces encouraged the formulaic and the realistic over the innovative and the metaphoric. Serious drama asked a panic-struck society to think about itself, while comedies and musicals sold forgetfulness and sensationalized the status quo. As a result, the majority of Broadway's successful fare in the thirties was scaffolding holding up nothing.

Only months after Miller moved to New York, a 20th Century–Fox executive offered him the eye-watering sum of $250 a month to move to Los Angeles and write screenplays. Miller turned him down. "I had higher ambitions," he said. Instead, for a relief check of $22.77 a week, he finagled his way into the Federal Theatre Project, a spin-off of the WPA, which would be closed down by Congress within the year for its perceived left-wing orientation. "The Federal Theatre Project introduced probably the only new form that was ever introduced into the American theatre: the living newspaper," Miller recalled. "It was a kind of collaborative mass art. There were no playwrights for these things, in the strict sense. There was a kind of Elizabethan quality, not in the writing but in the way these things were strung together. They were history plays in a new context. The style of the writing was less important than the style of presentation. They were enormously stimulating interpretations of what was going on." The Federal Theatre Project allowed for stage effects that were not possible in the cost-conscious commercial theatre. "You could put forty-five people on stage at $22 a week each. You were making work and the expense didn't matter," Miller said.

By then, Miller was, he said, "up to his neck in feverish anti-Fascism." As a student he had flirted with the idea of joining the Abraham Lincoln Brigade to fight against Francisco Franco. But "I was too appalled at the idea of not living to write a great play. Worst of all was the blinding prospect of informing my mother that I was off to war." To Miller, the Spanish Civil War was the event with the most powerful effect on his generation's sense of the world; it represented "the forced return of clerical feudalism" and "the death of the mind." He was incredulous at the daylight bombing of Guernica. "It was hard to sleep for weeks afterwards." (He wrote to FDR in protest—

a letter that, the White House informed him, was turned over to the FBI.) In 1939, while the United States and Britain looked on, Hitler annexed Poland and then Czechoslovakia. "I recall feeling myself surrounded in those times by a kind of drifting into cultural suicide and a self-blinded acceptance of murder in high places," Miller said.

It was in this atmosphere of alarm that in October 1938 he began writing *The Golden Years*, originally titled "Children of the Sun," an epic about Hernán Cortés's overthrow of Montezuma and the destruction of the Aztec Empire. Miller challenged himself to write a panoramic Elizabethan-style narrative and invented a new idiom, which alternated between prose and poetry. The play had twenty-two characters. "I can't imagine what I thought I was doing," he said later. "I was foolish to spend so much time on it. But once it began to draw on my heart I could not stop until it had sucked me dry."

Set in 1519 and subtitled "A New World Tragedy," the play was intended as an objective correlative for the collapsing Old World of 1939. A study of passivity and its risks, *The Golden Years* dramatizes the clash between a ruthless soldier of fortune and a dithering emperor fearful that his kingdom is in eclipse. (The play's first words—"My star seems bleeding"—are Montezuma's.) "Montezuma, like the Democracies facing Hitler, was as though hypnotized," Miller explained in a 1986 introduction to the play. "Weakened by self-doubt, he looks to Cortez, manifestly a brute and a conqueror, as one who may nevertheless bear within him the seed of the future."

Miller had seen reasonable, respectable, even heroic people, like Charles Lindbergh and his wife, Anne, react in the same way, returning from a visit to Nazi Germany only to declare it "The Wave of the Future." Miller's Montezuma cannot decide whether "Cortez" is an invader or Quetzalcoatl, the Aztec god who promised a Second Coming. "Are they men or gods?" he says of the conquistadors, adding, "It's true they've come calling commands, ruthless; but I've not stopped them and I will not raise a hand until I know; are they God's children, or mortal strangers coming for conquest?" When Cortez finally shows his hand, putting Montezuma in chains and threatening "to blow up your city and leave it in ashes," Montezuma agrees to pacify his people. "We must not live out our lives among ashes," he tells them. "Lay down your arms." Montezuma pays for this appeasement with his death and that of the Aztec civilization. As Cortez's looting soldiers melt the sacred Aztec relics into gold ingots, Montezuma tells him, "You are melting down a history." At the finale, with the boom of advancing cannons around him, Montezuma lies dying. His final words speak directly to an endangered Europe hesitating between showdown and surrender: "Let the history tell how an emperor died in search of the golden years. And by no hand but his own. For while his eyes were searching heaven for meanings and signs, a sword was pointing at his breast, and as it caught the light with such brilliant glare, it seemed to hold the sanction of the sun, and he dared not turn the killing blade away."

"I had never worked so long or so hard on anything in my life, and many, many were the times when I felt I had bitten off more than I could chew," Miller wrote to Rowe. "But I can write now and proudly that *Children of the Sun* is a beautiful play." A week after finishing it, never having read it through and fearing that it might be uneven, Miller gathered a few playwrights and professional actors for a reading. It was a hot night, and the play was three hours long. When they reached the end, Miller wrote to Rowe, "I looked around. I felt that even if the play were never produced I had my reward. They sat in solid silence for more than two minutes." He went on, "I thought at first they were waiting for someone to start the carping, but not so. The first word came from one of the playwrights, a rather cynical individual. He sat with his head in his hands, and in that position, he said, 'Jesus Christ,' which was good enough, and when he lifted his face he had tears!'"

"Despite its ideological breadth, the play is an actor's and director's holiday," Miller told Rowe. "I feel it will draw to it some interest." It didn't. Miller's bubble was soon burst by his agent, who could see "next to nothing in it" and didn't understand, he said, "why you wrote it in the first place." Nonetheless, for a while, Miller was buoyed by voices of admiration. The distinguished Group Theatre actor Morris Carnovsky told Miller that he would be "highly honored to play Montezuma" and passed the script to Harold Clurman and Clifford Odets, who never responded. Miller sent the play to the venerable dramaturg of the Theatre Guild John Gassner, who was impressed by it but cautioned Miller: "Try to understand the audience. What do they want to see in the theatre? That must temper your work. You must not be too hard on them, Arthur."

At the time, Miller fumed over Gassner's boulevard pieties, but later, alone, he understood that Gassner was as helpless as he was within the commercial system. "For a moment, I say all right, I'll comfort them," he wrote to Rowe. "I'll keep away from the conflicts, the important and wonderful crises in our lives. I'll warp what I see into comforting fantasy." He added, "How long can one shout and cry and roar laughing into a writing machine before the shouting and the crying and laughing become pantomime?"

With hindsight, it is hard to see the stilted exposition and stiff, psychologically unexplored characters of *The Golden Years* as nuanced drama. By May 1940, after thirteen months of work and many revisions, Miller was prepared to admit defeat. "Another hundred-odd pages for the file, and a year of my life," he wrote to Rowe. The many rejections had left him afraid "that I will never be able to write for our theatre." He was now twenty-four, still living at home, still unproduced. An acid thought had begun to force its way into his consciousness: "Have I justified my self-announced and self-appointed existence as a writer?" He felt like a ward of his father and brother: "The bed is soft, the house warm, and the food excellent. But somehow I feel a small size 14 chain around my 15½ neck, which is annoying me." For Rowe's benefit, Miller tallied up what he'd written in the two years since he "kissed Ann Arbor goodbye": two plays, a revue, five radio scripts, short stories, and three postcards. "Of it all, a four-minute radio sketch and a half-hour radio play have been accepted and produced. Net receipts, $200 less 10% commission plus $75 for the movie, equalling $255!" (Miller had written the narration for the first reel of an unfinished film documentary on Sergei Eisenstein.)

Miller had, however, profited in other important ways. He had learned to avoid costume drama. (He would return to the genre only once, sixteen years later, with *The Crucible*.) He had also understood the necessity of finding a theatrical idiom that bridged realism and symbolism, containing both the recognizable and the invisible. "I expect to write contemporary people and subjects and the dialogue will be much easier, and research will not be a problem at all," he told Rowe. The failure of *The Golden Years*—it was performed on BBC radio in 1987 but was never staged—had shown him the limitations of a young writer's solitude. Miller asked himself, "Can a man give his twenties, his rose-colored youth, to something and at thirty say he's through?" His answer was a staunch no. "I have always felt, and do now, but more intensely, that a writer must renew himself," he wrote to Rowe, quoting a line from another of his unproduced plays, "You've got to go out and collide with life." He went on, "Perhaps in this collision with life I will be flooded as I was in other years, years when I worked on trucks and warehouses, with insights into people that will overcome many objections to my work. That is, perhaps I do *not* understand the audience enough. . . . If this is true I will be able to bring to the theatre a heat and fire only if I feel it in myself. . . . So one way to re-attack, so to speak, is to store up more ammunition, otherwise I'm rapping at the portals with an empty gun." On August 5, 1940, filled with a new resolve to force himself into the world, Miller took a major step: he got married.

Mary Slattery was a tall, slender, forthright brunette, a lapsed Catholic from a reactionary lower-middle-class Ohio family, who put her faith in social change, not in the life to come. The couple had met in 1937 at a basement party at the University of Michigan, when Miller was a junior and Slattery a freshman studying psychology and planning to be a social worker. "When he asked for a date, I proposed a movie, but he didn't have any money," she said. "I treated him to the movies, and afterwards to malted milks." (It was a pattern of financial support that continued throughout their impecunious early years, when, to support them, she worked as an editor and a secretary.)

Unlike Miller, Slattery was a voracious reader and a good student. "She was very smart and cool," Miller's sister, Joan, recalled. Where Miller was passionate and dreamy, with the dramatist's habit of imagining all sides of a situation, Mary was resolute and exacting. "People were either right or wrong. . . . She saw things pretty black and white. You couldn't budge her," he said. He added, "At the time I admired it, because I was not that way. It was rock and water. I was the water. She was the rock." Slattery was Miller's first girlfriend and the first *shiksa* he dated. "We were mysteries to each other," he said. "She wanted a Jew-artist. And I wanted America." (When Miller's mother told her father, Louis Barnett, that Miller had married a gentile, he threw an alarm clock at her.)

Their Marxist faith was common ground and served them as a kind of "righteousness ticket," according to Miller. "Among its other benefits, it allowed you to suppress any contradiction that tended to cast doubt on socialism, and, as important, upon your own motives and virtue." Miller and Slattery kept separate apartments for the two years before their marriage; however, from the outset they coexisted in the same progressive universe, united in their expectation of a socialist revolution. They were married, without Miller's family present, by a Catholic priest outside the church, "not so much under the wing of the Church as under one of its feathers," he said. (The Miller family was informed afterward.) "Left to myself I would not have gotten married," Miller told his biographer Christopher Bigsby in 2001. "But I really admired Mary a lot. I had a great feeling of companionship with her. . . . She was really anxious to settle down, so I thought, well, it's probably a good idea." He went on, "Marriage, to me, didn't mean all that much, anyway. But I didn't want to lose her."

Marriage to Slattery, however, provided Miller with a kind of bulwark against doubt and the vagaries of the freelance life. She was his cheerleader, his sounding board, and his meal ticket—a true believer in his potential. "He needed somebody to adore him," the filmmaker Rebecca Miller, Miller's daughter from his third marriage, said of Slattery. The lovelight in Mary's eyes replaced the all-defining gaze of his mother, whom Miller called his "first audience." "I have never felt so solid, so at home in a house," he wrote to Rowe after three months of marriage. "In these times such a girl is a keel to an otherwise wayward ship." He added, "She demands nothing and yet gives everything—paradise."

About a week after their wedding, as part of his mission to break out of his little cave of consciousness, Miller waved goodbye to Mary and his parents at a Hoboken pier and set sail on the S.S. *Coppa Coppa*, a freighter bound for the Gulf ports and beyond. His solo honeymoon, he said, "felt weird even to me." He mused, "I loved [Mary] more in the leaving than if I had hung around merely dreaming of the sea." Unlike the Anglo-Saxon *perignatios*—ritual journeys of spiritual discovery—Miller's quest was a search more for material than for selfhood. Whereas his contemporary Tennessee Williams lived in a state of permanent flight and found inspiration in his sense of loss, Miller, who had begun as a reporter, was inspired by the world he observed. "Art was not a writer who made up stories. His material had to be experienced," Kazan said. "He had to have a living connection with a subject before he could make a drama of it."

But although he tried, in a failed play (*The Half-Bridge*) and an unpublished novel ("The Bangkok Star"), Miller couldn't make much sense of the characters and events he collected on his freighter trip. Nonetheless, when he reflected on the seafaring experience in an unpublished short story, recasting himself as the writer "Rufus Solomon" on a similar junket, Miller was forced to acknowledge a disabling self-involvement, which cast his wife as an extra in the epic of his literary endeavor. The unsayable thing he could admit neither in fiction nor in life was this: his marriage was an act of pragmatism, not passion. Miller's purest erotic connection was to his writing, of which he was at once protective and ashamed. "There was almost no space for me between sexuality and art, as though it were a sexual secret," he wrote in *Timebends*. He could surrender to the page far more easily than to another person. "My relationship to Mary and to all women was thin and cautious out of some fear that surpassed sex itself."

A year later, secluded on a friend's farm trying to knock out the first draft of a novel, he wrote to Rowe, "Swell here, alone with fine workshop. . . . Very stimulating, alone." The novel was to be called "The Man Who Had All the Luck"; Miller wasn't having much. Having failed to attract the interest of Broadway producers, he was forced to fall back on what he considered the "high quality pulp" of radio drama. His first radio play—a political satire titled *The Pussycat and Expert Plumber Who Was a Man*—was broadcast while he was at sea, but he was rejected for a Rockefeller fellowship (in the same year that Tennessee Williams received one). When the Library of Congress offered him a salary of $3,200 to interview the people of Wilmington, North Carolina, a boomtown that had been at one time a receiving port for the slave trade, Miller hesitated. "I don't want to leave here because for the first time my theatrical future is brightening and I don't want to leave town unless the production collapses," he wrote to Kenneth Rowe about his sea play *The Half-Bridge*, which the Theatre Guild was considering. It collapsed.

On December 7, 1941, a week after he returned from Wilmington, the Japanese bombed Pearl Harbor; four days later, Hitler declared war on the United States. Miller, who was a signatory of the pacifist Oxford Pledge at Michigan, nonetheless volunteered along with his brother Kermit for military service. Kermit was accepted into the Officer Candidate School in the army. Miller was rejected, due to a high school football knee injury. He then applied to the Office of War Information but was rejected again. "I seemed to be part of nothing, no class, no influential group; it was like high school perpetually, with everybody rushing to one or another club or conference with a teacher, and me still trying to figure out what was happening," he said. He felt, he admitted, "the inevitable unease of the survivor."

On December 9, Miller sounded a new call to arms in his notebook. "Why are you a revolutionary," he asked himself, and answered, "Because the truth is revolutionary and the truth you shall live by." He went on, "Tonight after more than four years of indecision and torment, after passing through the terrible gamut of bourgeois aspiration and bourgeois frustration and fear, I leave that world behind. And with it all that I have written and all I have tried to write and failed to finish. The last two works never completed themselves, for at last the mind has exhausted its memories. . . . Why should I continue to feign ignorance of cause? Why try to make heroes of the damned and the pathetic? Why strive for nothing but the scene that has passed? The hero today fights to the death for that which is to come. And now, in my strength, so do I."

The following spring, answering what he called "a wish for community," Miller took a job as a shopfitter's assistant for the navy, straightening steel and welding cracked nuts on depth-charge platforms under the Brooklyn Bridge, a fifteen-minute walk from home. Miller worked the night shift, breaking for lunch at midnight—a routine that left him the daylight hours to complete his novel and write radio plays, which became the source of an increasingly good living over the next couple of years. For Miller, who could turn out five or six scripts a year, writing radio plays was a "wonderful racket," "a kind of subsidy." (Devoting three months of his writing time to churning out the radio scripts, Miller said, he could earn between "ten to twelve thousand dollars": "I never had any illusions about it. To me, I was just carrying coal."

Since 1940 about a third of all broadcasting time was devoted to drama. It was a seller's market, and Miller found himself writing for two of the medium's best-produced and most prestigious shows: *The Columbia Workshop* and *The Cavalcade of America*, which produced mainly tales of historical figures and conflicts. The twenty-eight-minute productions were performed by the finest actors in the land and accompanied by a forty-piece orchestra—"They had orchestrations that thick, you'd think they were going to play the Ninth Symphony," Miller recalled. An as-yet unproduced playwright, he had the thrill of hearing his words spoken by such stars as Orson Welles (*Thunder from the Mountains*), Alfred Lunt and Lynn Fontanne (his adaptation of Ferenc Molnár's *The Guardsman*), Paul Muni (*The Eagle's Nest*), and Edward G. Robinson (*The Philippines Never Surrendered*). Miller got to be so expert at the job that he became a kind of emergency script writer for *Cavalcade of America*. "They would call me up and say, 'We've got this subject and we've got to go on tomorrow night.' They'd send a messenger over with a book. It would arrive at two o'clock in the afternoon and they had to be rehearsing the thing the next day at three," Miller recalled. He continued, "I would sit down—and these were not electric typewriters—and I could write the whole damn thing and get it off. I took great pleasure in being a good mechanic."

Competent though not inspired, these finger exercises in storytelling were rewarding in another way: they gave him confidence as a playwright. "I began to feel that I could somehow make this happen," he said. The narrative constrictions of radio—the need for brevity, clarity, vividness of phrase—helped him understand dramatic storytelling. "Less is better. Why? It's very simple. It's like a dream," he said, adding, "Dreams are very brief and some of them you never forget because they are very discreet. Nothing is wasted. No dream has excessive material. It all counts."

Miller managed occasionally to slip political observations into his radio scripts. "Isn't it time to unlock the kitchen and let women out?" a character says in *Toward a Further Star*, a play about Amelia Earhart. In *Buffalo Bill Disremembered*, he provided a neat metaphor for the nation's chronic historical amnesia about the sins of its imperial past: "I can't remember the truth anymore," Buffalo Bill says; "They even say there's a feller who's really Buffalo Bill and that I ain't." In *Thunder from the Mountains*, a radio play about the Mexican peasant leader Benito Juárez who became the country's president, Miller managed to include, despite the sponsor's resistance, the uncomfortable fact that Abraham Lincoln helped to arm the Mexican revolutionaries who seized power. He even wrote a propaganda piece—*That They May Win*—which encouraged people to buy war bonds and inform on anyone trading in the black market.

But Miller's prose was still too prolix and ungainly, his ideas undigested. "We have had lots of readings of AM's TMWHATL ["The Man Who Had All the Luck"]," a Doubleday editor wrote to Miller's agent. The editor found the novel "almost unique and fascinating," but added, "It is so uneven, such a mixture of the good and the bad, that in its present state we don't feel that we can undertake it." The editor asked if Miller would be interested in overhauling his manuscript. Miller wasn't. He decided to turn it into a play. "I have been bested time and again by writers who I know to be inferior," he wrote in his notebooks around this time. "I have had plays refused insultingly by managements who have gone ahead to buy some monstrosity or other. Had I no faith in my talent I should vent my hatred against these miserable people. But . . . I will go home and write."

In the early months of 1943, Miller's radio plays brought him to the attention of a Hollywood producer who was looking to make a screenplay out of *Here Is Your War*, a collection of columns from the front by America's foremost war correspondent, Ernie Pyle. For the extraordinary fee of $750 a week, Miller shelved both his navy shipyard work and his radio gig to tour a number of army bases interviewing young recruits for a film to be called *G.I. Joe*. The material Miller found among the enlisted men—racism, anti-Semitism, confusion about their mission—was much more complicated than the soldiering heroics the film intended to celebrate. Miller wanted to follow a dozen characters from boot camp to battlefield and have most of them killed in action, a body count that the Hollywood executives whittled down to one. "It is very hard to kill a good character, because the public seems to want pictures where nobody dies," Miller noted.

Although the film was subsequently made, seven other writers had a hand in it; none of Miller's work was used. His research, however, was preserved in his first published work, *Situation Normal* (1944), a book issued by the publishing house where Miller's wife was secretary to the editor-in-chief, Frank

Taylor. The anecdotal accounts, drawn from his interviews, were at once an acknowledgment and an appropriation of his brother's war experience. ("For: Lieutenant Kermit Miller—United States Military" was the dedication.) "The dedication of Arthur's army book was a form of vicariousness that lies at the heart of their relation to each other," Kermit's son, Ross Miller, wrote in "Relations," an unpublished memoir about the Miller clan. "A mutual cannibalizing of each other's experiences that is both the source of Arthur's art and the slow paralysis of my father's ambition." If the book brought news of the realities of the soldier's life, its combination of curiosity and pomposity also bore witness to Miller's own tongue-tied prose. "I am the wandering disembodied spirit which can enter the luncheon of the General Staff, and thirty minutes later, if the Colonel's story is not too long, be ensconced in the PX with some buck private who does not have very much use for the Colonel, or does have," Miller wrote. "The result is that serious things are often humorous to me, as they must be to any god, and funny things have stopped amusing me."

The promise of publication was not the only watershed moment of Miller's year. On September 7, 1944, he became a father for the first time. (Jane Miller was followed in 1947 by Robert Miller.) The sense of blessing reminded Miller of how lucky he was—which was also the theme of his unpublished 360-page novel: "the question of the justice of fate, how it was that one man failed and another, no more or less capable, achieved some glory in life." The original inspiration for *The Man Who Had All The Luck* was an anecdote, told to Miller by an Ohio cousin of Mary's, about a successful, buoyant, well-liked local who had killed himself. "Why should such a successful young man be drawn to his own death," Miller asked himself, "especially in the pristine countryside far from the crush and competitive pressures of the city?" Do we control our fate or are we fated? Are we ruled by caprice or by will? The metaphysical quandary stuck with Miller. To explain its allure he could point to recent history—the news of the Holocaust that was leaking out from Germany and the "fear of a drift toward fascism"—but there was a deeper, more personal and unconscious connection that would reveal itself over time as he transformed the novel into a play.

The innumerable rewrites, Miller said, "moved me inch by inch toward my first open awareness of father-son and brother-brother conflict." He continued, "One day, quite suddenly, I saw that Amos and David were brothers and Pat was their father. There was a different anguish in the story now, an indescribable new certainty that I could speak from deep within myself." In his story, Miller could say the unsayable: he had got himself away from his family, claimed his intellect, found a vocation, been excused from military service, and made a family. His luck had held and then some. By contrast, Kermit—the golden boy and would-be writer who had forgone his education so that Miller could have his, who had dutifully aligned himself with the father whose miscalculations in business had led them to three bankruptcies during the thirties—was now in harm's way in Europe, writing home about the "hellish cacophony, human screaming, rattle of gunfire . . . beyond my power to describe." The narrative tapped into Miller's fear of failure and his guilt over his success. "Perhaps I was refracting my own feelings of mysterious power gathering in me, contrasting it with its absence in others," he wrote disingenuously in *Timebends*, unable to point a finger at his brother and his father, whose trajectories were downward, while his was on the rise.

Because of all the fantastical accidents of circumstance that befall the young mechanic David Beeves, the hero of *The Man Who Had All the Luck*, Miller subtitled his play "A Fable." The eponymous lucky man—"wondrous, funny, naïve, and always searching," according to the stage directions—is a stranger to loss. "Everything I touch, why is it? Turns to gold. Everything," he says, as his apprehension escalates in proportion to his good fortune. Around him characters are buffeted and stymied by personal weakness, missed chances, lack of opportunity, miscalculations. David, on the other hand, who has no particular gifts and no particular ambition, goes from strength to strength. His young girlfriend's father, intent on preventing their marriage, is killed in a car accident; a crankshaft which is beyond David's skill to repair is mended thanks to a new neighbor; a highway built nearby turns his small gas station into a big business; even a mink farm into which he has sunk his considerable fortune is saved from going under and quadruples his money. Meanwhile, Amos, David's favored and more talented older brother, an aspiring Big League pitcher, can't get a break. "I ain't a trained man. You are. You *got* something. And you're going to be great. Because you deserve it," David tells Amos, who is so driven to make it in baseball that he practices throwing during the winter in the family cellar. But pluck is no use without luck. When opportunity knocks—in the shape of a visiting scout from the Detroit Tigers—Amos fails. When he is no longer in the cellar, and there are actual men on base, he panics and loses his legendary control. "I swear to God I don't get it," David says. "Everything is so hard for him." Amos quits—he won't fight for his future—and he ends up pumping gas at David's service station, waiting for something good to happen.

The Man Who Had All the Luck was too melodramatic and murky to be good. Nonetheless, the play was a significant advance in Miller's storytelling. "The overt story was only tangential to the secret drama I was quite unconsciously trying to write," Miller said later. "It became clear to me that I was not only reporting to others but to myself first and foremost." David's mink ranch venture is a stand-in for Miller's commitment to his own writing—a big financial gamble that is his way of fending off morbid fears of catastrophe. In David's case, the fear is triggered by his wife's pregnancy and his paranoid suspicion that she will have a damaged child. If something bad happens to the minks, David's magical thinking goes, then the child will be spared. (His wife, Hester, learns from the farm owner who first gave her husband the idea of raising minks that the feed is contaminated; she doesn't relay the message to David in the hope that the death of the animals will also kill her husband's obsession with work and turn his attention back to their marriage. "When will we sit and talk again? When will you pick up the baby . . . ?" she says, trying, and failing, to talk him out of his compulsive behavior. In the end, David spots the infected feed before it kills his minks, and Hester bears him a healthy son. "I'm not afraid of my luck anymore," he says. The play's redemptive last image has David ascending the stairs to be reunited with his wife and their newborn child. His trajectory is still on the rise but with a hint of approaching stormy weather: "As he mounts the stairs, a rumble of thunder sounds in the distance."

The storm in Miller's life came soon enough. *The Man Who Had All the Luck* was his first play to open on Broadway, at the Forrest Theater, on November 23, 1944, under the direction of Joseph Fields, who had a commercial pedigree as a writer of light comedy (*My Sister Eileen*) and musical libretti (*Gentlemen Prefer Blondes*). It closed after four performances. Five of seven of the daily critics brushed it off: "incredibly turgid . . . and stuttering" (*New York Herald Tribune*); "ambling . . . strangely confused . . . rather tiresome" (*New York Sun*). The laurel for disdain went to the high-handed George Jean Nathan of the *New York Journal-American* who wrote of "confidently expecting the final curtain to come down upon the spectacle of everyone on the stage squirting seltzer siphons at one another." Miller watched only the closing night of the fiasco, which he compared to "music played on the wrong instruments in a false note." Afterward he wrote, "It almost seemed a relief to get on the subway to Brooklyn Heights and read about the tremendous pounding of Nazi-held Europe by Allied air power. Some-thing somewhere was real."

Kermit Miller fought in that opposition to the last major German offensive on the Western Front, the Battle of the Bulge, which took place in mid-December, about two weeks after *The Man Who Had All the Luck* sank without a trace. Trapped in his foxhole by enemy fire, in blinding snow for a week, Kermit was one of the eighty-one thousand soldiers injured. He was evacu-ated to a field hospital with severe frostbite, facing the possible amputation of both feet, but, in defiance of the doctors, signed himself out before he was healed in order to rejoin his platoon. He would be awarded the Purple Heart and return a shell-shocked war hero.

Miller would also win the Theatre Guild National Award in 1944 for *The Man Who Had All the Luck*, recognition of sorts for his long, brave campaign to become a Broadway playwright. The unmooring experience had left him one of the walking wounded. With the forces of Broadway ranged so powerfully against him, Miller had no heart to continue the fight. The battle was not worth the prize. Life was too interesting to hang around writing play after play that nobody would stage. "I sim-ply decided I would never write another play," he said.

5

◆┼◆┼◆

Passion for Ignorance

We Americans are always trying to raise the standard
of living, and the same principle now seems to
apply to standards of hating.

—Richard Hofstadter, *The Paranoid Style
in American Politics*

"SO THEY DIDN'T KNOW you were a Jew till you told them?"
Gussie wrote to Miller in his first semester at Michigan. "Now
you can say in your inimitable way '*Ich hab sei alle in Drerd*'"—
Yiddish for, roughly, "I buried them all." She added, "Just show
them what a Jew can do when he tries."

Miller's coming of age coincided with the rise of fascism at
home and abroad, and anti-Semitism—"the poor man's snob-
bery," as it was often called—filled the American ozone. "The
Jews were the cause of every imaginable misfortune," Miller
said. "This ancient magical formula was not too hard for even
an idiot to grasp, and so the Jewish people, as they had been innumerable times since Christianity began, were up for sacrifice,

their destruction required before the promise of social progress for non-Jews could take place." He went on, "In short, the strength of anti-Semitism was its illogic, its supernatural nature."

To escape a certain kind of paranoid despair in 1930s New York, Miller developed, he said, "a hard shell." As a young man, he applied for the shipping clerk's job at the auto-parts warehouse Chadick-Delamater, encouraged by both the weekly fifteen-dollar salary and the fact that "unlike most ads this one did not specify 'Christian' or 'Gentile firm.' Or simply 'Chr.' or 'Cath.' or 'Prot.'" Even though most of the local parts dealers were Jewish, Miller was the first Jew the company had hired. "In my two years on the job I kept trying to imagine myself as really no different than the others," he said, "but some membrane persisted between me and them."

One Sunday, Miller joined a friend and his girlfriend for a weekend ride across the new George Washington Bridge to New Jersey. "As unshockable as I was at that time, I felt a blow inside my head on seeing a small sign at the driveway entrance to a country hotel that read: restricted clientele, Christian," Miller said. "Personally, I wouldn't have even dreamed of renting a hotel room, but the idea of being forbidden to so much as enter the place somehow exploded something in my brain. It was like being shot at. The hatred in that little sign was indigestible."

By 1944, when Miller decided to write a novel, it was impossible for him not to feel a mounting "sense of emergency" about anti-Semitism. His habitual optimism had been shaken by Kristallnacht. "Now the everyday slights and threats against me—and against Jews in general—began to swell as portents," he said. And although neither the New York papers nor the radio admitted "the Big Secret," Miller wrote, "the city was pulsing with hatred." "I myself had been taken for all sorts of people, and had therefore been exposed to the attitudes of people towards Jews when those people didn't think I was Jewish," he said. "It never ceased to astound me that this personal prejudice could be organized, as it was being organized by Hitler, to destroy a people and really to destroy a civilization." At the Brooklyn Navy Yard, where Miller worked the night shift, he was unnerved by "the near absence among the men . . . of any comprehension of what Nazism meant—we were fighting Germany essentially because she had allied herself with the Japanese who had attacked us at Pearl Harbor."

By the time America was at war, there were more than a hundred anti-Semitic groups purveying hate in the nation. Because of the number of Jewish academics in Roosevelt's cabinet, in racist quarters the New Deal was dubbed "the Jew Deal"; Roosevelt's real name was rumored to be "Rosenfeld," and his "polio" syphilis. Father Charles Coughlin, on his Christian Front radio show *The Hour of Power*—which, at the height of its popularity, reached thirty million listeners—proclaimed, "When we get through with the Jews in America, they'll think the treatment they received in Germany was nothing." At an America First rally in 1941, three months before Pearl Harbor, Charles Lindbergh warned Jews in America that instead of agitating for war, "they should be opposing it in every possible way for they will be among the first to feel its consequences."

In 1939, the S.S. *St. Louis*, carrying 937 Jewish refugees, was denied landing privileges on U.S. territory and forced to return to Germany. "This was a fairly prosperous, middle-class group of people and not what 'refugee' seemed to connote but even that seemed not to count," Miller said. Non-Jews and Jews, including Miller, feared an outbreak of anti-Semitism should the desperate passengers be allowed to disembark. The fear of a postwar depression stoked anti-Semitic feeling and played to the stereotype of Jews as vulgar and materialistic. A *Fortune* poll asking respondents if they had heard criticism of Jews in the previous month registered 46 percent yeses in 1940, 60 percent in 1944, and 64 percent in 1946.

* * *

If Miller had not yet found a way to say the unsayable in drama, in the silence around anti-Semitism, he saw a subject for provocation in his first published novel, *Focus*. Anti-Semitism, he noted, "was like some shameful illness that was not to be mentioned in polite society, not by gentiles and not by Jews." "The writing of *Focus* was an attempt to break through that silence," he explained, adding, "There had never been a novel which had anti-Semites actually talking about Jews the way they talked about them in life." He wrote *Focus* at full tilt, completing a draft in six weeks, knowing that publication was no dead cert. "Just putting down the words was a relief," he said.

The novel was Miller's first of many attempts to map the landscape of American denial. It opens with its blinkered common man, Lawrence Newman, startled out of sleep in his Brooklyn home by a Spanish-sounding woman shouting for the police. Newman stands crouching behind the venetian blinds of his front window, straining to see a couple who are grappling in the darkness just twenty feet from him. The physical details of the scene make a larger metaphysical point. Newman doesn't want to be seen, and he *also* doesn't want to see: "He backed away from the window, the woman screaming '*Police! Police!*' in her accent. He turned in the dark and went out of the room." As Newman gets back into bed—"dull again"—he rewrites the narrative in his mind: "Her accent satisfied Mr. Newman that she was abroad at night for no good purpose, and it somehow convinced him that she could take care of herself because she was used to this sort of treatment. Puerto Ricans were, he knew." In this first chapter, long before Newman meets and marries his wife, who nicknames him "Lully," his unwitting stereotyping signals the inertia of his inner life. He is not empty, he's vacant—a man entirely without curiosity. He is literally lulled. He can't—he won't—imagine the Other. Newman lives a lonely life with his mother, who is paralyzed. His paralysis, we see from the first pages, is moral.

On his own time, Newman, a personnel officer for a large unnamed corporation, plays the same "secret game" that he is paid to play at the office: he judges people by their appearance. On the subway riding to work, he watches the straphangers, filling in the features that he can only partially discern. His stereotyping is instinctive, an exercise in fictionalization: the Ukrainian ("He could not make out the man's eyes. Probably small, he supplied"); the black man ("Some day he must look into the various types of niggers"); the Jew ("Probably he alone on this train knew that this gentleman with the square head and the fair skin was neither Swede, nor German, nor Norwegian, but a Jew"). When Newman sees graffiti that reads "Kill Kikes," the furious scrawl does not inspire outrage or thought; instead it gives him a voyeuristic thrill, "as though he had just seen a bloody fistfight."

Newman is a shy man who has constructed a wall of order and routine around feeling; he never allows the threat of chaos to penetrate him. Likewise, when Newman's neighbor Fred, whom he meets on the subway, chats to him about how to "clean out the neighborhood"—specifically, get rid of Finkelstein, the local candy-store owner, whose relatives are rumored to be moving to their street, and who Fred suspects will lower the value of their real estate—Newman does not react. He is temperamentally passive; in his desire to get along, he is also morally inert. As he walks to his office, Newman calms himself with thoughts of the identical houses on his block. "The memory of sameness soothed his yearning for order," Miller writes, setting up a bubble of complacency only to burst it.

At work, Newman finds himself immediately in a mess. He has inadvertently hired a Jew. "It throws the whole office off," his boss tells him. He is sent to the optometrist to get glasses.

Back at home, Newman models his glasses in the bathroom mirror. "He was looking at what might very properly be called the face of a Jew. A Jew, in effect, had gotten into his bathroom," Miller writes. Newman not only looks Jewish to himself; even worse, he looks Jewish to others. "You know what they ought to do with people like you. They ought to hang yiz," Gertrude Hart, an Episcopalian applicant whom he mistakes for Jewish, shouts at him when he denies her a job. (She mistakes him for Jewish as well.) "Her malevolence was intimate," Newman, who is secretly excited by her passion, thinks. Miller writes, "He sat there unable to speak to her through his hate. . . . He was polite to an extreme and he could not say that he was not Jewish without coloring the word with repugnance for it, and thus for her. . . . For to him Jew had always meant impostor." With his new glasses, Newman fares no better with the corporate hierarchy, who want to hide him away in a back office. "We don't feel you'll make a good impression on people who come into the outer office," he is told. After twenty-five years of service to the firm, Newman quits rather than accept a demotion to back-room clerk.

By degrees, Miller pushes his anti-hero into the vortex of anti-Semitism. The novel's ambition, Miller said, was "to lift the prejudice out of the skull enough so that we could look at it, so that people could look at themselves not as Jews or Gentiles, but as people." Miller's narrative strategy is to weave a web of hatred around Newman and hoist the unwitting bigot on the petard of his own prejudice. Newman runs the gauntlet of bigotry—demotion, exclusion, denigration, humiliation—but he bounces back like a Semitic shmoo, refusing to acknowledge the violence. His neighbors keep their distance. He begins to feel the weight of otherness, "no longer anonymous" but "encircled" by "the darting eyes" of others.

Eventually, his self-consciousness metastasizes. In order to parry the objectifying gaze of prejudice, Newman begins to modify his behavior: the tone of his voice, his eating habits, the semaphore of his gestures. "Often to destroy any impression of close-fistedness, he left larger tips," Miller writes. "*He* was not his face," Newman thinks. "He was not this face which looked like it had grown out of another alien and dirty history. They were trying to make two people out of him! They were looking at him as though he were guilty of something, as though he would hurt them! They could not do that! They dare not do that because he was no one else but Lawrence Newman."

An adept of denial, Newman initially sheds the racist projections of his neighbors by identifying with the victimizers. He buys his Sunday papers from a non-Jewish street seller who has been imported by his neighbors to harass Finkelstein and force him off the block; he agrees to join Fred at a local anti-Semitic meeting; he paints his shutters the same green as that of the other houses on the street. But the suspicion that Newman is Jewish sticks to him like a bad smell. Even Finkelstein wonders, briefly, "Could it be . . . that his wife had always been right when she claimed that Newman was strictly a Jewish name?" One day, Newman wakes up to find garbage strewn across his lawn, the same Christian Front calling card that has been dealt to Finkelstein—who also received a written command to leave the street within five days.

In an infelicitous bit of plotting, Miller contrives to make Gertrude Hart—the vituperative job applicant whom Newman had rejected as Jewish—the person who interviews him at the Jewish firm where he finally finds work. Newman, who is drawn to Gertrude, is unable and unwilling to see that under her soft bosom lies a hard, pragmatic heart. "As a Jewess she seemed dressed in cheap taste, too gaudily," he thinks. "But as a gentile he found her merely colorful in the same dress, a woman who expressed her spirited nature in her clothes. It was as though she now had a right to her faults; as though her flair, her style, her abruptness no longer sprang from bad breeding . . . but from a rebellious mind . . . that dared to override the smaller rules of behavior."

By reintroducing Gertrude into Newman's story, Miller added alienation to mindlessness as part of the equation that results in anti-Semitism. "The Jew is seen by the anti-Semitic mind as the carrier of the same alienation that the indigenous people resent and fear because it is an alienation they feel in themselves, the same conniving exploitation," Miller wrote in his 1984 introduction to the reprint of *Focus*. "A not-belonging, a haplessly antisocial individualism that belies a fervent desire to be a serving part of a mythic whole, the sublime national essence. They fear the Jew as they fear the real."

From her first outburst at Newman when she is rejected, the reader understands, even if the credulous Newman does not, that Gertrude's moral compass is broken. Her desire to humiliate Jews stems from her own humiliated heart. The story she first tells Newman about herself—that she is a screen-tested actress and singer living with a Hollywood actor—is a grandiose tall tale that belies her profound disappointment. "I tried [for a screen test] but I was a typist and that's what those Jews out there decided I was going to be," she confesses to Newman after they get married. (Typically, "Oh" is the only response he can muster.) Gertrude's "actor" turns out to have been a dog manicurist and a follower of Father Coughlin, whose flamboyant hate-mongering becomes an outlet for her and Newman. "It felt like he was talking to me," she tells Newman, adding, "I could tell listening to him that he was on the level. . . . I'm not kidding, he gave me hope. I mean that there were still some honest people left."

The novel's watershed moment comes when Newman and Gertrude are refused a room at a country hotel. "Nobody makes a Jew out of me and gets away with it," Gertrude says, equally humiliated by Newman's passivity. "You should have spoke up instead of standing there. That's probably why Fred got sick of you. You never say anything." "I don't know what's happening to me," Newman responds, marking the beginning of an unmooring internal shift, then adds, "I guess the truth is that I wish the whole thing would blow over." Newman longs, Miller writes, "to go back to the old days when his hate had no consequence."

But Gertrude, who knows the racist landscape, understands that once the war is over and the expected depression sets in, anti-Semitic hatred will be coming their way. "You're going to see fireworks," she says, adding, "I'm going to be on the right side of it, and so are you." To prove his Christian bona fides to Fred and put an end to the vandalism of his property, Newman agrees, under his wife's pressure, to attend a Father Coughlin rally, where he is abused and beaten up by the inflamed crowd for not applauding. As Newman staggers toward home, Finkelstein finds him and attends to him at his shop. In that moment of connection, Newman feels a "sharp curiosity." He begins to think, to see beyond the stereotype. He starts to imagine Finkelstein's family, his point of view, his suffering. "It was as though all the tokens of the known world had been switched . . . as though all the things that had been true were now all catastrophically untrue. He felt he was going to throw up and cry," Miller writes. As he begins to recognize the humanity in Finkelstein, Newman perfectly exemplifies Oliver Wendell Holmes's comparison of bigotry to the pupil of an eye: "The more light you shine on it, the more it will contract."

Focus ends with a set piece of racist violence. When the couple are attacked by Christian Front thugs on their way home from a movie, Gertrude bolts for Fred's house to get him to call the gang off and Newman runs to the candy store, where Finkelstein is standing his ground with baseball bats. Together they fight off their attackers. Afterward, cleaning Finkelstein's blood-stained face, Newman is surprised by tears. The tears signal his awakening—a disenchantment that allows him to see Gertrude's failings and his own. He longs for light: "a swift charge of lightning that would with a fiery stroke break away the categories of people and change them so that it would not be important to them what tribe they sprang from." At the police station later, as he reports the incident, he's asked by the officer how many Jews live on the block. "There are the Finkelsteins on the corner," Newman says. "Just them and yourself," the policeman interrupts. "Yes. Just them and myself," Newman agrees. And with that, his vexed name takes on another meaning: he is a new man.

Focus brought news but not much literary nuance. "The protagonist's heroism has been clipped to his lapel like a delegate's badge at a liberal convention," Saul Bellow wrote in the *New Republic*. Nonetheless, Miller's first published work touched a nerve. The novel sold ninety thousand copies; it was also optioned for the movies. After eight years of hard scrabble, Miller had money and a name, though not in the arena he wanted. Novel writing was a solitary slog. "It's like singing and you're deaf. You never hear it. A playwright, like a composer, writes to hear it," he said. The form didn't "offer the same kick that comes from the direct experience of a confrontation with an audience." You never saw a reader give up on your book or enjoy it. Miller, who never wrote another novel, also found the form's lack of boundaries disconcerting. There were "no walls in the castle," he said. "It makes me nervous. I like to know where I am."

Buoyed by the success of the book, Miller decided to take one last crack at writing a commercial Broadway play. His ambition—"an excursion I was not at home in"—was to create, like Ibsen, a density of experience, "the past coming to life in the present." (In his early drafts, Miller even uses some of the names of characters in Ibsen's *The Wild Duck*.) "I wanted the audience never to think that this was written by anybody, to appear as a fact, almost a fact of nature." It would be a play "about which nobody could say to me, as they had with all the other plays, 'What does this mean?' I spent two years writing that play just to see if I could do it that way. Because I was working in a realistic theatre which didn't know anything else."

Six drafts and about seven hundred pages later, on January 29, 1947, *All My Sons* opened on Broadway, under the direction of Elia Kazan. By then, with the Depression over, the war won, and FDR dead, the American clock was being reset. Between 1945 and 1955, American per-capita income nearly tripled, in the greatest growth of wealth in the history of Western civilization. For the first time in fifteen years, Americans were free to live out the intoxicating guarantee of the Declaration of Independence: the *pursuit* of happiness. The collective mission of wartime—the destiny of *we*—gave way to virulent peacetime self-interest, the destiny of *me*. "Everything was up for grabs," Miller said, of the postwar mutation of the American character. "They were all for Number One. The death of Roosevelt was a major blow to the psyche of the country. The father was dead. It meant that the axis of concentration turned violently and very quickly away from the society to the self. It was a difference in the idea of the individual."

Between the gestation and the Broadway run of *All My Sons*, the world had changed. The United States, its hegemony reinforced by the A-bomb, might have emerged from the war as the dominant power, but the return to normalcy brought with it fears of dark outlying forces ranged against it. The Soviet Union, an ally only eighteen months before, was now an enemy and in control of Europe's Eastern bloc. After the Japanese surrender in 1945, Mao Zedong's Red Army had begun its takeover of mainland China, in a civil war that culminated in 1949 with the establishment of the People's Republic of China. Most significant, Russia had developed its own atomic bomb. America had won the war, but for many of its citizens it had lost the peace: "wrong allies, wrong enemies, wrong outcome," the historian David Caute noted. The groundswell of panic registered at the ballot box. In 1946, for the first time in thirty-one years, Republicans gained control of Congress and could now tap into the growing climate of fear to forge a new revisionist narrative. The period to which the play speaks—1946 to 1947—saw the creation of the CIA, the House Committee on Un-American Activities (HUAC), the Attorney General's List of Subversive Organizations, and the Federal Employee Loyalty Program. (Between 1947 and 1953, 4,765,705 federal employees had to fill out forms which in some cases initiated loyalty investigations.) "The nation was ready for witch hunts," David Halberstam wrote of the paranoia that accompanied the postwar boom.

When the curtain came up on Joe and Kate Keller's backyard, where a storm-toppled apple tree intruded on the otherwise tranquil "secluded atmosphere," it came up as well on a simulacrum of the radically transformed American moment, which was, according to Miller, "unhinged by fear": "The whole social dream of fraternity and justice was cancelled out. As always, forward motion in America meant the killing of the past." "The Big Conflict is between the forces of Honor, of Responsibility to your neighbor, of equality and democracy, of Christlikeness, of One-World-ism. Versus this, the Capitalist System, the competitive system, the jungle where one man exists only by the death (yes, sooner or later the death) of his neighbor," Kazan wrote about *All My Sons* in his director's notebook. "One thing is basic," he added. "The people are all good people, but they are in difficulty with this particular society, U.S.A. 1946."

"During the war I felt that the idea of social responsibility was at least a real factor in the mass public mind, that it was possible to deal with such an ethical concept on the stage without it appearing esoteric," Miller wrote. "But the play opened in peacetime when we were once again free to destroy each other without any social consequences, and thus the theme is again new, and even somewhat strange to some people." The etymological root of the word *individualism* is the Latin for "separate." To dramatize division, *All My Sons* engineered a collision of fierce competing notions of self and showed the fault lines that these different notions create in both the society and the psyche.

"Dramatic characters, and the drama itself can never hope to attain a maximum degree of consciousness unless they contain a viable unveiling of the contrasts between past and present, and an awareness of the process by which the present has become what it is," Miller said. The emotional impasto of *All My Sons* contains pigments from Miller's own past. In his first draft, Joe and Kate Keller were called "Pop" and "Mom." (Even the surname "Keller" echoes "Miller.") The uneducated Joe Keller—who has made his fortune during the war manufacturing airplane parts and whose loving son Chris is now his business partner—is cut from the outline of Isidore Miller, who went into business with his elder son, Kermit, a veteran and an idealist. Joe shares with Isidore a gregarious charisma; he is "a man among men," according to the stage directions. He also shares, as Kazan wrote, a "smothered guilt for which he is trying to gain forgiveness." Kazan added, "This also drives his anxiety to be liked, to be a host, to be the life of the block." Like Isidore, Joe exudes "a wonder in many commonly known things," according to Miller's stage directions. He is "a man whose judgments must be dredged out of experience and a peasant-like common sense." When Chris stalks off in a moment of principled outrage toward the end of the play, Joe's outburst echoes the cutthroat capitalism in which Isidore was marinated: "I should've put him out when he was ten like I was put out, and make him earn his keep. Then he'd know how a buck is made in this world." Even the game that Joe plays with a local youngster, Bert—he enlists him as a "policeman" and swears "on my honor" that there's a jail in his basement—replicates Miller's memory of his father's bonhomie, which he dispensed from his Brooklyn porch to neighborhood kids: "In a sudden fit of ennui, a few weeks ago, he said to a little boy passing by, 'I buy all kinds of cats' or a child will stop a stranger to ask what his business might be because my father . . . has persuaded the five-year-olds to 'stand guard and watch the block.'"

Kate Keller, likewise, exhibits some of Gussie's defining qualities: her superstitiousness, her devotion to her family and to controlling it, her repressed shame and disdain of her husband. "Don't underestimate either her cunning, her strength or her ferocity," Kazan noted of Kate, adding, "Kate and Joe are two tough hombres, no joke." But in his psychological assessment Kazan missed an essential aspect of Kate's behavior, one she shared with Gussie: her capacity for denial. "Gussie never admitted anything unpleasant," Kermit's son, Ross Miller, wrote. "There was a lot of social lying."

The masquerade of family loyalty is crucial to the impact of *All My Sons*. "Like other plays being written then, it concerned guilt, but not that of a person being falsely accused," Kazan said. "The guilt in Art's play was real. By not setting up an accusation that was to be disproved in three acts, the play dramatized a true moral confrontation. . . . The guilt uncovered was that of the hero's father, whom he loved." As it happened, while Miller was working on the play, the strong emotional attachment that he and Kermit had to their parents was also rocked by the exposure of a family secret. "If you think of Gussie as a gifted cover-up artist who is hiding a domestic crime, *All My Sons* is the District Attorney's closing argument," Ross Miller noted, adding, "I don't think that Arthur ever really came to terms with the effect of his mother's fibbing and her shame."

In 1946 Kermit returned to civilian life, only to learn that Isidore and Gussie had been in better financial shape than they had claimed after the Crash, when, according to Ross, Gussie "recruited my father to take over Izzy's role, effectively ruining his life." Ross later added, "Both brothers were lied to about the family's financial situation. Isidore and Gussie certainly had enough money to free my father from the mule work he was doing." Kermit, a man of almost pathological honesty, gave up his chances of higher education and his dreams of being a writer to help out. "Carrying two heavy sample bags all over Manhattan (indentured to his broken father and loving his martyred mother) prepared my father somehow to order men into battle," Ross said. Kermit joined the army and sent his combat pay home. Arthur also contributed to the parental coffers. Their parents' bad faith was unmooring. Once the truth was out, Kermit and Arthur stopped support immediately. "The fact that my father let me know about the betrayal indicates how serious an issue this was," Ross said, adding, "My father and his siblings avoided confrontation. He could accept anything but betrayal."

Within the Miller family, the betrayal played out less sensationally than in the Keller household; nonetheless, it was ruinous. "I believe that my father found it impossible, in the beginning of the hard times, to think that his parents would take advantage of him," Ross said. "If he had had this insight at the time he might have been a little kinder to himself, more forgiving of his own shortcomings." In 1946, Kermit underwent a series of ECT (electroconvulsive therapy) treatments for depression; he lived out his life as a carpet salesman. "My father's nobility of character drove Arthur crazy. How can you oppose a 'prince of a man,' who gives up his own ambitions to save others?" Ross said. Kermit repressed his anger. Arthur used his to fuel the fierce, reimagined version of events in his play. "I've been a good son too long, a good sucker. I'm through with it," Chris says at one point.

Chris "wants the father to help him fight the mother. The mother has a hold on the father. She knows his guilt. And in a way his guilt created her obsession," Kazan wrote in his notebooks, setting out the spine of the play. Joe, who has sold faulty airplane parts, is guilty not only of defrauding the government but of framing his neighbor and partner in order to save himself, his business, and his family. "You wanted money, so I made money," Joe tells Kate, blaming his ruthlessness on her materialism. The cost of Joe's actions is the lives of twenty-one airmen, plus that of his older son, Larry, who has been missing in action for two years and turns out, in the play's penultimate beats, to have killed himself out of shame. "If I had him there now I could kill him," Larry wrote in his suicide letter, which Chris reads out loud to his parents—a sort of broadcast from the grave. This awful revelation collapses the fortress of lies that Joe has built up to defend against his guilt. He pays for his shame with his life. "I'm not holding the father himself solely responsible," Miller said. "He's at the mercy of an ethic, of a group of forces which he obeys. His fault is that he didn't say no."

At first sight, the spacious green world of the Keller garden, with the shipshape seven-room two-story house in the background, is a scene of well-heeled normality. ("Fifteen thousand in the early days when it was built in the early twenties," Miller's stage directions are careful to point out.) The jovial opening conversations of the play may seem inconsequential, but the banter deftly establishes the ozone of new postwar affluence. "I got money again," announces Joe Keller, who reads the newspaper want ads "to see what people want" and to marvel at "all the kind of business goin' on." Doc Bayliss, Joe's neighbor, underscores the renewed capitalist swing of things, insisting that he'd never let his son follow in his own humanitarian footsteps. "Over my dead body he'll be a doctor," he tells Keller, adding, "I would love to help humanity on a Warner Brothers salary." "That's good, Jim," Keller, a big fan of profit, replies. At first, Chris, his son and new business partner, seems to be a chip off his father's capitalist block. With his heart fit to bursting with romantic idealism in act 1, Chris declares to the girl he intends to marry, "Oh, Annie, Annie . . . I'm going to make a fortune for you!"

The characters' badinage is dotted with references to the new material excitements in their lives: the toaster, the washing machine, the malt-mixer, golf, a dress "that costs three weeks' salary," the maid, even the baby boom. "It's so strange—Ann's not even married. And I've got three babies," the twenty-seven-year-old Lydia Lubey says, speaking of Ann Deaver, Larry's former fiancée, who is also the daughter of the partner, Steve, Joe framed for his crimes and sent to prison. Ann has returned to her old neighborhood after three years, half-expecting a marriage proposal from Chris—a prospect that is the drama's inciting incident.

If Ann marries Chris, Kate will be forced to give up the fantasy that Larry is still alive. Kate cannot, and will not, do this. "You're pronouncing him dead," Joe tells Chris. "Now, what's gonna happen to Mother. Do you know? I don't." Everyone is held hostage by Kate's virulent attachment to her belief. "Nobody comes back after three years. It's insane," Chris says to his father. But Joe, who is "frightened at the thought" of facing Kate with the truth, goes along with Kate's version of events, and thus fails a crucial parental obligation: he cannot protect Chris from his mother's madness. "You can't say that to her," Joe says. "You can talk yourself blue in the face, but there's no body and there's no grave, so where are you?" Kate acts benign, but beneath her hospitable veneer she is a kind of emotional terrorist. She uses the power of her injury—her severe headaches, her anxiety dreams, her grievous loss—to enforce a repudiation of reality. "Believe with me, Joe. I can't stand alone," she says at one point. Kate's morbid insistence makes a myth of Larry's future return and her loyalty to him. It also, crucially, makes a myth of her innocence.

Ann, by contrast, is sensationally disloyal to her imprisoned father. Believing him to be a criminal—"he murdered twenty-one pilots"—she has refused any contact, even through letters, since his incarceration. In shame, she has moved away from the neighborhood. As Ann explains to Kate, "He knowingly shipped out parts what would crash an airplane. And how do you know Larry wasn't one of them?" Kate immediately shuts her down. "Annie, I want to ask you never to say that again," she says.

ANN: You surprise me. I thought you'd be mad at him.
MOTHER: What your father did had nothing to do with Larry. Nothing.
ANN: But we can't know that.
MOTHER, *striving for control:* As long as you're here!
ANN, *perplexed:* But, Kate—
MOTHER: Put that out of your head!

In this thin-skinned exchange, the seed of Kate's complicity is neatly planted. She will not tolerate even the mildest offhand remark that links Larry's disappearance to faulty airplane parts. On her entrance—exuding an "overwhelming capacity for love," according to the stage directions—Kate is a spectacle of cosseting maternal care: for her missing son, for her neighbors, for the family. But what she shows to the external world is the opposite of what she does unconsciously to the internal one. Beneath her carapace of congeniality, she aggressively attacks the mental space of all around her. Her exhortation for thoughtlessness is almost biblical in its vehemence. "The trouble with you kids is you *think* too much," she says. Kate wants to simplify consciousness. With the force of her agitation and her superstition—"Don't be so intelligent. Some superstitions are very nice!" she says—Kate drives away unacceptable ideas, disallowing them even in idle conversation.

Her insistence on mindlessness—her enforced lack of curiosity, of clarity, of logic, and of receptiveness to others—is part of the orchestrated climate of denial in the Keller family's daily life, which the plot gradually exposes. "Dad and I are stupid people," she says later in the play; in fact, they, and those around them, make themselves stupid. The unquestioning Chris, for instance, no longer reads books, just book reviews. "I like to keep abreast of my ignorance," he says. Joe, too, wills himself to vacancy. "You have such a talent for ignoring things," Chris tells his father, who answers gnomically, "I ignore what I gotta ignore." One of the things Joe has to ignore is his wife's blind faith in Larry's return. "What do you want me to do?" Joe says, exasperated at Kate's morbid grief. She replies, "I want you to act like he's coming back. . . . Because if he's not coming back, then I'm going to kill myself." Kate's tyrannical behavior cows everyone around her and works as a kind of perverse loyalty oath—her family and her neighbors must swear allegiance to her view of things. "Mum's the word" is the tagline not just for the game between Joe and Bert but for the whole Keller clan. "Nobody in this house dast take her faith away," she says to Joe and Chris about Ann's loyalty to her missing fiancé, Larry. Life with Kate is a masquerade in which the mind disguises its own content, including its aggression.

In act 1, this discombobulation is epitomized in Joe's vivacious account for Chris and Ann's benefit of how, on returning home after being cleared of war-profiteering, he faced down the neighborhood's odium:

Picture it now; none of them believed I was innocent. The story was, I pulled a fast one getting myself exonerated. So I get out of my car, and I walk down the street. But very slow. And with a smile. The beast! I was the beast; the guy who sold cracked cylinder heads to the Army Air Force; the guy who made twenty-one P40s crash in Australia. Kid, walkin' down the street that day I was guilty as hell. Except I wasn't, and there was a court paper in my pocket to prove I wasn't, and I walked . . . past . . . the porches. Result? Fourteen months later I had one of the best shops in the state again, a respected man again: bigger than ever.

In Chris's idealizing eyes, his father is "Joe McGuts." Joe's practiced bravado works its magic not only on the youngsters ("Isn't Dad a great guy," Chris says to Ann, who seems to agree) but on Joe himself. Emboldened by their enthusiasm, Joe paints himself as not just a man of courage but a man of righteousness. He is Mr. Magnanimity. "Annie, I never believed in crucifying people," he says, suggesting that her father, after his release, should move "back to the block," then, later, that he would re-employ him. "He ain't my sweetheart, but you gotta forgive," Joe says.

What knocks Joe off his cloud is Ann's brother, George, a lawyer in a lather, who needs to be going almost as soon as he arrives, in act 2, by jet from New York. He is Miller's awkward deus ex machina, who puts the story right by exposing the Kellers' wrongs. George, who has just visited his father in prison for the first time, twists the play, and his sister, away from the idealized portrait of the Keller nuclear family, or the "Holy Family," as one neighbor bitches. George confronts the Kellers with their shame ("Your dad took everything we have") and with their process of denial ("You're a liar to yourself"). Under the pressure of George's interrogation, Joe accidentally admits that he wasn't sick on the day the faulty parts were shipped, thus implicating himself. The Kellers try desperately to spackle over the holes in Joe's story.

> GEORGE: She said you'd never been sick.
> MOTHER: I said he was sick, George.
> GEORGE, *going to Ann:* Ann, didn't you hear her say—
> MOTHER: Do you remember every time you were sick?
> GEORGE: I'd remember pneumonia.

By degrees, the masks of innocence drop away. When Chris finally announces his plan to marry Ann, Kate's practiced benevolence turns brutish; in the process her contempt for Joe is forced out into the open.

MOTHER: She's Larry's girl.

CHRIS: And I'm his brother and he's dead, and I'm marrying his girl.

MOTHER: Never, never in this world!

KELLER: You lost your mind?

MOTHER: You have nothing to say!

KELLER, *cruelly:* I got plenty to say. Three and a half years you been talking like a maniac—

Mother smashes him across the face.

MOTHER: Nothing. You have nothing to say. Now I say. He's coming back, and everybody has got to wait. . . . I'll never let him go and you'll never let him go!

CHRIS: I've let him go. I've let him go a long—

MOTHER, *with no less force but turning from him:* Then let your father go. Your brother's alive, darling, because if he's dead, your father killed him.

Kate, it becomes clear, has always known the truth about the faulty parts; her fanatical belief in her son's return preserves her hope not just for Larry's survival but for the survival of the family unit itself. To lose faith, as we will see, is to lose everything— son, husband, family, business, position. What Kate cannot admit, but Miller exposes, is that in her silence she is also culpable, an accessory to the crime. She wanted wealth; for her and for Joe self-interest trumped morality. Like Miller's mother, who married for money only to lose everything, Kate is done in by her own die-hard pragmatism. When Doc Bayliss observes, "Money-money-money-money. You say it long enough it doesn't mean anything," Kate smiles and "makes a silent laugh." "Oh, how I'd like to be around when that happens!" she says. At the finale, Chris rounds on her. "I'm like everybody else now. I'm practical. You made me practical," he says. Kate replies, "But what else can you be." Even in the play's last beats, when Larry's death is revealed to have been a suicide, Kate doesn't get it.

"Larry didn't kill himself to make you and Dad sorry," Chris says. "What more can we be!" Kate says. "You can be better!" Chris replies.

The unmooring moment brings to a head the struggle between social responsibility and self-interest. "Chris, I did it for you, it was a chance and I took it for you," Joe, for whom family is everything, tells his son. "I'm sixty-one years old, when would I have a chance to make something for you." Chris, "with burning fury," replies just before the curtain falls on act 2, "What the hell do you mean, you did it for me? Don't you have a country? Don't you live in the world?" No is Miller's answer: the Kellers don't have a country; they live in the kingdom of the self. Their spectacular selfishness is intended to dramatize the sin of separation that is engineered by capitalism. "This is the land of the great big dogs, you don't love a man here, you eat him!" says Chris, for whom the business goal of "making a killing" has suddenly taken on a punishing new meaning. He goes on, "This is a zoo, a zoo!"

The Kellers are not bad people, but they do bad things. They are literally and figuratively lost in their story. By extension, they are also lost in the middle-class American Dream— a narrative of abundance fanatically embraced in order to disavow the sins done in its name. Their ruthlessness embodies the spiritual atrophy of the American sweepstakes: as Thomas Merton wrote, "I have what you have not. I am what you are not. I have taken what you have failed to take and I have seized what you could never get. Therefore, you suffer and I am happy; you are despised, and I am praised, you die and I live; you are nothing and I am something, and I am all the more something because you are nothing."

Together, in their masquerades, the Kellers have defrauded both the government and their community, which they have robbed of trust. Their entire existence is exposed as counterfeit. When Chris expresses his outrage, Joe says, "What should

I do? Jail? You want me to go to jail?" He goes on, "Who worked for nothin' in that war. . . . It's dollars and cents, nickels and dimes. . . . What's clean? Half the Goddamn country is gotta go if I go." In this pivotal moment, Chris assumes the father's moral authority. Chris *does* want his father to go to jail; in fact, he insists on it. "This is how he died, now tell me where you belong," he says, flourishing Larry's suicide note. Chris, as Kazan wrote in boldface in his notebook, is "forced to be a hero." Although Kate remains blind to the moral implications of their actions—"The war is over," she says—Joe finally sees the light at the end of his tunnel, even though it's an oncoming train. Trying to comprehend Larry's suicide and the part he played in the deaths of the other airmen, Joe says, "I guess to him they were all my sons. And I guess they were. I guess they were." He goes into the house and shoots himself.

Seconds before the gunshot rings out, Chris tells Kate, "There's a universe of people out there and you're responsible to it." Joe's suicide acknowledges that responsibility. But at the end of the tale as in the beginning, Kate is the voice of the status quo ante. She "stands alone, transfixed," in the garden. Her husband has just taken his life, minutes after learning that their older son took his; her younger son is about to decamp to another city; and her own mendacity is exposed for all to see. Nonetheless, she meets this spectacle of devastation with denial and refuses to acknowledge either the violence around her or her part in it. "Don't take it on yourself," she tells Chris, embracing him in the play's last line. "Forget now. Live." Ironically, the curtain comes down on the sound of Kate hushing her child—a lullaby of self-interest, sung to the music of thoughtlessness.

Miller began *All My Sons* as his "final shot," he said, at being a playwright. "Every minute of it was going to work," he determined. "I wasn't going to rely on somebody else to make

it work." Miller was pulling to the theatrical equivalent of an inside straight. After his two-year slog, the first person to whom he
showed the finished play—then titled "The Sign of the Archer"—
was his theatrical agent, Leland Hayward, whose agency represented such talent as Fred Astaire, Ernest Hemingway, Katha-
rine Hepburn, Judy Garland, and Henry Fonda. Miller never
heard back from him. Confident about the play and furious at
the silence, he went to the agency, unbidden, to confront Hayward: "I said, 'I want my script back and all my other scripts.
I'm leaving this office.' Well, they went into a faint. He said,
'You can't be serious.' I said, 'I am serious. I've got to get on
with this thing.' He said, 'Give us twenty-four hours.'"

That meeting changed Miller's luck. Because of it, he acquired a new young representative, Kay Brown, who in the
mid-thirties had brought *Gone with the Wind* to the attention of
David O. Selznick and who now brought Miller's play to the attention of both the Broadway old guard—the Theatre Guild—
and a new producing company, "a fellow named Kazan who
was in partnership with a guy named Clurman." Both groups
wanted the play. Because he felt a personal and intellectual kin-
ship, Miller went with the upstarts. "Harold Clurman was, as
far I was concerned, God Almighty," he said. "He was the brain
of the Group Theater." Clurman, to whom the script had originally been sent, assumed that Miller wanted him to direct, but
his partner, Elia Kazan, was equally impressed. The play "had
a strength not found in the work of any dramatist of this time
except Lillian Hellman, but Art's play was warm hearted instead of hateful," he wrote. Miller was forced to choose between
them.

"Art admired Harold but felt closer to me," Kazan said.
Strategic and psychologically astute, Kazan helped his cause by
having Miller visit the set of *Boomerang*, a film noir he was directing, to watch him work. Miller was taken with the spirit on
the set and with the actors. Kazan even cast him as a suspect in

a line-up scene. The experience made a powerful impression. When it came time to cast the play, three of the *Boomerang* actors—Karl Malden, Ed Begley, and Arthur Kennedy—were in it. "I was really as green as I could be. I gave the play to a man I didn't know then and had heard only a little about and who himself had only begun to make his name," Miller said. But he soon concluded that Kazan was "quite marvelous." (He dedicated *All My Sons* to him.)

For Kazan, the play was a crucial stepping stone in his career. (Tennessee Williams, who saw *All My Sons* twice and thought it topped "any direction I've seen on Broadway," then offered Kazan *A Streetcar Named Desire*.) For Clurman, who had made his name in the thirties directing Clifford Odets, with whom he'd fallen out, "it was not an unimportant loss," according to Kazan. In the original production, Kazan focused on Chris, and his relationship with his father, as what he termed "the spine" of the play, an approach that he later realized was a mistake. "His spine doesn't inspire any stage action. It is a description and an analysis. A 'spine' should be a motor," he wrote. In fact, Kate is the play's real motor. "The war-profiteering aspect of *All My Sons* represents the play's material, not its meaning," Clurman insisted. "The mother, whose role in the explicit plot of the play is incidental, is the center of the play's meaning. She embodies the status quo or norm of our present day ethic and behavior patterns." Kazan's tack, which emphasized the moral melodrama of the script, made the play a hit, but it was the psychological subtext, which that first production skirted, that made the play enduring.

All My Sons opened to mixed reviews. "Two More Duds" was the headline of the *Herald-Tribune* review, whose critic conceded that Miller "had a feeling for the theatre," but that the subject matter was "at best confused." "Not Very Convincing" headed the *Daily Mirror*—a sour note that was echoed by the *Daily News* headline: "A Lot Goes On but Little Happens." "I experienced a curious lack of interest," the *News* critic, John Chapman, wrote, adding, "Long before they got through talking and Mr. Begley had shot himself I was ready to go home." But the most judicious and influential of New York's daily critics, Brooks Atkinson of the *New York Times*, gave both the play and its author the imprimatur of excellence. "The theater has acquired a genuine new talent," his review began. It ended with this: "In a performance with varying tone, rising pitch and dramatic design, they are acting an original play of superior quality by a playwright who knows his craft and has unusual understanding of the tangled loyalties of human beings." Atkinson's review ensured Miller a hit. "Without him, I'm not sure what would have happened," Miller said. Nonetheless, the sense of public approval was palpable. "I sensed a warmth in the world that was not there before."

"Seeing the audience held motionless in their seats, being hailed onto the stage after the show by an unheard-of demonstration, I remember the long years and their beginning—in your office," Miller wrote to Kenneth Rowe. He went on, "This whole thing is a very strange experience. The idea of sitting at home and suddenly realizing that a thousand people are, at that very moment, listening to all my lines. . . . Quite weird. . . . My child has left home, thank God . . . after all the idiots who have lived on in my desk drawers."

Miller was now suddenly earning two thousand dollars a week on Broadway and feeling morally disgusted, "that I was making money without working." His sudden renown—later that year he won the first Tony Award for Best Playwright and beat out Eugene O'Neill and *The Iceman Cometh* to win the New York Drama Critics' Circle's Best Play Award—only fueled his guilt. "Such guilt is a protective device to conceal one's happiness at surpassing others, especially those one loves, like a brother, father or friend," he said. To mollify his ambivalent feelings, he took a sixteen-dollar-a-week job at a box factory in

Queens, putting beer-box dividers into wooden crates. It was, he said, "a moral act of solidarity with all those who had failed in life." It was also a valedictory gesture: good-bye to anonymity and hello to success. He now had a name, an income, a pedigree, and an audience. "I didn't need to write another well-made play to keep from starving," he said. After a week of working shoulder to shoulder with the salt of the earth—"these people were totally depressed"—Miller quit his factory job and embraced his new identity: Broadway playwright.

6

All the Wild Animals

"I still feel kind of temporary about myself," Willy
Loman says to his brother Ben. I smiled when I wrote
those lines in the Spring of 1948, when it had not yet
occurred to me that it summed up my own condition
then and throughout my life.

—Arthur Miller, *Timebends*

I can't bear to be a separate person. Separateness from
our fellow men is a human non-sequitur.

—Arthur Miller, *After the Fall*

"GET THE HELL OUT OF TOWN and start on your play,"
Kazan told Miller in the wake of *All My Sons'* acclaim. The new
play Kazan was referring to was *Death of a Salesman*, a phenomenon that changed both their lives. *Death of a Salesman* opened
on February 10, 1949, and its impact was seismic. "By common
consent this is one of the best dramas in the whole range of

American drama," Brooks Atkinson raved in the *New York Times*. Tennessee Williams wrote to his agent, Audrey Wood, "I received five complete sets of Arthur Miller notices, more than I ever received for any play of my own. Everybody seemed most anxious that I should know how thoroughly great was his triumph." He added, "I hope that I was pleased over it."

Miller's sensational success owed a lot to Williams's theatrical pathfinding. According to Miller, the lambent, lyrical voice of Williams's *The Glass Menagerie* (1945) had not only "planted the flag of beauty on the commercial theatre"; it had "granted a license to speak at full throat"—a license that inspired Miller. As it happened, *All My Sons* had introduced Williams to the muscular direction of Elia Kazan, to whose rising star Williams quickly hitched his wagon, sending him *A Streetcar Named Desire* (1947). ("You have the dynamism my work needs," Williams told Kazan.) Miller attended the pre-Broadway tryout of *Streetcar* in New Haven. "After the performance he appeared to be full of wonder at the theatre's expressive possibilities," Kazan recalled. "He told me he was amazed how simply and successfully the non-realistic elements of the play—'*Flores! Flores para los muertos!*'—blended with the realistic ones."

"*All My Sons* had hardly started its run when I became dissatisfied with it," Miller said. He found the play's thematically organized structure "too exclusive." "It didn't leave me time for the offhand expression of feeling." To Miller, *All My Sons* was "a kind of sonata. In a sonata you don't fool around. You have certain laws of motion you follow. I had always wanted to break up those laws of motion, and I felt a license to do it now." Soon after *All My Sons* opened, Miller began writing *Death of a Salesman*, "which was organized not around the theme so much as it was around a dream," he explained. (In his director's notebook for the play, Kazan wrote, "It must have the vividness of an OPPRESSIVE NIGHTMARE.") In college, Miller had started a play with the same theme as *Salesman* but had given it up because, he said, "I couldn't find a way to include the dream, the texture of Willy's mind." It is no coincidence that Miller's working title for his prospective new play was "The Inside of His Head." Where Williams's work was an exploration of the imperialism of the self, Miller's was about society's effect on shaping the self. "A person comes to a point where he has to say, 'What do I do now? What am I doing this for? Why and what is making me do it? Am I doing this for myself?' In other words, to conceive of himself and, once he starts to do that, he gets into an area where he becomes a social individual. I mean, the machine, the engine, is no longer purely personal. You're joining with mankind in some generalization about yourself. And we don't do that on stage. At least, we haven't."

When it came to postwar society's obsession with self-realization—that "long delayed but always expected something that we live for"—Williams's plays defined the manic side and Miller's the depressive. Willy Loman, the eponymous salesman, is both a messenger and a victim of competitive capitalism. His wild mood swings—from exhilaration to exhaustion, from optimism to suicide—were the first sighting on the American stage of the fracturing self, a self oppressed by its own machinations. As embodied in the set by designer Jo Mielziner, a sort of spatial split-screen of notional rooms, Willy's dissociation was a correlative for the emerging division in the national frame of mind—a split between the ideal and the paranoid, which increasingly sought refuge in the comforts of materialism and conspiracy theories. The Red Scare, the proliferating suburbs, and television were just a few of many new social realities that signaled a psychological retreat from reality. "Deferral and the refusal to think about a phenomenon are forms of dissociation," the psychoanalyst Christopher Bollas writes, adding, "Dissociation is itself a form of shock."

Onstage, however, Willy's sociological relevance was overshadowed by the profound wellspring of loss he tapped into.

"There was too much crying going on in the audience for my comfort," Miller recalled. "The stringent quality of the play was its social theme. It was being drowned in tears of pity for Willy. When you're crying, you can't see straight." Miller had no interest in theater that wrapped itself exclusively in what he called "the shroud of introspection." He saw himself as working in the illumination business, throwing "light on the condition of man as a social animal. That's where our fate is, and that's where the great plays are written."

The success of *Death of a Salesman* thrust Miller into a new realm. "I'd spent my life on the outside and now I was on the inside, where all the dangers and the wild animals live," he said. Almost instantly, to the world and to himself, "Art Miller" became "Arthur Miller," tugged by the unmooring gravitational pull of his new fame. "Medals! Ribbons! Christ sake, I'll put them all on some day and look like a Russian ice skater," he wrote to Kazan only two months after the play's debut. "I don't know what the hell is wrong with me. I keep refusing to do things and go places, and still I haven't eaten at home but twice a week for a month." He was dining with Thomas Mann, opining about tragedy and the common man on the arts pages of the *New York Times*, partying with the cast and the New York critics, and worrying about the Pulitzer (he won it), confounded to find his name in gossip columns. He was giddy at the news that *Salesman* would be the first play ever chosen as a selection by the Book of the Month Club and that Simon and Schuster was rushing a quarter of a million paperback copies into print—this, along with the movie sale to Columbia Pictures, brought his estimated earnings on the play to an astonishing two million dollars. "I tell ya, kid, Art pays," he wrote to Kazan.

Miller and Kazan were bound together in the enterprise of triumph. Each saw the other as a building block to creative fulfillment. ("The professional standing of a director depends on the plays he's able to attract," said Kazan, who with *A Streetcar Named Desire* and *Salesman* to his credit was midwife to the most defining plays and playwrights of America's postwar theater. "Kazan / Kazan / the miracle man / Call him / As soon as you can" became the Broadway mantra.) Kazan had already set his sights on a new artistic challenge. Just before starting rehearsals on *Salesman*, he had finalized a deal with 20th Century–Fox to direct six original pictures over ten years. His hope, he said, "was that I might have something unique and personal to do in films. If I could bring fine writers like Miller into the movies . . . I might do work no one else in this country had yet done." Miller was interested in the movies, too; after he told Kazan about his experience working in the Brooklyn Navy Yard, they planned a film about the waterfront.

The Miller-Kazan partnership had been sweet from the start. "I immediately felt close to Art," Kazan said of the playwright, who became "like a member of my family. I saw him almost daily and usually at my home." (Even to Kazan's smart, starchy, outspoken wife, Molly, who served as in-house dramaturg to her husband, Miller was "Artie.") He and Kazan shared a deep mutual understanding. "We were soon exchanging every intimacy," Kazan said. Both were men of ferocious energy and unabashed ambition. Both were children of the Depression. Both were leftists who had flirted with communism. Both had struggled with problematic salesmen fathers who were bewildered by the arts and wanted their sons to work in business. Both were the undisputed darlings of their mothers, who had encouraged their creativity. And, perhaps crucially, both had marriages that were, in Kazan's words, "unsteady." Kazan was an unrepentant womanizer who saw promiscuity as a catalyst for creativity; Miller was a puritan who struggled under the moral weight of his marital vows. "During the production of *All My Sons*, I thought him rigid with inhibition," Kazan wrote. "When he embraced a young woman in friendship—not in any way a 'come on'—he did it turned sideways, with the side of his body against the front of hers, usually he'd turn in another direction, not at her."

Salesman was life changing for both men. "We all puffed up," Kazan said. "We became convinced of our ability to do anything we chose to do." This sense of potency and its inevitable "touch of arrogance" was especially noticeable in Miller, who had a new voracity for work and for life. He was suddenly the most observed of all observers. His eyes, according to Kazan, "acquired a new flash"; his carriage took on "a hint of something swashbuckling." He affected a pipe, and was accorded the role of public intellectual, which suited his newfound grandiosity. The success also gave oxygen to his dramatic imagination. "There come moments—quite suddenly—when without knowing at all what I am going to write, I see a whole vision of the main character, and feel a power over the entire universe, as though it were waiting for me to set forth this man," he wrote to Kazan. "He was at his best during this time, still searching, still unsure of himself, not yet Lincolnesque," Kazan said. But to others who competed for Miller's literary limelight, like his Brooklyn neighbor Norman Mailer, Miller's loftiness made him "sufficiently pontifical to be the first Jewish Pope, who puffed upon his pipe as if it were the bowl of the Beyond and regaled sophisticated New York dinner parties with tedious anecdotes of his gardening and his well-digging[;] he was a Hamsun and Rolvaag of the soil, a great man!—one had to listen."

Miller had grasped fame's live wire—"a new power, a power to make real everything one is capable of imagining"—and as painful as it would prove to be, he couldn't let go. The acclaim, the awards, the attention, the opportunities coming his way tipped the already precarious balance of power in his marriage. As he and Mary made their way home at 3 a.m., after *Salesman*'s opening night, something else rode with them: "I sensed in our silence some discomfort in my wife and friend over these struggling years. It never occurred to me that she might have felt anxious at being swamped by the rush of my new fame, in need of reassurance. I had always thought her clearer and more resolved than I. Some happiness was not with us that I wanted now, I had no idea what it might be, only knew the absence of it, its lack—so soon. In fact, the aphrodisiac of celebrity, still nameless, came and sat between us in the car."

The power of Miller's growing renown was matched in private by the power of Mary's growing recrimination, a distrust that had begun years earlier when Miller naively confessed his adulterous thoughts for a war widow he'd met on a road trip as a way of showing Mary how much he loved her. That moment was, he wrote in a fictionalized version in his unfinished novel, "The Best Comedians," "the last day of her innocence . . . the final moment after which she would never again be young, or a believer, or really his wife." Miller now had a public and a platform. Power made him sexy. He was attractive to the world, and more attractive to himself. He no longer needed Mary as a sounding board or as a bulwark. In "The Best Comedians," he portrayed the shifting sands of their relationship. In one scene, Miller describes the writer coming out of his room with a sheaf of papers, sitting his wife down in a chair, and reading the day's writing to her: "He would look up and wait for her word. 'I like it,' she would say, feeling both the wave of his power pleasurably engulfing her, and slowly over the years a realization that she was only his audience, that he was really talking to himself with her." The wife, in the novel, decides that she will no longer "pamper" her husband:

> She would listen to anything he had to say but she would be
> a disservice to him if she ever again let him think he could
> go on ignoring her or paying even less than full respect and
> attention to her, and still have her worshipping him as he
> demanded. Her job, she saw, and she saw it with pride and

some sense of having a thankless task which her own fidelity had laid upon her—her job was to lead him as well as she could to his own maturity. . . . Some extremely deep and intelligent people regarded him as a genius, and not merely as a writer, but as a person. He did have a weird kind of integrity in a lot of things.

The avalanche of post-*Salesman* acclaim confirmed Miller's belief, often repeated in letters, that "a hand had been laid on him." (Even his mother referred to him as "God's chosen.") Miller saw himself as a moral man, but fame's centripetal force drew him into turbulent emotional water, buffeted by the conflicting challenges of being good and being great. Success opened his eyes and awoke his appetites. "It made Art reckless—albeit in a cautious way—with certain constraints on his personal life and curious about experience that lay outside the bounds of his behavior up to that time," Kazan said. Inevitably, Miller strayed "from the courtroom of his home," as Kazan put it. Mary blamed Kazan for what she saw as Miller's slide into moral turpitude. "Art is acquiring all of your bad habits and none of your good ones," she told the promiscuous Kazan, who was so startled by her indictment that he wrote it down. "At home all is well, unwell, well, by turns. I am wearing out the threshold of the doghouse," Miller wrote to Kazan in 1950, adding, "But she's right—and I'm right, too. It will all be for the best, however, if we both end with an increased feeling of power." Mary took courses at Vassar, "to reconstitute herself," as Kazan said. "Art admired her for this. In time—for a time—they reconciled," he added. Both aggrieved parties went into psychoanalysis, a process that for Miller opened up a Pandora's box of repressed feelings, which put him on edge and left him, according to Kazan, unable to write. "He was longing for something nameless, a condition I recognized in my own life," Kazan said. "What did he want? It wasn't complicated. Call it fun, a new experience, ease of mind and heart, relief from criticism, happiness. His life, he told me, seemed to be all conflict and tension, thwarted desires, stymied impulses, bewildering and unexpressed conflicts."

Miller's mood in 1949 was "a persistent dread that we were being cut from our past and entering darkness." To assuage his anxiety, he "put himself to work," writing a screenplay about corruption on the docks in the Red Hook section of Brooklyn— "Brooklyn's Sicily"—just ten blocks from where he lived. On one of his spirit-raising strolls around Brooklyn, he had noticed a large, chalk-scrawled graffito: "DOVE PETE PANTO"—"Where is Pete Panto?" Over the next few days, he saw the same words written on trucks, brick walls, the windows of empty stores. When Miller dropped into a local longshoremen's bar to ask the question "Who *is* Pete Panto?" he was stonewalled. One of the drinkers followed him out of the bar to confide that Panto was a young longshoreman who had tried to organize a rank-and-file uprising against the racketeers who ran the union and controlled the waterfront. He was now sleeping with the fish. The longshoremen's palpable fear of even speaking Panto's name, let alone mentioning his murder, seemed to Miller yet another symbol of the toxic, surreal American moment. Michael Ferrera was the name that Miller gave to his fictional renegade longshoreman, who, if he didn't resemble his creator physically, did fall in line with his righteous political mission: "A hand had been placed on him, making him the rebel, pressing him toward a collision with everything that is established and accepted." In his notebook, Miller sketched his character: he is "the strange, mysterious, dangerous thing—the genuinely moral man. He is one with all the others, has received no more than they, but feels it more. Why?"

The screenplay of "The Hook" did not answer that question; it merely stated it. "I'm gonna live like a man. I'm gonna fight for my rights. . . . I'm gonna be an example, so the men here should know there's a guy here he ain't ascared to open his mouth," Ferrera hectors his band of exploited workers, who are fighting to rid the union of corruption. The rambling 152-page screenplay made up in length for what it lacked in complexity. The longshoreman shake-outs and the racketeer shakedowns were novel subject matter, but the story had no traction. The dialogue and the characterization seemed rushed, undercooked. "I felt Art had done a half-ass job finishing the script, that it was not 'ready to go,' and would require considerably more work," Kazan said. "But I was determined to do it next and was convinced that if we could set up a production and if Art and I could work together for a few weeks, we'd have a good screenplay." In January 1951, trailing clouds of theatrical glory and with the studio percolating with excitement over Kazan's just completed film version of *Streetcar*, the pair arrived in Hollywood on the Super Chief, as cocky as Kings of Spades. They were intent on selling "The Hook" as a new kind of neo-realistic American film. But what was meant as an idealistic challenge to the notion of public corruption ended up turning Miller's own moral convictions upside down.

One day during their stay, Kazan took Miller to 20th Century–Fox, where *As Young as You Feel*, a comedy written by Paddy Chayefsky and directed by Kazan's former film cutter Harmon Jones, was being shot. Kazan wanted to reacquaint himself with an actress he'd met the year before with her agent, who had just died. "She hadn't even gone out with anyone since his death," Kazan, always with an eye for sexual adventure, said. "So I wondered if I shouldn't look her up." There, in the crepuscular gloom of the soundstage, Miller first laid eyes on Marilyn Monroe. She was being filmed from behind "to set off the swiveling of her hips, a motion fluid enough to seem comic," Miller remembered.

When Monroe finished the scene, she came over to Kazan and embraced him. From where he stood in the shadows behind Kazan, Miller could see that Monroe was weeping under her black-lace veil, which she lifted to dab her eyes. She was confiding to Kazan, he explained later, that her fifty-five-year-old agent and protector, Johnny Hyde—who had believed in her, wanted to marry her, and got her choice cameos in *Asphalt Jungle* and *All About Eve*—had died in the hospital calling her name. His family had barred her from entering the room. Kazan motioned Miller over to meet Monroe. The name that cinematographers gave to the subliminal power of Monroe's presence through the lens was "flesh impact"; in person, Miller felt the same wallop. "When we shook hands the shock of her body's motion sped through me," he said. "A sensation at odds with her sadness and all the glamour and technology and the busy confusion of a new shot being set up."

Monroe's captivating, studied looks—her blue-grey eyes, her alabaster skin, her blond hair piled up on her head—were in total contradiction with the mess of her internal world. On-screen, she was a vivacious picture of equipoise, a seductive promise of delight. Off-screen, she was all disarray, a waif haunted by the doom that was her blighted family inheritance. When Miller met Monroe, she was in a particularly dark place. After *As Young as You Feel*, she had no work lined up. She was stymied. Hyde's death meant that she had no one to protect her or to find her small but quality parts with good directors, like John Huston and Joseph L. Mankiewicz. Although Hyde had been a partner and a senior agent at William Morris, no one at the agency now would take her calls. (She had overdosed after Hyde's funeral.) Her contract with 20th Century–Fox was up in May, and it was doubtful that the head of the studio, Darryl F. Zanuck, who disliked her and thought her "just a freak," would renew it.

When she embraced Kazan on the set, Monroe was aware that she was greeting a show-biz powerhouse. Kazan, too, understood the politics of the encounter. After listening to her distraught lament, he asked her to dinner. "I wouldn't say a word, I said, just be with you, then take you home," Kazan recalled telling her. Monroe declined, then later found Kazan in the studio cafeteria and thanked him for his kindness. Kazan asked her out again, and this time Monroe accepted. Both were pros at playing the Hollywood game, both understood that Hollywood's currency of exchange was sex. "All young actresses in that time and place were thought of as prey, to be overwhelmed and topped by the male," Kazan said. "A genuine interest, which I did have, would produce results." A few days later, they began a year-long affair. "The girl had little education and no knowledge, except the knowledge of her own experience; of that she had a great deal, and for an actor, that is the important kind of knowledge," Kazan, who referred to Monroe as "a stray cat," said.

Many of Kazan's nights with Monroe were spent at the producer Charles Feldman's Tudor mansion in Beverly Hills, with Miller sleeping down the hall. According to Kazan, Miller, who had been barred from marital intimacy, "was starved for sexual release." The sun and the fragrant Los Angeles air loosened his libido, only to leave him stalled on all fronts. Twentieth Century–Fox and Warner Brothers turned down "The Hook." Miller spent most of his days by Feldman's pool, swimming laps and trying unsuccessfully to work on rewrites. As he and Kazan palled around Los Angeles trying in vain to sell the screenplay, Monroe was brought along as a kind of "mascot," according to Kazan. "We were essentially a threesome, and there was fun of various kinds for all of us," Kazan recalled. They went on picnics and browsed bookstores. (Miller bought Monroe a copy of *Salesman*.) "Marilyn" was a playful character Monroe could call up out of herself—a sensational presence who decoyed (and excused) a sensational absence. She had a show-stopping body but an untutored mind; she was full of wonder and shame. As hungry for knowledge as she was for fame, inevitably she took to her companions like a bass to a top-water lure. "I was still seeing her at night," Kazan recalled. "But she had a violent crush on Arthur. I wasn't sure how much time Arthur was making with her. He was not an aggressive man in this area. Marilyn had stars in her eyes when she talked about him." The pair dubbed Monroe "Miss Bauer," and as a prank took "Miss Bauer" along as their "secretary" when they pitched "The Hook" to the hard-bitten, foul-mouthed Harry Cohn, the head of Columbia Pictures. Cohn's first verdict on the script was "Burn it"; however, although he was convinced that the film "wouldn't make a dime," he saw an opportunity to snare Kazan for his studio. "I'll go in with yiz, pervaded yiz don't make any money unless it makes money. I mean if yiz are so fucking idealistic, right?" Miller recalled Cohn saying. As the script awaited vetting by Columbia's labor-relations man and the FBI, the trio partied.

Almost every night during their stay, Feldman, a suave divorcé who had produced Kazan's film version of *A Streetcar Named Desire*, threw a party. "The all but announced themes of these evenings seemed to be sex and money," Miller observed. One of these parties was held in Miller's honor. Kazan had promised to take Monroe—named only as "Kazan's date" on the guest list—but then made other arrangements with an actress Darryl Zanuck was urging him to use in *Viva Zapata*. Kazan asked Miller to stand in for him with Monroe.

"I was never alone with her for five minutes—although Mary never believed this and is incapable of believing it. But it is the truth," Miller wrote to his parents in 1956, explaining the origins of his relationship with Monroe, which had by then become international tabloid fodder. "She was unknown then, having appeared in a few pictures but not as a star. I had certainly never heard of her. To everyone else, apparently she was the sexy dame. To me she had a face bathed in tears, was scared to death, and could barely talk above a whisper." To a man of conscience with a passion for justice and empathy for the dispossessed, Monroe's story was as extraordinary as it was compelling. "You couldn't help being touched," Kazan wrote to his wife in 1955. "She was talented, funny, vulnerable, helpless, in awful pain, with no hope and some worth and not a liar, not vicious, not catty, and with a history of orphanism that was killing to hear. She was like all Charlie Chaplin's heroines in one."

Monroe's loveless childhood was a never-ending tale of unmooring loss. She was rejected by her father ("he left while I was getting born—without ever seeing me"); neglected and finally abandoned by her schizophrenic mother, who twice tried to kill herself; boarded out to a series of strangers; and shunted between foster homes and an orphanage. "You see, I was brought up differently from the average American child because the average child is brought up expecting to be happy," she said. Every humiliation seems to have been lavished on Monroe. She was molested by her aunt's husband at eleven, sexually assaulted by her cousin at thirteen, a high school drop-out at fifteen, and married at sixteen (which ended, she said, "my status as an orphan"). Speaking of her guardian, Grace McKee, the one empowering figure in her early life, who was a film cutter and her mother's best friend, Monroe recalled that when she was eight, McKee was the first person who ever patted her head or touched her cheek. "I can still remember how thrilled I was when her kind hand touched me," she said. She added, "As I grew older I knew I was different from other children because there were no kisses and no promises in my life. I often felt lonely and wanted to die. I would try and cheer myself up with daydreams. I never dreamed of anyone loving me as I saw other children loved. That was too big a stretch for my imagination. I compromised by dreaming of attracting someone's attention (besides God), of having people look at me and say my name."

Although Monroe was used to being handed around at these Hollywood affairs like nuts at Christmas, when Miller took her to Feldman's party he was courteous. He insisted on picking her up from her house. Miller also listened to and seemed to see Monroe. He paid her the respect of taking her seriously. "Men do not see me, they just lay their eyes on me," Monroe said. (Maggie, Monroe's stand-in in *After the Fall* [1964], says more or less the same thing to Quentin, who is Miller's mouthpiece, leading Quentin to confide to the audience, "The honor was that I hadn't tried to go to bed with her! She took it for a tribute to her 'value,' and I was only afraid! God, the hypocrisy.") In the haute bourgeois luster of Feldman's mansion, Monroe seemed to Miller a "strange bird in the aviary, if only because her dress was so blatantly tight, declaring rather than insinuating that she had brought her body along and that it was the best one in the room." Watching Monroe work that room, her low-cut bodice pitching her forward "like the prow of a ship," the former wife of John Huston, the actress Evelyn Keyes, confided to Miller, "They'll eat her alive." "The air around her was charged," said Miller, who felt charged himself with "something secret . . . a filament of connection." Monroe's pain called out of Miller a protectiveness that kept his desire hidden from him. "I gave her comfort. She had a bomb inside her. Ignite her and she'd explode," he said.

For Monroe, Miller's gentle, stalwart regard felt "like a cool drink when you've got a fever." She was twenty-five and unknown; he was thirty-five and famous, already beginning to assume the gravity of a great man. As Monroe later wrote to him, "Most people can admire their fathers, but I never had one. I need someone to admire." At Feldman's party, Monroe kicked off her shoes and spent most of the evening with Miller, talking on the sofa while he massaged her feet. "For reasons which I have never understood I told her what I thought—that she would be a great star, and that she had in her a kind of sensitivity which, if she worked at it, could make an actress out of her too," Miller wrote to his parents about their long conversation at the party. Those words, coming from a Pulitzer Prize–winning playwright, spoke directly to Monroe's great need, as well as to what Kazan saw as her fatal contradiction: "She deeply wanted reassurance of her worth, yet she respected the men who scorned her because their estimate of her was her own." For Miller, whose plays plumbed complex psychologies, Monroe's allure was her paradoxical nature: she was beautiful and vulnerable, naive and knowing, intelligent and vacant, unabashed and shy, pragmatic and dreamy, detached and attentive. "Life—I am both of your directions," she wrote in a poem.

By the time Kazan arrived late back to the party from his *cinq-à-sept* to reclaim his "date," Miller and Monroe were on the dance floor. "How happy she was in his arms!" Kazan said. "All her doubts about her worth were being satisfied in one package." As the pair swayed together in the low light of Feldman's living room, Kazan noticed in Miller's eyes "the lovely light of lechery." "I hadn't known he had it in him," Kazan said, adding, "He didn't read like the constricted man I'd known."

A few days after the party, trapped between desire and duty, Miller cut short his Hollywood stay and forced himself back to New York before Cohn had handed down his final verdict on "The Hook." "I knew that I must flee or walk into a doom beyond all knowing," he wrote. It was "a retreat to the safety of morals, to be sure, but not necessarily to truthfulness," he said. Kazan and Monroe came to the airport to see him off. "The sight of her was something like pain," Miller recalled. He kissed Monroe on the cheek to say good-bye. She gave a startled intake of breath. Miller started to laugh at this overreaction "until the solemnity of feeling in her eyes shocked me into remorse and I hurried backwards toward the plane." On the plane home, the scent of her perfume was still on his hands. "I knew my innocence was technical merely," Miller said.

In February 1950, almost a year before Miller and Kazan pitched their screenplay in Hollywood, Senator Joseph Mc-Carthy delivered a stump speech in Wheeling, West Virginia, during which he held up a list of 205 alleged Communists in the State Department. In the journalistic feeding frenzy that followed, the number dipped from 205 to 57 and then to 4. Nonetheless, McCarthy was the flame that lit the fuse of public paranoia that the right wing had been laying down for years, "spreading fear of uttering any opinion that could be remotely interpreted as left or even liberal, let alone pro-Soviet," said Miller, who saw McCarthy as "the last act, not the first—of America's reactionary retreat from its core values of freedom of speech and assembly." The Red Scare, of which McCarthy became a figurehead, shook the nation. "The old political and moral reality had melted like a Dali watch," Miller said. "Nobody but a fanatic, it seemed, could really say all that he believed."

Miller certainly couldn't. In 1951, with the news of the trials of Alger Hiss and Julius and Ethel Rosenberg dominating the front pages, the House Committee on Un-American Activities turned its attention for a second time to Hollywood and the infiltration of Communists in the industry. The movie studios, which owed their profits to the goodwill of the paying customers, at first refused to cooperate but finally gave in to the new push for purification. "This unleashed a veritable holy terror among actors, directors and others, from Party members to those who had the merest brush with a front organization," Miller recalled.

Miller got his first taste of "the howling gale of the far right," as he referred to the new delirium, when Harry Cohn finally got back to him about "The Hook." Cohn agreed to take on the film, provided that Miller made some strategic changes. At the suggestion of the FBI, to whom Cohn had taken the unusual precaution of showing the script, the union crooks and their gangster protectors would need to be changed to Communists. "I knew for a fact that there were next to no Communists on the Brooklyn waterfront, so to depict the rank and file in revolt against Communists rather than racketeers was simply idiotic," Miller said. Without explaining his reasons to Kazan, who had declined to direct Tennessee Williams's *Rose Tattoo* on Broadway in order to direct their film, Miller withdrew his script. "What was Art protecting—his script or himself?" Kazan asked in his memoir, adding, "Maybe Art had been rattled by his marital situation and the distress it was causing him." Maybe also, having just made his name, Miller did not want it tarnished by the studio's promised investigation of its employees' politics. Miller's brother Kermit had been a member of the Communist Party, and as he admitted in his HUAC testimony in 1955, Miller himself had attended meetings with Communist writers back in 1947. He had drawn right-wing flak a couple of years earlier as one of the luminaries speaking against the emerging Cold War at the ill-fated 1949 Waldorf Peace Conference (Cultural and Scientific Conference for World Peace). Along with Charlie Chaplin, Marlon Brando, Langston Hughes, and about forty-five others, Miller was featured in a *Life* magazine article about the gathering under the boldface headline "Dupes and Fellow-Travellers." "There were nuns on their knees around the Waldorf-Astoria praying for the souls of those within, and enormous, loud, and violent picket lines of various patriotic organizations," Miller recalled, adding, "It did a great deal to destroy me." From that point on, Miller said, "I was beginning to believe that a tremendous underground change was going to take place in this country, and I was scared of it." The day after Miller withdrew "The Hook," Cohn wired him in Brooklyn: "IT'S INTERESTING HOW THE MINUTE WE TRY TO MAKE THE SCRIPT PRO-AMERICAN YOU PULL OUT."

"Amazing kind of spaghetti was being cooked here, you

couldn't follow one thread more than two inches," Miller said. In the climate of increasing suspicion and confusion, he felt "treed." In late 1951, when the film of *Death of a Salesman* was about to be released, Columbia Pictures asked Miller to sign an anti-Communist statement, which he declined to do. But he could not stop the producers from making a twenty-five-minute disclaimer intended to precede the screening of *Death of a Salesman*, which "explained that Willy Loman was entirely atypical, a throwback to the past when salesmen did indeed have some hard problems. But nowadays selling was a fine profession with limitless spiritual compensations as well as financial ones." "Why the hell did you make the picture if you're so ashamed of it?" Miller asked the producers, after a screening of the intended prologue. Miller threatened a lawsuit; the disclaimer was never shown. But Miller could not shake the taint of Communist affiliation. The cultural frame of mind had become so paranoid that to imagine writing a play about it "was like picking your teeth with a ball of cotton wool," said Miller, who was drawn to the subject matter while feeling he "lacked the tools for it." "I was sure that the whole thing would soon go away, but it didn't," he recalled, adding, "I began to despair of my own silence. I longed to respond to the climate of fear."

"I tell you friend," Miller wrote to Kazan as early as 1949. "They will hang us all without so much as raising their voice. We have to be proving how anti-Communist we are every waking minute." Three years later, the HUAC investigations proved him right. Miller may have been reluctant to acknowledge his political past, but Kazan was not. In the mid-thirties, for eighteen months, Kazan, the "Proletarian Thunderbolt" of the Group Theatre, had been a member of the Communist Party. He had quit in disgust at the Party's plan to take over the Group Theatre. He knew that he would be called before HUAC. He also knew that he "couldn't behave as if my old 'comrades' didn't exist and didn't have an active political program." He added, "There was no way I would go along with their crap that the CP was nothing but another political party, like the Republicans and the Democrats. I knew very well what it was, a thoroughly organized worldwide conspiracy."

Kazan was called before the Committee twice: first in January 1952, then again in April. As the most successful director on Broadway and already an Academy Award–winning film director, he had a stature in American popular culture that was unique. He was a plum witness at what was in essence a degradation ceremony, in which the Committee served as "a kind of national parole board whose job was to determine whether the 'criminals' had truly repented of their evil ways," as Victor Navasky points out in *Naming Names*. In other words, the process was not a quest for evidence; it was a test of character. In his January appearance, which was behind closed doors and not under oath, Kazan answered all questions but refused to give names. In April, under mounting pressure from the studios, he decided to inform.

Miller wanted to dissuade Kazan from naming names. On his way to Salem, Massachusetts, to research a play about the witch hunts, which he saw as parallel to HUAC's investigations, he stopped off to see Kazan at his 113-acre Connecticut estate. Months earlier, Miller had asked him to read Marion Starkey's *Devil in Massachusetts*, about the witch hunts, a subject Miller had been interested in since college and which excited him now as an apt metaphor for the time. "It was taken for granted—although Miller later denied it to HUAC—that he wanted me to direct it," Kazan said. "We were the perfect team." As they walked in the woods, Kazan explained that he could not see sacrificing his career for something he no longer believed in. "There was a certain gloomy logic in what he was saying," Miller recalled. "Unless he came clean he could never hope, at the height of his creative powers, to make another film in America, and he would probably not be given a passport to work abroad either. If the theatre remained open to him, it was not his primary interest anymore; he wanted to deepen his film life, that was where his heart lay, and he had been told in so many words by his old boss and friend, Spyros Skouras, president of Twentieth Century Fox, that the company would not employ him unless he satisfied the Committee."

At the end of the mournful afternoon, as Miller was getting into his car, Molly Kazan, who was as outspoken as she was analytical, rushed out of the house and into the drizzle to have a few words. Miller could see agitation in her eyes. Molly was fiercely on her husband's side. (She wrote Kazan's explanation of his decision, which appeared as an ad in the *New York Times* two days after his testimony.) She informed Miller that the United Electrical Workers union was in the hands of Communists, that he had lost touch with the country, and that all the people who lived on their road in Sandy Hook approved of the Committee. Miller said he didn't agree with the decision to name names. Then, to extricate himself from the awkward moment, he mentioned in passing that he was on his way to Salem. Molly, who had read *The Devil in Massachusetts*, immediately understood that his mission was to write a play. "You're not going to equate witches with this!" she said. "Those witches did not exist. Communists do."

The rift between Kazan and Miller was emblematic of the deepening emotional schism in the land. The breaking of charity between people epitomized by the hysteria of the 1692 Salem episode was now being replayed across the republic. In Salem, it seemed to Miller, people had been forced to sin against themselves or die. Americans now were committing a similar sin of omission: not protesting what they knew was wrong. "We weren't executed here," Miller said. "We died another way." As he drove north to Massachusetts, Miller was beset by emotional contradiction. He still felt "brother-love" for Kazan, "as painfully alive in me as it had ever been." Alongside that, he was chilled by "the undeniable fact that Kazan might have sacrificed me had it been necessary."

On April 10, for the second time, Kazan came before the House Committee on Un-American Activities. In his first January appearance, Kazan had not given names, now he did. The day after Kazan's ad ran in the *Times* explaining his position, Molly Kazan wrote Miller to continue their sour disagreement, which had begun when Kazan first explained his political quandary to Miller in their walk in the woods. "Dear Artie," she began, throwing down the gauntlet about his Salem play. "I love you because facts disturb you. Fact. There are no witches. . . . Fact. There are Communists. Fact. It is difficult to find out who they are. . . . Fact. A faulty and patchwork analogy isn't a taking off point for a good, healthy, strong statement." She added, "Why do you pick this? Nothing's an accident? S. Freud."

"Indeed, there are no witches," Miller began his long, trenchant reply. "The point is there are none now either, and this committee's mentality, and the atmosphere which it has engendered after almost fifteen years of ceaseless propaganda, are such as to throw perfectly honest people into a kind of nameless fear which is utterly destructive of a sane order of life." Miller went on to explain the historical facts of the fatal year in Salem, which had nothing to do with witches but everything to do with a battle between two hardened factions "over a vast and very important tract of land whose title lay in doubt. Eleven families abutted on this tract and . . . formed the contending factions." The mayhem of accusation turned Salem into a community in which the "righteous" projected onto others the rapacity which they could not accept in themselves. "It is not an analogy I am after," Miller wrote to Molly Kazan. "It is the process of fright which can overtake a community until it strikes in fury at every shadow."

Miller's letter continued:

I am aware that you do not believe this process is at work among us now. It is not an analogy at all, but the naked process itself; indeed, it was so naked in its operations in Salem, so stripped of all but the machine of fear itself, that though thousands of people were burned at the stake in the French province of Lorraine, and four hundred in Sweden not long before the Salem tragedy, it is the Salem experience that has become the classical one here and abroad.

As I told Gadg [Kazan's nickname] many times before I even knew he had been summoned by the Committee, I agreed with his intention to testify as he did at the private session. I agreed because I still conceived that such a course could be taken while still preserving one's integral viewpoint. But as I said to him in the woods two weeks ago, it would be morally wrong for him to do or say anything out of fear rather than conviction. I believe, Molly, that his second testimony was the testimony of fear; and I owe it to both of you as well, to add that his statement in the Times is in many particulars morally untrue, and it is fear that has wrung these untruths from him. I intend in this play to examine fear. I, who have found Gadg closer to me than any other friend, had a profound and weeping interest in this subject.

No, there are no witches; and there are Communists. Is it worthy of mankind, however, to act toward the one as though they were the other? Or to enhance the prestige of a committee that has demonstrated a hundred times in the past its design to empower Legionairism, chauvinism, and the inherent violence of super-patriotism? Is it through such men, who demonstrated to Gadg himself their own lack of honor through the promise they broke [the Committee leaked sealed testimony] that light is to be brought to the people? I do not believe it.

After he testified, in left-wing circles Kazan went from cultural prince to pariah overnight. "I seemed to have crossed some fundamental and incontrovertible line of tolerance for human error and sin," he wrote. He was threatened, abused, and shunned. He changed his telephone number and hired a bodyguard for his wife and family. (The ructions in Hollywood when he was chosen, four decades later, in 1999, to receive the Honorary Academy Award for Lifetime Achievement, demonstrated that in some parts of the show-biz community Kazan had still not been forgiven.) Even though he could continue to work, the crisis had made him a contractual cripple; he was relegated to the bottom of the studio heap. As Kazan put it, he was "on a great social griddle and frying."

Two days after Kazan's testimony, Tennessee Williams sent him an expanded draft of *Camino Real* to direct. Although most of the theater community rushed to judgment, Williams did not. "I take no attitude about it, one way or another, as I am not a political person and human venality is something I always expect and forgive," he wrote to a friend. Miller, however, could not forgive. Before the testimony, at the end of their walk in the woods, according to Kazan's diary, Miller had put his arm around Kazan and said, "Don't worry about what I'll think. Whatever you do will be okay with me. Because your heart's in the right place." Kazan wrote, "It was like the truth of a pop song title. There was no doubt that Art meant it and that he was anxious to say this to me before we separated. We parted on affectionate terms."

But after Kazan's testimony, Miller cold-shouldered him. Over the next few years, various friends tried to engineer a reconciliation. "Gadg mourns your loss with unending sorrow," John Steinbeck wrote to Miller in 1955, adding, "It's wasteful that two such men should be apart. Please do something to mend this break. . . . I beg you to give it a chance. I beg you." In 1956, at an Actors Studio benefit, Marilyn Monroe briefly reunited them. Taking Miller's hand, she walked him across the room, took Kazan's hand, and put their two hands together. Then, she cradled both their hands in hers. "There was silence in the room. The music stopped. Conversation stopped," the actress Madeleine Sherwood recalled. "Marilyn said, 'It was the most wonderful moment of my life when those two men accepted that I had put their hands together.'" But the gesture was cosmetic. Although they would collaborate one more time, on *After the Fall* (1964), for all intents and purposes, the pall over their friendship never lifted. "I would never really feel toward him quite what a friend should," Kazan wrote of Miller. "Nor, I imagine, he toward me." Kazan's testimony and Miller's subsequent silent treatment put paid to what Brooks Atkinson had once called "the Kazan-Miller era of American theatre."

7

Collisions

The playwright is at the mercy
of the moment in a terrible way.

—Arthur Miller

My world seemed to be colliding with itself, the past
exploding under my feet. And on top of everything
else I was once more under attack.

—Arthur Miller, *Timebends*

As HE DROVE TOWARD SALEM, Miller was unsure whether he "would really write about the outbreak in 1692." Over the centuries, the settlement, which took its name from the Hebrew word for peace (*Shalom*) and was, according to Miller, the scene "of one of the strangest and most awful chapters in human history," had become shorthand for violent, hysterical paranoia. Founded on a remorseless Puritan creed whose discipline helped it to battle the wilderness, the community purged its repressed thoughts, decades later, by embracing God and eliminating all those suspected of being his enemies among its inhabitants. Lunacy reigned. As proof of guilt, the Salem judges accepted "spectral evidence." "If I swore that you had sent out your 'familiar spirit' to choke, tickle or poison me or my cattle, or to control my thoughts or actions, I could get you hanged unless you confessed to having had contact with the Devil," Miller wrote. Denying the existence of witches could cost you your life, he added, given the Bible's exhortation "Thou shalt not suffer a witch to live." "There had to be witches in the world or the Bible lied," he wrote. Terror infected every corner. In the end, nineteen people and two dogs were hanged, and one man was pressed to death. "Salem became a sort of asylum, a mass confessional where the population gathered every day . . . to hear the latest secrets of their neighbors' subconscious lives. And when they had heard, they executed certain individuals and felt a great temporary relief," Miller said. He added, "It was as though they poured into these victims all their guilt, and then destroyed their guilt."

At the curtain rise of *The Crucible*, we see an agitated household gathered around the bedside of the young, comatose Betty Parris, who seems to be under a weird spell ("She sleeps and yet she walks"). At the time of *The Crucible*'s incubation, in the summer of 1952, in a *New York Times* essay titled "Many Writers: Few Plays," Miller diagnosed a similar sleeping sickness—a "lizardic dormancy," he called it—among his fellow playwrights, who also appeared spellbound. "The creative mind seems to have lost its heat," he wrote, as a challenge both to himself and to others to be daring in dark times. He went on, "Is the knuckle-headedness of McCarthyism behind it all? The Congressional investigations of political unorthodoxy? Yes. But is that all? Can an artist be paralyzed except he be somewhat willing? . . . This is no time to go to sleep." The play that Miller was writing explored exactly this kind of toxic symbiosis, in which the terrorized create the very thing they fear. The society's denial of reality—its magical thinking—leads to implosion from within. In this sense, *The Crucible* enacts one of the dictionary meanings of its title: "a situation of severe trial in which different elements interact, leading to the creation of something new." The new idea at the heart of Miller's moral melodrama involved the dynamics of terror, how it can kill thought as well as people.

According to the laws of both cinema and stage, action is character: the greater the pressure on character, the greater the revelation of personality. Behavior is psychology in action. The same holds true for communal identity. In the case of *The Crucible*, that pressure—the catalyst that triggers Salem's collective paranoid anxiety—comes not from the so-called witches, who are merely emissaries of the unknown, but from the unknown itself: the virgin American wilderness, which lurks at the very edge of the Salem settlement. From the villagers' point of view, this vast, impenetrable terra incognita is the habitat of all real and imagined threats: "the last place on earth not paying homage to God," as Miller writes in his "overture" to the play, "the Devil's last preserve, his home base, and the citadel of his final stand." Pilgrim life was strict and somber. The fierce rigor of Salem's residents was, at first, a defense against the forbidding and forbidden territory around the village. "Abominations are done in the forest," Reverend Parris says when he first takes fright. In the play, the forest is offstage, but the transgressing young women who ventured into the woods to frolic naked and practice sorcery make the anarchy of the wilderness palpable, in all its erotic and barbarous power.

"Will you wake, will you open up your eyes?" the distraught Reverend says to his daughter, Betty, in the play's first beats. Sight, and the lack of it, are at the heart of the play. Parris fears for Betty's life, and so does Betty, who was among the renegade teenagers her father accidentally discovered cavorting in the woods. She is petrified, literally frozen by her sin. Her hysterical paralysis, in which her mind has shut down, fore-shadows the paralysis of her fundamentalist community: people who are so wedded to their orthodoxy that they cannot, will not, "cope with the evidence of their senses," as Miller said. The villagers fall under a kind of collective spell, a negative hallucination in which they cannot see what is literally in front of them. The Salem tragedy—"one of the few dramas in history with a beginning, a middle, and an end," according to Miller—gave him both the accumulating momentum of a solid structure and a deracinating psychology, in which the mind is made progressively useless.

The play's first act is an accumulating whirlwind of accusation and explanation. What exactly went on in the woods? Who has cast this spell on Betty, for which there seems to be no cure? In the play's first beats, Betty's cousin Abigail alludes to the perception that her mysterious ailment may be the work of the devil. "Uncle, the rumor of witchcraft is all about," she tells Reverend Parris. "I think you'd best go down and deny it yourself." Abigail's advice is not at first absorbed by the pragmatic, unpopular minister, whose immediate thought is to cover up the scandal of their midnight frolic, which could be used as ammunition by his village enemies. "And what shall I say to them? My daughter and my niece I discovered dancing like heathen in the forest," he asks, adding, "They'll ruin me with it." What begins as a prospect of malicious gossip escalates by degrees to a nightmare vision that so contaminates the village that by the end of act 1, both the trespassing girls and the terrorized towns-people are sucking "at the Devil's teats," as Miller puts it. Danger is everywhere. Panic and suspicion disrupt and divide the pious community.

At the core of this indigestible, metastasizing terror is a kernel of reality. Abigail, an orphan and servant girl "with an endless capacity for dissembling," according to the stage directions, has been released from her service in the household of

Elizabeth and John Proctor and lives under her uncle's roof. Overcome by her desire for John Proctor, with whom she had an affair, Abigail has coaxed Tituba, Reverend Parris's Caribbean servant, along with the other servant girls, into the woods to practice voodoo. "You drank a charm to kill John Proctor's wife," Betty, woken by Abigail, accuses. Under threat of death, Abigail orders Betty and the other girls to keep to their agreed-upon story. But although Abigail is nimble in answering Reverend Parris, she cannot seem to wiggle free of his agitated inquiries. Through the forest murk, he glimpsed the girls' revels, and Abigail's suave explanations cannot dispel what he has witnessed—a naked body gamboling in the forest, a dress on the ground, chanting in tongues. When the Reverend asks Abigail bluntly if she was "conjuring spirits last night," she says, "Not I, sir." Then, forced into a corner, she ups the ante. "Tituba and Ruth," she whispers confidentially in her uncle's ear. "You have discovered witchcraft," one of the villagers immediately exclaims, upon hearing Abigail's admission. In the architecture of anguish that Miller expertly builds, this moment is the play's tipping point. The naming of names has begun.

A free-for-all of accusation follows. Everyone must choose between confessing to having seen the devil and death. The villagers are frightened quite literally out of their minds. In this hallucinatory realm, anyone can be called out on a whim. Logic is displaced. Words, explanations, reason go unheard. The mind is rendered useless. "Their names, their names!" Reverend Parris urges Tituba, who, to save herself from hanging, has confessed to seeing witches. *The Crucible* flushes out into the open the psychic jujitsu by which the panic-struck force onto others all their repressed hate and hurt. In this process, the accusers and the confessors turn themselves into radical innocents. "Look at her God-given innocence," Reverend Hale, a witch hunter who has been summoned, says at the sight of the stricken Betty on her bed, adding, "We must protect her, Tituba, the Devil is out and preying upon her like a beast upon the flesh of the pure lamb. God will bless you for your help."

At this point, Abigail, "enraptured, as though in a pearly light," cries out, "I want to open myself!" And she begins to name names. "I saw Sarah Good with the Devil. I saw Goody Osburn with the Devil. I saw Bridget Bishop with the Devil." This stage-managed epiphany of purification raises Betty from her bed. She joins both the company of innocents and the chorus of accusation, "calling out hysterically and with great relief," the stage directions say. "Let the marshal bring irons!" Reverend Hale shouts, as the accused are ushered out of sight, as well as mind. "A drama cannot merely describe an emotion; it has to become that emotion," Miller said. Here, at the end of act 1, as the voices "rise to a great glee," thought dies. Victims and victimizers lose all contact with their authentic selves. The stage picture *becomes* the terrorized mind releasing itself from both its turbulence and its aggression.

As in all terrorized communities, the villagers' rush to judgment defends them against their indigestible fear. A new narrative is quickly constructed to seal off the contamination and the persecuting anxiety that accompanies it. In *The Crucible*, that narrative takes shape before our eyes. "Theology, sir, is a fortress: no crack in a fortress may be accounted small," Reverend Hale tells John Proctor, the play's flawed hero, who refuses to go along with the new version of things. "The world is gone daft with this nonsense," Proctor says to Hale. "There are them that will swear to anything before they'll hang: have you never thought of that?" (Of course, not-thinking is psychologically essential to the strategy of fear that the play delineates.) Proctor is significantly *not* an innocent. In his transgression with Abigail he gave in to lust. Where the young women deny reality, Proctor, by contrast, owns up to his sins. The women project their guilt onto others; Proctor admits his and tries to repair his marriage. Over the course of the play, Proctor becomes Miller's model of authenticity: he will not repudiate his knowledge of experience or feelings. Where most of Salem's citizens are spell-bound, denying their own consciousness, Proctor is the mes-senger of disenchantment, embracing complexity, ambiguity, and guilt.

Proctor, who is both visionary and victim, is Miller's link from the seventeenth century to his own. "When irrational ter-ror takes to itself the fiat of moral goodness, somebody has to die," Miller said. The ecstasy of sanctimony that characterized the Salem denunciations presaged by almost three centuries the maelstrom of exclusion inspired by the Red Scare: "the old friend of a blacklisted person crossing the street to avoid being seen talking to him, the overnight conversions of former left-ists into born-again patriots." These ructions were the outward and visible signs within the community of a shift in power, a shift that is illustrated most sensationally in the play by Mary, the Proctors' family servant and the most tentative of the forest revelers—"I only looked!" she bleats—who becomes part of the inquisition and "a mouse no more." Described in the stage di-rections as "a subservient, naïve lonely girl," Mary is reborn as an innocent with startling clout. "I'm an official of the court," she boasts to the Proctors, impudently abandoning her house-keeping chores to answer the call of her righteous civic duty. As Proctor moves to beat her for her insolence—"I'll whip the devil out of you"—Mary stops him in his tracks. "I saved her life today," she says, pointing to Elizabeth. At a stroke, Proc-tor's world is turned upside down.

Proctor is both Miller's spokesman and his simulacrum. On his research visit to the Salem archives, where he read through the transcripts of the trials, Miller came upon a sharply observed moment in the examination of Elizabeth Procter, Abigail Wil-liams, and Amy Putnam, written "in primitive shorthand" by Reverend Parris, one of the instigators of the witch hunt and the villain of the play: "Both made offer to strike at said Procter;

but when Abigail's hand came near, it opened, whereas it was made up into a fist before, and came down exceedingly lightly as it drew near to said Procter, and at length, with open and extended fingers, touched Procter's hood very lightly. Immediately, Abigail cried out her fingers, her fingers, her fingers burned."

That singular recorded gesture jogged "the thousand pieces I had come across . . . into place," Miller said. "I was sure that John Proctor had bedded Abigail, who had to be dismissed most likely to appease Elizabeth." Proctor—"a sinner not only against the moral fashion of his time, but against his own vision," according to the stage directions—connected Miller to both his hidden, frustrated desire and his fraudulence. "My own marriage of twelve years was teetering and I knew more than I wished to know about where the blame lay," he said. "That John Proctor the sinner might overturn his paralyzing personal guilt and become the most forthright voice against the madness around him was a reassurance to me, and, I suppose, an inspiration: it demonstrated that a clear moral outcry could still spring even from an ambiguously unblemished soul." Miller added, "A play began to accumulate around this man."

"Is there no good penitence but it be public?" Proctor asks at one point. *The Crucible*, which Miller dedicated to his wife Mary, was a public gesture of both political and personal repair. "I had to guess that Art was publicly apologizing to his wife for what he'd done," Kazan said. Proctor laments the chill atmosphere of repressed recrimination in his household ("Oh, Elizabeth, your justice would freeze beer!"). By the finale, Elizabeth has owned up to her punishing *froideur* ("It needs a cold wife to prompt lechery. . . . Suspicion kissed you when I did. . . . It were a cold house I kept!"). With his refusal to point fingers to save his life, Proctor wins back not only his wife's love but his own dignity.

Implicit in Miller's principled stance as a public intellectual was his moral rigor; his reputation for goodness was central to his identity. Like Proctor, he was a flawed man of conscience, "burning in [his] loneliness," having sworn off contact with his own enamored orphan, Marilyn Monroe. After their initial meeting in Hollywood in 1951, Miller wrote to his parents, he and Monroe exchanged only a couple of letters and then had no contact at all until 1955. "I was trying to make my marriage work then. I had no hope, but I was bound to try." At home, like his onstage counterpart, Miller walked on eggshells, trying to earn a forgiveness that never came. He was embattled, contending with the demands of both his wife and his talent. If Miller was not quite the cheater his wife suspected, by his own admission he did have a mistress—his writing. "You get this absolutely crazy concentration on the work. You don't hear anything anymore. In all justice to Mary, she was talking to the wall. I was really obsessed with developing new kinds of plays and I didn't know how to do that and function in any other way. . . . I was doing that my whole waking life."

In the year that it took Miller to complete *The Crucible*, he came up with nineteen different titles for the play, not including Mary's jokey suggestion, "Death of a Salem." The producers announced the play to the press as "Those Familiar Spirits." But by Christmas Eve 1952, four weeks before the Broadway opening, they'd settled on *The Crucible*. Jed Harris, Miller's snobbish new director, liked the title because he felt that most of the audience wouldn't know what it meant. "He connected it with the cross, the crucifixion, which is fine," Miller said. "I wanted something that would indicate the burning away of impurities, which is what the play is doing."

Harris, at fifty-two, was as close as Broadway could come at that time to a director with the prestige of Kazan. He was a hit maker—he had premiered George S. Kaufman and Edna Ferber's *The Royal Family* (1927) and Ben Hecht and Charles MacArthur's *The Front Page* (1928), among others—but from another era, no longer the enfant terrible of Broadway though still a terrible infant. He was broke and all too aware that this was his last chance at the brass ring. Where Kazan was emotional, psychologically astute, confident, and collaborative, Harris was cool, undermining, fearful, and high-handed—"I want to be cremated and have my ashes thrown in Jed Harris's face," George S. Kaufman once quipped—an old-school Broadway megalomaniac whose commercial successes were mostly forgotten but whose legend of malice lingered on. "He had fought with practically everybody who was anybody in the Broadway theatre," Miller said.

Now it was Miller's turn. At first Miller was impressed by Harris's erudition and energy. "Jed was a charming man living at the raveled edge of his self-control, and I suppose that was the source of his authority. We tend to obey the crazy," he wrote. Miller felt that Harris's "tremendous visceral force" would help a play that was so emotional in story and theme. Soon enough, however, Harris's demands for shared royalties and co-authorship took the shine out of Miller's eyes. (Harris was not beyond pulling pages out of Miller's typewriter to rework them.) "He couldn't read a newspaper without telling you it needed a rewrite," Miller recalled. He came to distrust Harris, and Harris was not shy about voicing his doubts about Miller. On the train to Wilmington, Delaware, where *The Crucible* was having its world premiere, Miller spoke to a *Times* reporter about theocracy and diabolism, until Harris cut in: "What gives me a pain is this conception of Arthur as a big social thinker, a man sitting like a sort of Brooklyn Ibsen, sitting thinking about the society." He added, "*Art Schmart* . . . if this play is any good, it can only be good for one reason. As a theatrical experience." On the opening night in Delaware, where *The Crucible* got nineteen curtain calls, there were cries for "Author! Author!" Miller, who was watching from the rear of the stalls, started down the aisle. Harris strolled out from the wings and took the author's bow.

The enthusiasm of the Delaware first-nighters did not dispel Miller's anxiety about the production. He knew that Harris, who disliked the emotionalism of Kazan's directing, had imposed too formal a shape on his play. Actors were directed to address the audience, instead of each other. Laid out like the noblemen around a table on the Dutch Masters cigar box, an image Harris frequently invoked during rehearsal, the stage pictures were static. Harris had toned down the tumult and the terror to make a tidy, commercial play. "I knew we had cooled off a very hot play which therefore was not going to move anyone very deeply," Miller wrote. "It was not a performance from within but a kind of conscious rendering." By the time the play's twenty-five actors reached New York, according to Miller, their performances had also lost wattage, "dried up from the tryout ordeal. They couldn't maintain a level of life."

The Crucible opened at the height of the McCarthy storm. "It was the real high tide, and there I was spitting in the teeth of it. God knew how they were going to react," Miller recalled of the Broadway opening night. In his own disingenuous depiction of the moment, he stood in heroic isolation, shouting into a reactionary gale. "What I had not quite bargained for was the hostility in the New York audience as the theme of the play was revealed; an invisible sheet of ice formed over their heads, thick enough to skate on," he wrote. Throughout Miller's life, as he told it, the rejection of that opening-night crowd— "the audience clucked but they didn't applaud"—extended to him as well. "People I had known for fifteen years walked out in the intermission or at the end, and I was standing there, and they never said hello to me," he told the press. "They didn't want to have anything to do with me."

The *New York Herald Tribune* reported otherwise: "Before the curtain rose, the audience sat in such expectant silence that one got the impression of being in a cathedral. Then, in the second act when the curtain was lowered for two minutes between scenes, these same spectators let loose a barrage of sustained applause rarely heard during the course of a dramatic offering. The bravos resumed at the play's close and repeated cries of 'author' finally brought Mr. Miller from the wings."

Miller made a myth of the hostility, not the huzzahs. Rejection was also his prevailing memory of the critical reaction. Although there were some wounding responses—"The world has made this author important before he has made himself great," Eric Bentley wrote in the *New Republic*—most playwrights would have been pleased with the mixed reviews Miller complained about: "another powerful play" (*New York Times*); "the author has written with compassion and felicity . . . a powerful play, conceivably the most interesting of the year" (*New Yorker*); "Miller brings shrewd theatrical gifts: he knows how to make a point plain, how to give it bite, how to make its caustic and cauterizing language ring out on stage" (*New York Herald Tribune*). Still, the glare of *Salesman*'s recent huge success cast a shadow over *The Crucible*, which made it difficult to see the play clearly. "The critics were insulated from it by virtue of suspicion that it was a defense of Communists at a time when it was unpatriotic to defend Communism," Miller said. *The Crucible* was judged not as good as *Salesman*, too cold for some, too polemical for others. And in one case, even too unfair to witches. "Several of my friends are witches," William Brower wrote to Miller on March 7, 1953. "They and I resent bitterly your implied portrait of witches in your play. It is people like you who make witches and witch-hunters unpopular. Just because some witches have led improper lives, you have no right to show witches in an unfriendly light." To Miller's great disappointment, the Broadway production closed after 197 performances. "They hated it," he said. "And they hated me for reminding them." In fact, the public reaction was something worse than hate—indifference.

Over the years, *The Crucible* would become by far Miller's

most popular play. (When he last added up the play's paperback sales, in a 1996 *New Yorker* essay, he found that it had sold "more than six million copies." "I don't think there has been a week in the past forty-odd years when it hasn't been on a stage somewhere in the world," he said.) At the time, however, despite the fact that *The Crucible* won the 1953 Tony Award for best play, none of the critics handed it the laurel of greatness or saw beyond its connection to the Red Scare to its deeper meanings. "If *The Crucible* is still alive today it can hardly be about McCarthyism," Miller noted, adding, "Its underlying reference is to political paranoia."

Eighteen months after its disappointing debut, *The Crucible* was revived Off-Broadway, directed by Paul Libin. By then McCarthy was dead, and the Red Scare had abated. Audiences and critics were ready to receive Libin's warmer, more fluid Off-Broadway version. No words of the play were changed. "But it all seemed different. Of course it did: it was seen through a different historical moment, and it *was* different," Miller said, adding, "The critics were able to look at it as a work of art, and they themselves were not being forced to face their responsibility toward mankind."

In the year and a half between *The Crucible*'s collapse in 1953 and its resurrection in 1955, Miller was rudderless. "It was not easy to go back to the desk again," he recalled. Despite the play's commercial failure, he judged it an artistic success. "I could not help thinking in 1953–4 that time was running out not only on me but on the traditional American culture," he said. "I was growing more and more frighteningly isolated, in life as in theatre."

The Crucible may have been dedicated to Mary—"Just a story about a bad marriage," Clifford Odets quipped about the play—but its message worked no magic. Miller had long viewed Mary, he said, as "a vindictive, punishing woman": "Whenever

I am quietly desperate, when I am able to function at a low level, whenever I am close to feeling that my life is a thoroughly quiet surrender. . . . It is precisely at these times that she appears to me to feel most secure and satisfied," he wrote in "The Best Comedians." "I see this and cannot bear to accept it as true of her because then it would be simply that I must cut myself down to make her feel secure. And if that's so, then I don't belong with her." Things grew so sour and hate-filled that Miller contemplated "other ways than writing to make a living." To his mentor Kenneth Rowe, he confided, "I write my life, as you know, and when life becomes a lie it is no longer possible to write or to live either."

The play he wrote during this period, *A View from the Bridge*, was "written out of desperation . . . with my teeth clenched." An incident soon after Miller had finished *A View from the Bridge* dramatized the emotional quicksand he had stumbled into, and the sense of guilt that sucked him deeper and deeper in. At the home of the composer Elmer Bernstein, in front of Miller, Mary started to detail the plot of his new play. "I was very resentful that she had presumed to do that, which was beastly of me, because she was proud of me," Miller told his biographer Christopher Bigsby. "But such was my absolute control of my work that I didn't want anybody talking about it until I was ready to release it. That will give you an idea of how violent my self-absorption was. She had a tough row to hoe. Imagine living with a guy like that." Miller's self-denigration showed how deeply he had internalized Mary's complaints, but his intuitive response also registered the aggression in Mary's act. Despite her apparent enthusiasm for the play, Miller felt robbed. She had taken his story. "She is trying to cripple me, as she has for years. But I won't be crippled," he wrote to his parents in 1956, in a letter about his impending divorce.

Although Marilyn Monroe had been out of sight since she and Miller had waved their good-byes at the airport in 1951, she had not been out of mind. Monroe, Miller said, "had taken on an immanence in my imagination, the vitality of a force one does not understand but that seems on the verge of lighting up a vast surrounding plain of darkness." Miller had written his memory of her into an unfinished play, "Lorraine." In his writing notes for *The Crucible*, Abigail has a sexual imperialism and voracity far beyond her age or experience. "If your wife had what I have under my dress, she'd be what I am," Abigail says to Proctor in an unused exchange. "There never were a husband didn't linger at my bed to say goodnight. . . . I alone, I am the truth, for I am what they want. I am what women hate and envy." In his notebook, Miller emphasized Abigail's faith in her sexual charisma. "Abigail has absolute conviction that John's love for his wife is a formality and that she will get him when it's all over," he wrote. "She is on the offensive, against his, and all, male hypocrisy." So, too, was Monroe, who even in her new-found stardom and her new marriage to Joe DiMaggio still fantasized that Miller was part of her manifest destiny. She is quoted in Donald Spoto's biography as having the following conversation with her friend, the movie reporter Sidney Skolsky, in 1954:

"I'm going to marry Arthur Miller."

"Arthur Miller? You just got home from a honeymoon. You told me how wonderful Joe was, how happy he made you, and what a great time you had! Now you tell me you're going to marry Arthur Miller. I don't understand."

"You will. You'll see."

For a long time after their first meeting, Monroe kept a photo of Miller by her bedside. Full of curiosity but with no structure to organize her learning, Monroe felt an intellectual inadequacy that only added to her shame-filled insecurity. Inspired by Miller, she began taking courses at UCLA. She imagined Miller seeing one of her movies in New York. Her letters to Kazan, with whom she continued to have an affair for another year after Miller was out of the picture, were full of concern about him. "Try to cheer him up," she wrote. "Make him believe everything isn't hopeless."

Between their parting and their reunion four years later, much more had changed for Monroe than for Miller. In 1952 five of her films were released; by 1955 the unknown starlet whose feet Miller had massaged on a Hollywood couch had become a figure of universal attention. Monroe was on a first-name basis with the world. She was "Marilyn"—that bright idea of herself and her greatest theatrical creation, who distracted both the world and herself from misery. "I can't forget all the unhappiness . . . but I'd like to try," she said. "When I am 'Marilyn Monroe,' I don't think about 'Norma Jean.'" In her guileless kewpie-doll persona Monroe's gaiety and her grief somehow coalesced. What was caught by the camera lens was a playful, unforgettable paradox: innocent and rapacious, credulous and cunning, desirable and detached. Her oblique attitude toward emotion—the ability to both feel and comment on what she was feeling—made her sexuality funny and unthreatening. "To put it briefly, she had a quality no one else had on screen, except Garbo," said the director Billy Wilder, who worked with her on *Some Like It Hot* and *The Seven Year Itch*. By 1953, Monroe had been on the cover of *Life* and was *Playboy's* first ever Playmate of the Month. She had played opposite Jack Benny on his television show and turned the scandal of early nude calendar shots into an international conversation. Her fan mail ballooned from five thousand letters a week in 1952 to twenty-five thousand the following year.

Her legend was also burnished by her two-year romance with "Joltin' Joe" DiMaggio, baseball's superstar, who became involved with her the year he retired from the New York Yankees. It was a publicity bonanza. DiMaggio, a good Catholic boy who had also not finished high school, was shy, loyal, conventional, and a physical specimen. "He moves like a living statue," Monroe said. Although DiMaggio disliked Hollywood, her movie roles (he didn't think she was talented and wanted her to quit the business), her provocative clothes, and the clamorous attention she attracted, they married in 1954. Monroe married for protection; she didn't reckon on possession. A romantic and dutiful lover, DiMaggio proved punishing and disdainful as a husband, a monster of jealousy and emotional abuse. She claimed that he ignored her, sometimes refusing to speak to her for days. On occasion he also slapped her around. Monroe, who had never seen DiMaggio play baseball, dubbed him slyly "Joe the Slugger." "He wanted me to be the beautiful ex-actress, just like he was the great former baseball player. We would ride into the sunset forever," she said when they divorced after eight months of marriage. "I wasn't even thirty, for God's sake." The news of the divorce, the Associated Press reported, "hit Hollywood like an A-Bomb," and proved, as Oscar Levant quipped, "that no man can be a success in two national pastimes."

According to Miller, Monroe "refused to take one nickel from DiMaggio, even though she could have held him up for a fortune." "I'm not interested in money. I just want to be wonderful," she said. By the time of the divorce, she was making $750 a week and was a singular box office sensation, the most famous screen personality since Jean Harlow. But she was a powerhouse without the power to manage her own creative destiny: she was not getting the parts, the control, the pay, or the respect she wanted. "I knew there was more I could do, and more that I was. Nobody was listening to me," she recalled. She decided to shed her screen persona as the Beatific Bimbo, whose breathy voice mocked the stereotype even as it ravished. "I want to be an artist not an erotic freak. I don't want to be sold to the public as a celluloid aphrodisiac." In search of an education and a new artistic identity, she decamped to New York and the Actors Studio. "I never had a chance to learn anything in Hollywood. They worked me too fast. They rushed me from one picture to another. It's no challenge to do the same thing over and over again," she explained, adding, "I want to keep growing as a person and as an actress. . . . After all, if I can't be myself, what's the good of being anything at all."

Monroe's move was bold; for someone as fragile, unmoored, and fearful as she, however, it was fraught with danger. She needed support and guidance. She looked for it first in her friend the photographer Milton Greene, who briefly became her manager and at whose Connecticut home she lived for a time. A movie industry tyro—"He just didn't have it," Miller said later—Greene set up, in exchange for half her profits, Marilyn Monroe Productions, which produced *The Prince and the Showgirl* before it collapsed. Greene also renegotiated Monroe's lucrative contract with 20th Century–Fox which allowed her to make four independent films over seven years, and to have approval of script, director, and cinematographer, plus a hundred-thousand-dollar salary and a percentage of the gross.

Monroe also fell under the spell of Lee Strasberg, the powerful artistic director of the Actors Studio, who effusively praised her talent and gave her private lessons. Strasberg convinced Monroe to go into Freudian analysis, as well as to employ his wife, Paula, as her on-set drama coach. ("She didn't know anything more about acting than a cleaning woman," Miller said.) For a time Monroe also moved into her guru's family home. It was at the Strasbergs' spacious apartment in the Dakota on Central Park West that Miller re-met Monroe in June 1955.

Earlier in the year, Monroe had been introduced to Miller's university compadre, the playwright and poet Norman Rosten, who was also a Brooklyn resident. Rosten told Miller that she was in town. "I still did not see her because I was going to hang on to the bitter end and beyond. But I could not write anymore," Miller told his parents. When Miller and Monroe were reunited at the Strasbergs both were at emotional crossroads. "I had lots to do. I was preparing for a new stage in my career. But Arthur didn't have much to do. In a way, I felt sorry for him," Monroe said. To Miller, Monroe had always been "a whirling light." At their reunion she seemed as bright as ever. "It was wonderful to be around her," Miller said. "She was simply overwhelming. She had so much promise. It seemed to me that she could really be a great kind of phenomenon, a terrific artist. She was endlessly fascinating, full of original observations, and there wasn't a conventional bone in her body." The next day he asked Paula Strasberg for her phone number.

The rest was more or less headlines.

8

Blonde Heaven

Most marriages, after all, are conspiracies to
deny the dark and confirm the light.

—Arthur Miller, *Timebends*

Marilyn seemed without expectations,
which felt like freedom.

—Arthur Miller, in *Arthur Miller: Writer*

THE EGGHEAD AND THE HOURGLASS. The Genius and the Goddess. The Great American Brain and the Great American Body. The tabloid press turned the Miller-Monroe romance into a saga of sensational opposites; in fact, in many ways, when they met again both were hungering for the same elusive things: inspiration and validation. Each saw in the other a form of redemption. Around the time of their reunion, Miller, trying to dissect his marital stand-off with Mary, his "living challenge," had his protagonist in "The Best Comedians" wonder, "There must be a woman in the world . . . who would . . . want to know what I feel and who would tell me what she feels. I cannot possibly be so totally disgusting."

Monroe's gaze reinvigorated the deflated writer, who again fell under the spell of her radiance. She seemed to drink him in, too. She accepted him and amused him, and, as Norman Mailer observed in *Marilyn*, opened up "this tall and timid hero of middle-class life, as guarded in his synapses as a banker," to a liberating new world of feeling and fun. To Miller, who had lived so long in an emotional desert, Monroe was a kind of oasis. To Monroe, who was rudderless, Miller was a kind of anchor—a father figure (she nicknamed him "Papa"), a teacher, a guide, a solid, substantial man whose stature bolstered her fragile sense of her own worth.

"You aren't there"—Monroe's constant complaint to the men in her life, according to her friend Norman Rosten—did not apply to the attentive Miller, who clung to her like Ishmael to his coffin. And Monroe's adoration was oxygen to Miller's ego. Publicly, he was transformed by the international attention paid to their romance from a loner to a celebrity; privately, he became a kind of savior. As a child Miller had been unable to remedy his father's humiliation at his own ignorance or to overcome his depressed mother's sense of unfulfillment; with Monroe, who was so emotionally impoverished and so grateful for his attention, his messianic urge could finally be satisfied.

The glory of her transformation could reflect on him; likewise, Monroe's complexity and wide experience—"she is enough new experience to last him a lifetime," Mailer wrote—could enrich and unleash his own stymied creative powers. "I began to dream that with her I could do what seemed to me would be the most wonderful thing of all—have my work, and all that implied, and someone I just simply adored," Miller said. If Miller, as he later realized, was being "idealized beyond all human weakness" by Monroe, the inverse was also true. In Monroe's brokenness, Miller saw bravery; in her questing, he saw poetry;

in the sexual degradation that she parlayed into ascendance, he saw a proletarian heroine. "You're a victory," Miller's stand-in says to Monroe's in *After the Fall.* "You're like a flag to me, a kind of proof, somehow, that people can win." The ghosts of their past had been eradicated by the brilliance of their present. "So be my love as you surely are," Miller wrote to her during their courtship, adding, "I believe that I should really die if I ever lost you. It is as though we were born the same morning when no other life existed on this earth."

Their affair began in April 1955. At first the couple would meet at safe houses: the Milton Greenes' in Westport, Connecticut, the Strasbergs' Fire Island retreat, the Rostens' summer place on Long Island's North Fork, and Monroe's apartment in the Waldforf Towers in Manhattan. Sometimes Monroe took a taxi to Brooklyn Heights so they could stroll along the Esplanade and the streets of his youth, or they rode bikes through Manhattan. As Monroe came to occupy him more and more, Miller found himself stuck between the rock of desire and the hard place of marriage. "I was alternately soaring and anxious that I might be slipping into a new life not my own," he said. "My will seemed to have evaporated." Miller wanted to leave, but he could not go. The quandary was resolved by Mary Miller. Having learned of the romance, she kicked Miller out of their home in October, the month he turned forty. Miller moved into the bohemian Chelsea Hotel on West 23rd Street in Manhattan.

Monroe's divorce from DiMaggio came through on October 31. But Monroe, who once characterized her relationship to DiMaggio as "a crazy friendship with sexual privileges," continued to see him even as she was falling for Miller. She also had other things to occupy her time: the Actors Studio, psychoanalysis five times a week, and the negotiation of a new, more favorable contract with 20th Century–Fox. She put no pressure on Miller; in fact, she urged him not to divorce on her account. Monroe, who was frequently humiliated in the press, did not want to be labeled a homewrecker. Before Miller and Mary had made their divorce public, Monroe was cornered by reporters asking about a possible affair. She replied disingenuously, "Why would I do that? He's a married man."

"I have come alive at last, and I mean to keep myself that way," Miller wrote to his parents about his relationship with Monroe. She was both a gift and a gamble, and the pragmatic side of Miller liked the odds. He also liked the attention his association with her brought him. Commercially speaking, as Mailer observed, their romance was the "equivalent to five new works by [Tennessee] Williams." In addition to being, in Mailer's words, "a diamond mine for any playwright looking for a big play," she was the Treasury: Monroe's new studio contract gave her a weekly allowance of five hundred dollars as well as a hundred thousand a film (nearly a million dollars in today's money). At the time of his divorce—the uncontested decree was granted on June 11, 1956, not for Miller's adultery but for Mary's "extreme cruelty, entirely mental in nature"—Miller was taking a beating from Mary's lawyers. "The hatred in her heart, which she has had for years, is now taking the form of this nonsensical warfare," he wrote to his parents, calculating that he'd have to earn forty-three thousand dollars a year to pay the alimony. (Miller's settlement included eleven thousand a year until Mary remarried. She didn't.) He added, "To live anywhere but on the Bowery I will have to make a good deal more than that. . . . I am agreeing to this settlement so that I can proceed with my life."

On May 9, 1956, Miller wrote to his parents, "While I want to marry her [Monroe] someday, I can't say when it will be." Fifty-four days later, on June 29, they were married. Although Miller imagined that to others Monroe might appear to be "a notorious and evil woman," to his mind, she had "more courage, more innate decency, more sensitivity and love for humanity than anyone I have ever met." Many in Miller's cohort were bemused at his naïveté. "That's a wife?" the set designer Boris Aronson exclaimed. Kazan was also astonished at the notion of the marriage. "Marilyn simply wasn't a wife. Anyone could see that," he said.

On February 28, 1955, Miller had completed a draft of a one-act verse play he titled *A View from the Bridge* (his first title was "Under the Sea"). The play opened on Broadway on September 29 as part of a double bill with *A Memory of Two Mondays*, another one-acter he had begun in 1952 while working on *The Crucible*. (The production ran for 149 performances.) "This is the gullet of New York swallowing the tonnage of the world," Alfieri, a lawyer, who serves as the chorus to the tragic tale, says at the opening, describing the working-class Italian enclave on the seaward side of the Brooklyn Bridge where the drama takes place. He adds, "I am inclined to notice the ruin in things, perhaps because I was born in Italy."

The ruin in question is the longshoreman Eddie Carbone, a palooka with no purchase on language or on his own psyche, who is destroyed by his unexamined desire for his teenage niece Catherine, whom he and his wife, Beatrice, have raised. When Catherine falls in love with one of the two illegal immigrants who are living with them—cousins from the old country— Eddie's only way to keep her from getting married is to report the cousins to the Immigration Bureau. By dropping the dime, Eddie betrays his wife, his niece, his relatives, himself, and, by extension, his entire tribe. He's a dead man walking.

Miller called *A View from the Bridge* a "probe." In his exploration of the unraveling of Carbone's forbidden desire, he was not only testing the theater's narrative possibilities but ruminating on the consequences of his own roiling, hidden feelings, in which both betrayal and desire figured. "When I wrote the play I was moving through psychological country strange to me, ugly and forbidding," he said. By using the act of informing as the tragedy's inciting incident, he was also publicly answering Elia Kazan, whose film *On the Waterfront* (1954) had just won the Academy Award for Best Picture. The movie covered the same territory as their abandoned joint project "The Hook"; it also drew, as Miller had, on Malcolm Johnson's 1948 Pulitzer Prize–winning *New York Post* articles about waterfront corruption. Kazan, who won an Academy Award for Best Director, had chosen, however, to dramatize the informer as a hero. "I was telling the world where I stood and my critics to go and fuck themselves," he wrote in *A Life*, adding, "As for Art Miller, the film spoke to him and to Mr. John Wharton"—Miller's lawyer. "I would in time forgive them both—but not that year."

Of Miller's decision to stonewall him after his HUAC testimony, Kazan wrote, "It would have been nice if Art, at this moment, while expressing the strong disapproval he felt, had acknowledged some past friendship—or even written me a few words, however condemnatory." In *A View From the Bridge*, Miller answered back. Where Kazan made his hero a victim of systemic corruption, Miller depicted Carbone as a deluded victimizer. Denounced in his neighborhood and in his home ("You got no more right to tell nobody nothin'! Nobody! The rest of your life, nobody!" Catherine tells him), Carbone dies calling for respect. "I want my good name, Marco. You took my name!" he tells one of the cousins he betrayed. "Animal! You go on your knees to me," Marco says, before stabbing Carbone to death.

"What I think is interesting about *A View* is that it develops a process of human action which holds true for a great many individuals and nations too," Miller wrote to the advertising agency for the play. "It is the process of seeing a disaster approaching in a friend, in a relative, in yourself, perhaps a terrible thing coming closer and closer, and you are unable to reason it away or wish it away or pray it away. Under such circumstances it is not a question of saying someone is bad or good; it is simply that you see a person revealed." He added, of Carbone, "After you've reasoned with life and deceived it and blinded yourself to it and hidden from it, it is still there and the only thing that finally matters is the quality—not necessarily the goodness but the quality of your confrontation with it. Underneath the rest, this is what I was after in this story."

At the suggestion of Peter Brook, who directed the play's British premiere, on October 11, 1956, Miller rewrote *A View from the Bridge* as a two-act prose play. By then the ructions in Miller's private life had tempered his righteous indignation concerning Kazan. In the one-act version, Eddie Carbone is shown no mercy; he dies a humiliating, debased, and deluded death, calling out Catherine's name. In the two-act version, in the last beats of Alfieri's ambivalent envoi, Miller seems to speak across the footlights to Kazan. His rueful weasel words play both as a way of forgiving Kazan his trespasses, and, by extension, allowing Miller to forgive himself for his own. "Even as I know how wrong he was . . . I confess that something perversely pure calls to me from his memory—not purely good, but himself purely, for he allowed himself to be wholly known. . . . And so I mourn him—I admit it—with a certain . . . alarm."

For both Miller and Monroe, 1956 was a watershed year. In February, fortified with a new contract and new artistic control, Monroe went back to work at 20th Century–Fox on *Bus Stop*. In April, Miller set off for Reno, to sit out the required six weeks for a quicky divorce, in a cabin about forty miles north of town overlooking the prehistoric Lake Pyramid, where "there is no living soul nor tree nor shrub above the height of the sagebrush," he wrote to Kenneth Rowe. A few weeks before heading west, Miller had written coyly to Saul Bellow, who was already in residence in Reno with soon-to-be wife No. 2, Sondra Tschacbasov, to ask about places to stay:

I have a problem, however, of slightly unusual proportions. From time to time there will be a visitor who is very dear to me, but who is unfortunately recognizable by approximately a hundred million people, give or take three or four. She has all sorts of wigs, can affect a limp, bulky coats, sunglasses, but, if it is possible I want to find a place, perhaps a bungalow or something like, where there aren't likely to be crowds looking through windows. . . . I need hardly add that this is just barely entre nous, only for the reason that I would rather not crowd [John Foster] Dulles off the front pages until next Winter.

A sense of thrill and self-inflation come through Miller's swagger. In Nevada, Bellow became Miller's next-door neighbor, as well as his frequent dinner companion. "He talked non-stop about Marilyn," Sondra Bellow recalled. "Her career, her beauty, her talent, even her perfect feet. He showed us the now famous photos by Milton Greene—all quite enlightening since neither Mr. Bellow nor I had ever even heard of her before this."

At this point in his career, commercially, Miller had hit still water. Although *The Crucible* and *A View from the Bridge* would, over the years, become staples of the American repertory, initially they were succès d'estimes, or, rather, successes that ran out of steam. "Such was the hubris of the time," Brooks Atkinson wrote years later, recalling the premiere of the one-act double bill, "that the plays were produced solemnly like major works of art, as if Mr. Miller were already a classic." In fact, Miller was struggling. Even a screenplay that New York City had commissioned about street gangs and the urban problem had been canceled because of his "questionable political background." The American Legion and the Catholic War Veterans had lodged a complaint with the sponsoring city body, citing Miller's links to "subversive organizations." Of the eight city commissioners, or their deputies, responsible for green-lighting Miller's twenty-five-page treatment, seven voted against. "I'm not calling him a Communist," said one of the members of the City Youth Board who voted in the majority. "My objection is he refuses to repent." "City Crime Film off in Red-Taint Battle" read the headline in the *New York World-Telegram and Sun*, which ran an editorial suggesting that perhaps the film could be made if Miller's name were removed.

But now that he was playing a part in the saga of Monroe's life, Miller took on a new amperage. He may have deplored the publicity scrum, but some part of him was also excited by the psychic imperialism of stardom. From Hollywood, on one of her nightly phone calls to a Nevada pay phone, Monroe told him that President Sukarno of Indonesia had refused to attend a gala cocktail party unless she was present. "She goes to meet him," Miller wrote to Bellow. "He asks, 'You are going to marry Mr. Miller?' She shrugs. He giggles, says, 'I think that will be very fine.'" Miller was living at a new velocity; giddiness now mixed with gravity to become part of his metabolism. Miller's plays aspired to disenchant; Monroe's celebrity turned them both into magical figures who fed the culture's spell of distraction. Miller's plays were no longer the news; *he* was. In early June, a New York *Daily News* reporter found him in his Pyramid Lake bunker. Miller wrote to Bellow, "The next day the front page of the *News* had us about to be married. All hell breaks loose. The phones all around never stop ringing. Television trucks (as I live!)—drive up cameras grinding, screams, yells. I say nothing, give them some pictures, retire into the cabin." Just the day before, Miller had arranged for Monroe to join him in his lunar landscape. "I called her and cancelled her visit," he told Bellow. "Imagine if [the reporter] had got here a day later! ALORS!"

Miller's new life was beginning. He could put his old private life behind him but not his political one. In early 1956, when the New York gossip columnists first got wind of the romance, Walter Winchell alerted his readers to "the fact that America's best-known blonde moving picture star is now the darling of the left-wing intelligentsia, several of whom are listed as red fronters. I don't think she realizes it." The FBI, which had recently compiled a ninety-five-page file on Miller, now began one on Monroe. In May, on his radio show, Winchell told Mr. and Mrs. America, "The House Committee on Un-American Activities is going after Broadway Commies again. Proceedings are on the way. One of Marilyn Monroe's new romances, a long-time pro-lefto, will be asked to testify."

On June 8, 1956, three days before Miller had completed his Nevada residency and could be officially divorced, he was served with a subpoena compelling him to appear before HUAC, which had recently opened public hearings on "the fraudulent procurement and misuse of American passports by persons in the service of the Communist conspiracy." Miller was seeking a passport to go to England to join Monroe on the set of *The Prince and the Showgirl*, the first film to be produced by her own company. In 1954 he had been refused a passport to go to Brussels for the premiere of *The Crucible;* there was no certainty that the refusal would be reversed. Given her dependence on Miller, Monroe, too, was in trouble: How could she leave for England without him? From her sequestered sidelines she cheered on her Great Man. "He's got to tell them to go fuck themselves, only he can do it in better language," she told her friend the actress Susan Strasberg.

On June 21, Miller appeared before the House Committee, with the renowned Washington lawyer Joseph Rauh by his side. There was no doubt that he was stepping into a theatrical arena. But whose theater was it? Prior to his public romance with Monroe, the Committee had shown no interest in interviewing Miller; now, as the whole Red Scare was beginning to bore the American public—"People feel that this subject has had it," Miller said around this time—the publicity surrounding Miller's appearance drew attention back to the Committee and its crusade. At 10 a.m., as Miller took his seat in the caucus room of the House Office Building, he recalled in *Timebends*, "The large number of reporters present (including I. F. Stone, perhaps the hardest working and best reporter in Washington) and especially the unprecedented appearance of more than twenty foreign journalists all seated at a long table far from me."

Miller had an audience and a stage. Ironically, the night before, over drinks with Monroe at Rauh's home, he'd learned that the congressional sideshow didn't have to go on. "How would you like to not have to go into the hearing tomorrow?" Rauh had asked him, after taking a call from the office of Representative Francis Walter, the chairman of the Committee. If Monroe agreed to pose for a photograph with the congressman, the political interrogation would be canceled. "I burst out laughing," Miller, who was eager to confront the Committee, wrote. In 1954, Miller had written a fierce satire of McCarthyism in the *Nation* titled "Every American Should Go to Jail: A Modest Proposal for Pacifying the Public Temper." Now it was his turn to walk the walk. Before the day's official proceedings began, Miller read a prepared, combative statement to the press, which concluded:

> If Arthur Miller is now a disgraced person: if my past and present antagonism to jingoism, monopoly capitalism, and the brick-headed reaction of veterans groups and the lunatic fringe—if this makes me unfit to speak through my plays to the People, then I leave it to history as to who is "American" and who her enemy. . . . I shall hold to an image of man free of irrational fears, conscious of his power to create goodness, and in control of machines that now enslave him. If that quest is now prohibited in America as treasonable then I belong in jail, for I will go on with it. I give fair warning. I will go on with it until the end.

Miller seemed to be spoiling for a fight. But instead of box-
ing the Committee's ears off—as Paul Robeson and the screen-
writer John Howard Lawson had done—he courteously bobbed
and weaved around their clumsy punches. "The slightly amazing thing to me is that I never felt scared at all," he wrote to
Bellow. "Something's snapped in me—the connections of fear.
I guess I have reached that ancient and dangerous stage when
one just doesn't give a shit."

The hearing began with an account of Miller's passport
history—for a month and a half he had been waiting for the
State Department's response to his current application—but
it soon veered into an examination of his political past. "Mr.
Miller was eager to talk about his present views, and the committee kept turning him a deaf ear," Mary McCarthy reported.
The dogged congressional questioning yielded garrulous answers from Miller, who treated the Committee like an audience
at an author's Q&A. He invoked Socrates, the Spanish Civil
War, and anti-Semitism in prewar Brooklyn. He talked at length
about what had kept him in the Communist orbit until 1948.
Was he against the Smith Act, which made it a crime to speak
of or advocate the overthrow of the government? "I am not
here defending Communists. I am here defending the right
of an author to advocate," Miller said. Did he believe that one
should be allowed to write a *poem* advocating the overthrow of
the government? one bewildered congressman wanted to know.
"I would say that a man should have the right to write a poem
just about anything," Miller replied. And what about his views
on Ezra Pound? Did he know Elia Kazan? And was he aware
that one of his own plays—*You're Next*—had been produced by
the Communist Party? "I take no more responsibility for who
plays my plays than General Motors can take for who rides in
their Chevrolets," Miller said.

After a long and fruitless game of cat-and-mouse, the Committee slowly got down to the real purpose of the stage-managed

loyalty test: getting Miller to corroborate the names of suspected Communist sympathizers. The strategy was to make betrayal seem like a norm of good citizenship. As Mary McCarthy put it, "It was not necessary that Mr. Miller *be* an informer; he was merely being asked to *act* like one, to define himself as the kind of person who would interpose." But first the Committee asked him why he wanted a new passport, which gave Miller, either consciously or unconsciously, the chance to drop the only name of the afternoon.

"The objective is double," Miller said. "I have a production which is in the talking stages in England of *A View from the Bridge* and I will be there to be with the woman who will then be my wife. That is my plan." (In New York, Monroe, who was listening to the hearings, called the Rostens in Brooklyn. "He announced it before the whole world! He told the whole world he was marrying Marilyn Monroe—me!" she said. "Can you believe it! You know he never really asked me. I mean, *really* asked *me* to marry *him*. We talked about it but it was all very vague.")

What Miller did next made him a heroic legend not just to Monroe but to the American left. Unlike almost all the previous prominent personalities, who, when asked to name names, had either complied with the Committee or claimed the Fifth Amendment, which protected them from self-incrimination, Miller politely replied to the chairman that he could not in good conscience do as they asked. "I want you to understand that I am not protecting the Communists or the Communist Party," he told the Committee, then echoed John Proctor's speech in *The Crucible*. "I am trying to and I will protect my sense of myself. I could not use the name of another person and bring trouble on him." Miller went on: "I will be perfectly frank with you in anything relating to my activities but I cannot take responsibility for another human being. . . . My conscience will not permit me to use the name of another person. . . . My

counsel advises me that there is no relevance between this question and the question of whether I should have a passport."

Miller's assertion of private scruples was of no interest to
the Committee, or, at first, to the press. The next day's headlines involved not his current actions but his political past: "Arthur Miller Admits Helping Communist-Front Groups in the
40's" (*New York Times*), "Marilyn's Fiancé Admits Aiding Reds"
(*Chicago Tribune*), "Miller Admits Aiding Reds, Risks Contempt"
(New York *Daily News*).

By late that afternoon, a scrum of reporters had backed
Monroe against the wall of her Sutton Place apartment in New
York. What kind of wedding did she want? they asked "Any
kind," Marilyn said. What attracted her to Miller? "Everything!"
she said in her breathy voice. "Haven't you seen him?" In Washington, where gravity still ruled, at the same hour, Francis Walter was already tossing cold water on the romantic news. "Despite
June and Cupid, this man will be dealt with just as everybody
else who appears before this Committee," he said. Miller was
granted a temporary six-month visa to travel to England. On
July 25, however, in a vote of 379 to 9, the House of Repre-
sentatives cited Miller for contempt; he was given a suspended
sentence of thirty days in prison and a five-hundred-dollar
fine. (In 1958 the U.S. Court of Appeals reversed the decision,
the last move in a political fiasco that ended up costing Miller
about forty thousand dollars.) By then, the Monroe-Miller union
was occupying the national attention. In the public imagination Miller's somewhat rambling confrontation with HUAC
had elevated him to "the risk-taking conscience of his times."
Among left-wing liberals, like the ever-competitive Lillian
Hellman, who had also been defended by Rauh but had taken
the Fifth, Miller's performance seemed overrated. Of his claim
to the Committee that in writing *The Crucible* he had "been to
hell and back and seen the devil," Hellman quipped, he "must
have gone as a tourist." On June 29, 1956, only eight days after

his testimony, Miller tied the knot with Monroe in a civil ceremony in White Plains. Two days later, with about thirty friends looking on, they married again, in a Jewish ceremony, at the Connecticut home of Miller's agent Kay Brown. (Monroe's conversion, according to Miller, took a couple of hours with the officiating Reform rabbi.) The wedding party then moved on to Roxbury, to celebrate at Miller's home with champagne and shellfish. Reflecting later on the marriage, Miller said, "It was an attempt on my part and on hers to transcend the barriers between two kinds of living—the one which was more sexual, the other more intellectual." Only months earlier, Monroe, exhausted from struggling through the production of *Bus Stop*, had wept on the phone to Miller in Nevada. "Oh, Papa, I can't do it," Miller recalled her saying. "I hate Hollywood. I don't want it anymore. I want to live quietly in the country and just be there when you need me. I can't fight for myself anymore." In Miller, Monroe had found her protector and her healer. "She looked to me to keep everything happy," he said. As Kazan saw it, "Art gave Marilyn a rose-tinted view of her future, that of an elite actress, doing serious work. He promised to write a film for her." Monroe now seemed to have everything she'd always wanted, including in-laws.

On July 13, with twenty-seven suitcases in tow only three of which were his (excess baggage charge: $1,500), Miller and Monroe set off for London and their working honeymoon. Pandemonium surrounded their New York take-off and their London touchdown at Croyden, the old wartime airfield, which was then London's main airport. "She shattered a thousand years of British imperturbability," Miller said of their arrival. More than seventy British bobbies had cordoned off the four hundred shouting reporters and photographers. "There was little else in any newspaper the next day, and on certain other days too during her months in England," Miller said, adding, "Marilyn was among them, a goddess risen from their cold sea." The adoring couple, both dressed in white, posed for the press holding hands; the gold wedding ring Monroe wore was inscribed "A to M. Now is Forever." A thirty-car caravan led them into the Surrey countryside, an hour outside London, and up a long gravel path to Parkside, a grand Georgian manor next to the queen's own Windsor Great Park, where they would live for four months with seven servants at their service. "Arthur was going to make my life different—better, a lot better. If I were nothing but a dumb blonde, he wouldn't have married me," Monroe said.

9

Love's Labour's

Innocence kills.

—Arthur Miller, *Timebends*

"I WONDER IF MAYBE there was just too much hope: we drank it, swam in it. And for fear of losing it didn't dare look inside," Miller wrote in his last play, *Finishing the Picture* (2004), still trying to fathom his marriage to Monroe forty-eight years on. Certainly when the pair stood before the clamoring British press in the airport canteen in 1956, resplendent in the glow of their white outfits and their collective promise, to the world and to themselves they were the culture's power couple, poised, in their own minds, at a watershed moment, "each of us doing our own work side by side, drawing strength from each other," Miller said.

They had joined forces, but with little understanding of the energies their union yoked together. Miller had earned the sedate renown of a Broadway grandee; he knew nothing of the deracinating momentum of superstardom. In the ardor of their whirlwind romance, ravished by Monroe's practiced and compelling gaiety, he had failed to engage with the deep, anarchic currents of what she called her "terror beyond fear." Kazan, too, used the bomb analogy: "She had a bomb inside her. Ignite her and she exploded." "Art, by comparison, was an innocent, and out of his depth," he observed.

From the outset, Monroe craved Miller's adoration and played to it. "He saw me as so beautiful and innocent among the Hollywood wolves that I tried to be like that," she said. As Miller confessed to his parents a month before the wedding, they had not had much "continuous time" together: a rookie mistake. Their romance had been conducted in fits and starts, between long, work-enforced absences, which were oxygen to their desire. (While Monroe was shooting *Bus Stop*, Miller, in breach of Nevada's divorce law, would sneak to Los Angeles to shack up with her at the Chateau Marmont on her weekends off.) He believed in Monroe's potential as a great actress—"She has a talent beyond most dreams," he said—but until their trip to England, he had seen her only on-screen and never at work.

Now, unlike Joe DiMaggio, who had never believed in Monroe's art or appeared with her in public, Miller stood on parade at all public occasions—her knight, her shelter, her talisman of transformation. Monroe, Kazan said, "went for the drug of reassurance." And Miller was that drug, her contact high. He was beside her the day after their arrival for a press conference at the Savoy Hotel, where four thousand people lined the Strand for a glimpse of her; he was there to squire her to a ball for the British talentocracy, which Terence Rattigan, who adapted his play *The Sleeping Prince* into the screenplay of *The Prince and the Showgirl*, threw in her honor; and he was with her when Harrods closed to the public so that she could shop without fear of being mauled by fans. And as *The Prince and the Showgirl* hit rough water, he was there to help steer her through it, in vain as it happened.

The Prince and the Showgirl was the first production of

Monroe's new company. By choosing Sir Laurence Olivier, the greatest British actor of his era, to be her director and co-star, Monroe was demanding respect for her own acting abilities. Olivier, in agreeing, at fifty, to play opposite Monroe, was betting on his box-office appeal as a male lead. Monroe's regard for Olivier verged on awe. Prior to her arrival at Pinewood Studios, she had torn up his original contract, which gave him 25 percent of the film's profits and her 75, and made it a 49–51 split in her favor. "He, she said, is a great artist and she is just a beginner," Miller reported to his parents. "It would be wrong to take so much more than he."

From the beginning, as Norman Rosten—who, with his wife, Hedda, had been imported for the Millers' emotional support—observed, "Arthur was plunged into a world of daily crises, unspoken antagonisms, endless decisions, and the necessity of providing Marilyn with almost constant support." Monroe's retinue included a cook, hairdresser, bodyguard, makeup man, masseur, two publicists, and, most important, Paula Strasberg, her acting coach (and stand-in for her acting swami, Lee Strasberg), who became in short order a spanner in Olivier's directorial works. Paid $2,500 a week for "her puddings of acting philosophy," as Miller called them, Strasberg fed Monroe a constant stream of affirmation about her greatness and Olivier's competitive envy. Miller thought her "poisonous and vacuous": he hated Monroe's "nearly religious dependency" on her almost as much as did Olivier, who dubbed Strasberg "the beast." Olivier was so infuriated by her intrusiveness that he banned her from the set only to have her reinstated by Monroe under threat of a walk-out.

Monroe was late to the set on the first day, and Olivier's suave welcome came across to her as patronizing. From that moment, according to Rosten, "She was on guard, suspicious, sullen, defensive with flashes of anger breaking out." On the second day of shooting, when Monroe was three-quarters of an hour late, Olivier insisted that she apologize to Dame Sybil Thorndike, who was playing the Dowager Queen. When, later that week, Monroe felt that Olivier had denigrated her talent by saying, "All right, Marilyn, be sexy," she stalked off the set. "He looked at me as if he had just smelled dead fish," she fumed to her maid. "Like I was a leper, or something awful. He'd say something like, 'Oh, how ravishing, my dear.' But he really wanted to throw up."

Monroe paid Olivier back with self-indulgence and insolence, addressing him as "Sir Olivier," and looking to Strasberg for direction. "She doesn't really forget her lines. It's more as if she never quite learnt them," Colin Clark, a director's assistant and Monroe's minder, wrote. One scene, in which she had to eat caviar and sip champagne, took thirty-two takes and two cans of caviar; Monroe also insisted on real champagne, not juice, and increasingly slurred her words.

"When the monster showed, Arthur couldn't believe it," Monroe later said. Before her husband's eyes, Monroe's cheerfulness and optimism vanished and were replaced with a spectacle of sleep-starved, drugged collapse. "She was like a smashed vase. It is a beautiful thing when it is intact, but the broken pieces are murderous and they could cut," Miller wrote in *Timebends*. Monroe was, he said, "bedevilled by feelings she could not name." The depth of her darkness was heartbreaking and disorienting; it was as if the cruel betrayals of her upbringing were being re-created in her struggles with the production and her own business partner, Milton Greene, who she discovered had been cheating her. "She had idealized Greene's ability to set up her financial life and now felt deceived; she had idealized Olivier as a grand artist without egoistic envy of her, a kind of actor-escort or father who would think only of safeguarding her; I too was crumbling because I could not smash her enemies with one magic stroke," Miller wrote.

As distressed as he was by his wife's anguish, Miller was also perplexed by her unprofessional behavior. "To me no film was worth this kind of destruction, while to her a performance was almost literally worth a life," he said. When he tried to cajole her out of her paranoia about Olivier or her pill popping—"the little suicides each night"—Monroe accused him of trivializing her torment. He was encountering a new rigidity in Monroe, which brooked no disagreement or ameliorating word. "Once she made a judgement in relation to people, she was adamant (one of her less appealing traits)," Rosten noted. "She demanded the loyalty of her friends in this judgement. 'If you're my friend, you can't like anyone I dislike' was her motto." Miller's defense of Olivier played into Monroe's irrational fear of abandonment. "She was felled by my stubbornness, everything was over; if she was so opposed she could not be loved," he explained. In her eyes, Miller had failed to protect her. In his eyes, he had extricated himself from the disapproving tyranny of his first marriage only to be trapped, four months into his second marriage, by another kind of tyranny, submission to the weak.

In August, in the middle of this turbulent psychological stand-off, Miller went back to America for a few weeks to see his children. Monroe's New York psychiatrist and Lee Strasberg himself flew in to help support her in his absence. Before his departure, whether unconsciously or by design, Miller had left out his notebook, which Monroe read. The incident, which Miller does not mention in *Timebends*, seems to have broken the spell of their romance. To his notebook, he had confided the sour feelings he had had to repress in order to get a hearing with his wife. "It was something about how disappointed he was with me," Monroe tearfully told Lee Strasberg. "How he thought I was some kind of angel but now he guessed he was wrong. That his first wife had let him down, but I had done something worse. Olivier was beginning to think I was a troublesome bitch and that he (Arthur) no longer had a decent answer for that one."

* * *

When the couple returned to America in late November it was with more guilt than glory. "England, I feared, had humbled both of us," Miller wrote. The big magic of their talent had failed to transform their lives. "We were as we were before, but worse; it was as though we had misled one another. She had no resources to rally against our failure." Miller hoped that once they were settled in their Connecticut farmhouse and their Sutton Place apartment they could rediscover the sweetness and trust they had originally kindled in each other.

Monroe made a stab at being a conventional housewife, redecorating and rearranging rooms in which she was never quite comfortable. Miller tried to get back to his writing routine—rising at 5 a.m. and working until 11—though this was harder now that he kept Monroe company through her sleepless nights. Shuttling between two homes and two domestic rhythms also made it difficult for Miller to get work done. The solitude that he needed for his craft was not a match for Monroe's metabolism. She longed for distraction and excitement—social contact, noise, attention. "It would have been easier for me with a more party-going kind of man, but that would be easy for one side of me," she said.

"I'd say out of five we had two good years," Miller said. "But her addiction to pills and drugs defeated me. If there was a key to her despair I never found it." Monroe's mood swings were hard to read or to fathom. "When she's high, a sweet chime of music surrounds her," Norman Rosten, who spent the summer of 1956 with the Millers in Amagansett, Long Island, recalled. "When she's low, she moves to another plane, withdrawn, private." Even within the window of their good years, Miller recalled once having had to restrain Marilyn from jumping from their Sutton Place window. In Amagansett, depressed after miscarrying an ectopic pregnancy, she overdosed on Nembutal and had to be rushed to the hospital. Monroe, who'd had twelve abortions, wanted to give Miller the family they had dreamed of. But doubt had seeped into their relationship. "That's what I want most of all, the baby, I guess, but maybe God is trying to tell me something," Monroe wrote to Rosten, adding, "I'd probably make a kooky mother. I want it, yet I'm scared. Arthur says he wants it, but he's losing his enthusiasm."

Monroe had been Miller's heroine; now she transformed into his child. "The kids were here until a month ago," he wrote to a friend. "It took some adjusting but they, with Marilyn, are all together now, my three children." The new note of condescension was hard to miss. Miller, who was heavily invested in the idea of himself as a moral man, doubled down on his dutifulness. He was, as Norman Mailer wrote, "her god, her guard, her attendant, and her flunky." For himself and for the public, Miller's show of attentiveness kept alive the idea of Monroe as a powerhouse and him as an angel of repair. By helping her be the actress and the integrated person she wanted to be, he could do for her what he had never been able to do for his stalled family—vanquish humiliation and shame. He was determined to make good on his vow to write Monroe into a serious work, a paean to her "greatness of spirit . . . a crazy kind of nobility that the right role might release." He set about expanding and adapting a story he had published in *Esquire*, "The Misfits: Chicken Feed—The Last Frontier of the Quixotic Cowboy," into a screenplay that would be a vehicle for Monroe.

Still, the union that Miller and Monroe had imagined as a shelter became, by degrees, a kind of prison. "I have come out of the cold," Monroe said in the first year of their marriage; by the third year, the chill had settled back in, and her stalwart knight had become yet another male abandoner. "He stays as far away as he can. Gets up before she does and usually doesn't say two words to her all day," their New York maid reported. Miller required privacy; Monroe needed attention. "Every morning he goes into that goddamn study of his and I don't see him for hours and hours. I mean what the fuck is he doing in there," she complained to friends. Increasingly, Miller was living with Monroe "in the third person," as Rosten observed. Even his erudition, which had at first excited Monroe's desire for self-improvement, now only increased her sense of lack. "I don't think I'm the woman for Arthur," she told friends. "He needs an intellectual, somebody he can talk to. . . . He makes me think I'm stupid. Gee, he almost scares me sometimes."

By 1958, Monroe was at the high point of her career, shooting *Some Like It Hot*, but her marriage was floundering. "I have a feeling this boat is *never* going to dock," she wrote to Rosten. "We are going through the Straits of Dire. It's rough and choppy but why should I worry I have no phallic symbol to lose." Miller did. He quarreled loudly with her on the set. "With Arthur it all seemed sour," the director, Billy Wilder, said. "And I remember saying at the time that in meeting Miller at last I met someone who resented her more than I did."

A week after the film wrapped, Monroe had a second miscarriage. A few days later, in a newspaper interview, Wilder was asked if he would make a third film with Monroe. "I discussed this project with my doctor and my psychiatrist, and they tell me I am too old and too rich to go through this again," he quipped. Miller rounded furiously on Wilder. "I cannot let your vicious attack go unchallenged," he telegraphed. "You were officially informed by Marilyn's physician that due to her pregnancy she was not able to work a full day. You chose to ignore that during the making of the picture." By telegram the same day, Wilder replied to Miller's accusations of cruelty and injustice:

> The fact is that the company pampered her, coddled her and acceded to all her whims. The only one who showed any lack of consideration was Marilyn, in her treatment of her co-stars and her co-workers right from the first day, before there was any hint of pregnancy. . . . Her chronic tardiness and unpreparedness cost us eighteen shooting days, hundreds

of thousands of dollars and countless heartaches. . . . This having been my second picture with Marilyn, I understand her problems. Her biggest problem is that she doesn't understand anyone else's problems. . . . Had you, dear Arthur, been subjected to all the indignities I was, you would have thrown her out on her can, thermos bottle and all, to avoid a nervous breakdown.

In March 1957, before Monroe started shooting *Some Like It Hot*, Miller had pitched *The Misfits* to Wilder. Miller thought of the screenplay as an "Eastern Western." In his eyes it was a meditation on the "dislocation of people of my generation" who had "lost any orientation politically or socially, for that matter." In the original story, three free-wheeling cowboys wander through their aimless days in the Nevada desert, enjoying their freedom, living hand to mouth from odd jobs, including wrangling wild horses by airplane and truck to sell as dog meat. In this well-told tale, the focus is on the men's strong feelings for one another, and the character of Roslyn—the forty-year-old lover of one of the cowboys, Gay Langland—is an incidental figure who is referred to but never appears. In the movie, the story becomes an exploration of the men's strong feelings for her. Roslyn appears as a kind of answer to each man's emotional prayers; the movie was an answer to Miller's. He needed a hit, and he needed to consolidate his marriage. Monroe needed a role that would stretch her and confirm her in the eyes of the world as a serious actress.

In the film, Roslyn takes up with Gay (played by Clark Gable), an older, stoic divorcé who has left his wife and children. The character was based on a cowboy Miller had met in Reno. While writing, to make up for the fact that Gay felt "too distant from me," Miller said, "I transferred some of my background." In fact, he invested Gay not only with his own personality—"respectful, ardent, humorous, and above all, kind"—but with his emotional predicament. "I must perhaps dramatize her awareness of his *distinctive* kindness in the beginning, as opposed to her [former] husband's sadism," Miller wrote to Wilder. Gay, he went on, "is at a dawning crisis in his life. An adventurer ought not to grow middle aged. For the first time he finds himself afraid it will not be he who walks away from the relationship, but the other. The solution for him is to assert his skill, his craft; as well, to earn money of his own instead of living on hers." Gay coaxes Roslyn to join him on a hunt for wild horses. "He conceives the mustang hunt to win her back, to dominate her, to bedazzle her, to assert his strength before her again and thus to conquer and dispel her uneasiness and its threat of dismissal for him," Miller explained.

Both the story and the film end on a note of tentative hope. "The love between them is viable, holding them a little above the earth," Miller writes in the story's last beat. At the end of the movie, as they drive down a bumpy road into the night, Roslyn asks Gay, "How do you find your way back in the dark?" "Just head for that big star straight on," he answers. "The highway's right under it: take us right home." *Home* is the movie's last word as the couple disappear into "absolute silence."

The first draft of *The Misfits* was finished in October 1957. Miller thought of it as a gift to Monroe. But by the time the cameras rolled, on July 18, 1960, it had become an epitaph. Miller and Monroe were lost to each other. "There's no communication between us anymore, and I feel so inferior around him. He seems so distant," she said in 1959, a year before embarking on an affair with her co-star Yves Montand on the set of *Let's Make Love*, a film whose dialogue Miller had punched up. The affair became humiliating headline news. "I was sympathetic to Art, not her," Kazan said. "I knew how unprepared he was for that kind of tension. I also knew the degree of anger and vengeance she'd felt; it had been unremitting and without pity." Within weeks of completing *Let's Make Love*, Monroe started shooting *The Misfits*. According to Monroe's biographer Barbara Leaming, Miller, who was also the film's executive producer and had a lot riding on the project, had done everything to ensure that Monroe would show up on time to begin the film. "He had kept her in New York until the last minute. He had dealt with her agents. He had haggled with the studio. He had endured her rages," Leaming writes. By then the project, begun as an act of empathy, was received by Monroe as one of exploitation. Her hero had become the enemy, as Rosten noted, "a representative of the movie industry, using her much the same way as the others."

At the outset of their romance, Monroe perceived Miller as a great artist who was above the show-biz merry-go-round. She spoke of a desire to play Grushenka in *The Brothers Karamazov;* Lady Macbeth, Lee Strasberg suggested, was within her range. Miller had promised to write a play that showcased her as the serious actress he was sure she was. But the role of Roslyn turned out to be not so much an advance as a replica of "how he saw me before we broke up," she said. "She is that girl . . . whose childhood has never ended," Miller explained to the French director René Clement, to whom he had sent the *Misfits* screenplay. "She is a poet without words who must always make those about her uneasy until they have hurt her. . . . She is lyrical, abrupt, passionately sympathetic. It is not a world for such a girl once she is past sixteen." Roslyn was not so much a departure as a return, a role that trapped Monroe into playing the illusion that had betrayed them both. For Miller, the screenplay was an act of resuscitation; for Monroe, it was a suffocation. The film was, in a sense, a cinematic rehearsal of the divorce she would soon seek from Miller.

On every page of the script, Monroe found Roslyn quoting her real life back at her. In the opening scene, for instance, Roslyn's landlady, Isabelle (Thelma Ritter), helps her rehearse her remarks to the Reno divorce judge; the lines were taken whole cloth from the proceedings of Monroe's divorce from Joe DiMaggio. In another scene, Gay's observation, "You're the saddest girl I ever met," and Roslyn's reply, "No one ever said that to me," was an actual exchange lifted from Miller and Monroe's romance. And when Isabelle tries to console Roslyn with "At least you had your own mother," the family history Roslyn details is specifically Monroe's: "How do you have somebody who disappears all the time? She'd go off with a patient for three months." Even the dilapidated house that Gay and Roslyn haphazardly renovate—an echo of Miller and Monroe's unfinished Roxbury farmhouse—contains visual reminders of the past that Monroe was trying to put behind her. Taped on Gay's closet door are pin-up shots of Monroe. "Don't look at those," Roslyn says. "They're nothing. Gay just put them up as a joke."

"She doesn't like me. How could she? I didn't save her, I didn't do the miracle I kind of promised. And she didn't save me, as she promised. So nothing *moved*, you know?" says Paul, Miller's stand-in in *Finishing the Picture* (2004), of the balky film star who is refusing to emerge from her trailer. He adds, "I'm afraid of her now—I have no idea what she's going to do next." Monroe's capriciousness toward Miller began well before she stepped on the set of *The Misfits*. Months earlier, when demanding rewrites on the script, she got Miller into a three-way telephone conversation with Norman Rosten, who was also a playwright and a poet. Rosten recalled the conversation:

> "I want this speech rewritten," she said harshly on the phone. "Are you there, Arthur?"
>
> His voice, controlled, at the edge of anger, "I'm here."
>
> "Well, what are you going to do about it?"
>
> "I'm going to think about it."
>
> "Norman agrees with me."
>
> I cut in. "I didn't agree, Marilyn. I agreed to read the screenplay which I did. If Arthur asks my opinion on certain

scenes or speeches, I'll tell him." She was silent. I could hear her frustrated breathing. Always the gentleman and coward, I said, "Look, it's a draft, I'm sure there'll be more work on it. I mean, it's not final, is it?"

Miller replied listlessly. "It's a draft."

. . . I continued, "Maybe that section can be trimmed. If Marilyn has specific objections—!"

"I object to the whole stupid speech," she said. "And he's going to rewrite it!"

She was giving him the business, making him eat the Hollywood shit as they made her eat it for so long. She was fighting the pain and humiliation of another rejection, of one more failure in love. . . . She knew too, that Miller wanted the film made even if it meant continuing the fiction of their marriage. Yes, she could be vengeful.

"She treated Miller very badly on the film," said the photographer Eve Arnold, who was one of the army of nine Magnum photographers, including Henri Cartier-Bresson and Inge Morath, to cover the production. The movie was filmed in extremely high temperatures, with many shooting days postponed because Monroe was late or too drugged and exhausted to work. (For a two-week period in August the production shut down completely while Monroe detoxed at the West Side Hospital in Los Angeles.) "She was incapable of rescuing herself or of being rescued by someone else. It affected her work," said John Huston, who directed the movie and was "absolutely certain that she was doomed." "We got through it," Miller said of the filming, which ended forty days behind schedule on November 4, 1960. "I made a present of this to her, and I left it without her. I didn't even ride home with her on the last day."

Two weeks later, Monroe sued for divorce. Both viewed the marriage as a calamity. In the divorce proceedings, Monroe blamed Miller for the collapse, calling him "cold and unresponsive." "He's a cold fish," she told the press. "I thought he was

Lincoln, but Lincoln had a great sense of humor. Arthur's got no sense of humor. I'm living with a dead man. You know the most frightening part? He reminds me now of a Nazi."

Miller had hung in longer than any of Monroe's other spouses. He had tried to be the hero she was looking for, someone who could convince her that she was not alone in the world. Nonetheless, on his watch she'd had three breakdowns and three suicide attempts. Monroe's resentment was as indigestible to Miller as her behavior. "I spent four years doing nothing except *The Misfits*. There was no gratitude. It just increased her contempt," he said. His naive messianic fantasy had been that inhabiting the role of Roslyn would somehow transform Monroe. She and Roslyn faced the same dilemma; Roslyn resolved it. "I hoped that by living through this role, she too might arrive at some threshold of faith and confidence," Miller said.

But his sentimental version of his disillusioned wife—his refusal to allow Monroe's darker story into the film—infuriated her and made the script feel more of a betrayal than a blessing. "He could have written me anything and he comes up with this," she said. "If that's what he thinks of me, well, then, I'm not for him, and he's not for me." Monroe "needed Arthur to love her in spite of all the shameful things she had done," Leaming wrote. "Marilyn saw the script as proof that he had never really accepted her." The film, in Monroe's eyes, had become about cowboys and horses. "They don't need me at all. Not to act—just for the money. To put my name on the marquee," she said. Even Monroe's big bow-wow acting moment—Roslyn's furious outburst over the roping of the horses—was trivialized in long shot, robbing the scene of its gravity. "I guess they thought I was too dumb to explain anything, so I have a fit—a screaming, crazy fit. I mean *nuts*," Monroe said. "And to think Arthur did this to me. He was supposed to be writing this for me, but he says it's his movie."

*   *   *

The Misfits, which was Miller's first screenplay, was conceived as an attempt to make what its producer, Frank Taylor, called "the ultimate motion picture." The credits were top heavy with major American talent: Miller, Huston, Gable, Montgomery Clift, and Monroe in her first serious role. In addition to the publication of Miller's script, there would be a book and a documentary film about its making as well as the nine Magnum photographers, working a shift or two a week to cover every nook and cranny of the set. Although there were moments of great excitement (the wrangling of the mustangs), great beauty (the lunar Nevada landscape), and great fun (Monroe's deft handling of a paddle ball), the four-million-dollar black-and-white film struggled to navigate Miller's high-minded critique of the decaying West and his high-blown dialogue.

"We're all blind bombardiers. I can't make a landing and I can't get up to God," Guido, a mechanic and pilot, played by Eli Wallach, says. *The Misfits* also had trouble landing. The fizz that seemed to be missing on-screen was also absent from much of the critical response. "If there is a right tone in which to play the Miller script, the director, John Huston, hasn't found it," Pauline Kael wrote in the *New Yorker*, calling the movie both "erratic" and "unlucky." The *New York Times*'s Bosley Crowther found *The Misfits* "curiously congealed." Roger Angell, writing in the *New Yorker*, dismissed it as "so sentimental as to be unintelligent." Angell continued, "When, at the end of the picture, Mr. Gable's rueful cowboy, the last of the Western giants, ropes and wrestles down the last free mustang and then cuts him loose, we realize with disappointment that we have been on the Plains of Allegory all along and that the drumming of hooves does not obscure the clack of the author's typewriter."

When Miller cleared out the study in their Sutton Place residence, he took everything but Monroe's photo, which hung on the wall. Leaving her photograph behind was easier than leaving her behind, a process of evacuation that would take a lifetime. (His works *After the Fall*, *Ride down Mt. Morgan*, *Everybody Wins*, and *Finishing the Picture* all return to her and the turmoil of their marriage.) Miller had endured more than the usual marital licking. If the pair hadn't divorced, he said, "I would be dead." He had been traumatized by Monroe's madness and by his own stupidity. The attrition of those harrowing lost years, he felt, had changed both him and his writing. "I hope and believe I'll have a play again soon," he told a friend in the summer of 1961, by which time he was in a relationship with the photographer Inge Morath, who would become his third wife in 1962. "For various reasons, I suppose, my stuff seems to bear little relation to what has gone before. I feel like a beginner and all that wonder."

10

Darkness Visible

If you cannot get rid of the family skeleton,
you might as well make it dance.

—George Bernard Shaw, *Immaturity*

"FOR WHAT CAN'T BE PUT INTO WORDS" was how Miller inscribed his brother's copy of *After the Fall* (1964), his first play after a nine-year hiatus. Eight years earlier, still full of ambition for a political theater, he had proclaimed, "I can no longer take with ultimate seriousness a drama of individual psychology written for its own sake, however full it may be of insight and precise observation." Now, in this autobiographical cri de coeur, Miller had written exactly the kind of subjective play that his earlier works had been pitched against.

After the Fall may be flawed as a drama, but it is extraordinary as a map of Miller's internal geography, "the most personal statement that I've made," as he finally admitted in 1987. Miller's friend and sometime director Harold Clurman saw the play as a singular step in Miller's evolution both as a man and as an artist. "The play's auto-criticism exposes him to us; it also liberates him so that he can go on free of false legend and heavy halo," Clurman said, adding, "Had he not written this play he might never have been able to write another."

Miller had been through a kind of emotional war; now he was trying to survive the anguish of the aftershock. Trauma, Freud declared, is helplessness experienced. By that measure, Miller was certainly traumatized. He was reeling from the collapse of his second marriage and Monroe's death in January 1962. He was not writing well or living well. "Arthur was in bad shape trying to make it on his own," his nephew Ross Miller recalled. "He clearly wanted my parents around, especially my father. I remember him attempting to cook for us, trying to pay attention to someone other than himself."

The force that turned Miller's life around was Inge Morath, the intrepid, cultured Austrian photographer whose stand-in he introduces at the opening of *After the Fall* as "Holga"—her arms full of flowers, speaking of Salzburg and Mozart. The first time Miller met Morath, during the filming of *The Misfits*, he thought her "shy and strong at the same time." She turned out to be Miller's luck. In every emotional and intellectual way, Morath was the opposite of Monroe: independent, purposeful, well educated, well read, secure in her career, easy in herself, and relaxed in the company of artists and intellectuals with whom she'd come of age carousing in Europe. Morath was never tempestuous or needy. "He doesn't like being disturbed when he's working, but neither do I," she said of Miller. This equality of enterprise and emotional autonomy generated a liberating intimacy. "There was some new permission," Miller wrote in *After the Fall*. "There was suddenly no blame at all but that . . . we each were entitled to . . . our own unhappiness."

Morath had joined the famous Magnum Photos agency in 1953; she was one of only two women in the distinguished collective. On the set of *The Misfits*, Monroe had refused to be photographed with Miller; nonetheless, Morath had managed to capture their unbridgeable isolation in one haunting image, which shows Miller in a shadowy bedroom corner watching Monroe, in the opposite corner, as she leans out the window into the bright day. A diaphanous curtain billows behind her, separating her torso from the rest of the room and from Miller.

Only after the shoot, back in New York and going over contact prints, did Miller get to know Morath. Within a few months, she was calling their relationship "serious." She accompanied Miller to President Kennedy's inauguration in January 1961, and to his mother's funeral that March. "She brought me Europe," Miller liked to say, but Morath did more than that. She brought him buoyancy. "Inge savored life as only one can who has nearly been killed," Miller wrote, adding, "It was hard to think of an American who was as cheerful as she." Morath exuded the charm of the well loved. As a photographer, according to Miller, she had "a way of disarming men of power" with her "romantic playfulness." Her flirtatiousness and good-humored intelligence almost immediately disarmed Miller. As *After the Fall* dramatized in its final beat, she was a totem of hope:

> HOLGA: Hello!
> *He comes to a halt a few yards from her. A whispering goes up from all his people. He straightens up against it and walks toward her, holding out his hand.*
> QUENTIN: Hello.

Morath called herself "a traveller with a camera." "For Inge, to see a valise was to start packing," Miller said. She was fluent in seven languages. After the war, as a translator, journalist, and finally photographer, she had lived in bohemian circles in Vienna, Paris, and London. (What attracted her to Miller, she said, was his "European awareness," although "it wasn't in his work at that moment." Morath was well born and well educated. (Her scientist parents had been Nazi sympathizers.) But the nightmare of the world war—homelessness, deprivation, and destruction—had robbed her of her teenage years. Toward the end of the war, she was drafted into service in an aircraft factory in Berlin. When the factory was bombed, she joined the exodus of workers, setting off on foot for her parents' home in Salzburg, 455 miles away. Starved, strafed, sleeping rough, saved by a stranger from throwing herself off a bridge in despair, Morath lost all sense of how long the trip took her, but she made it home. Her survival gave gusto to how she lived and how she later photographed the life around her. Her images bore articulate witness to her humanity and her resourceful spirit. "We all had one very strong thing in common," she said of her Magnum cohorts. "We all wanted to help bring a better world about."

Morath, who "loved to work," had found her first, short marriage, to a much-married, bisexual English writer, Lionel Birch, "infinitely dull" and "a waste." And she was wary of Miller's grief. "Arthur was in despair and sought my company. But at the time I just wanted to get away—I had no desire to console a Marilyn Monroe victim," she said of the first year of their romance. Miller was even more ambivalent about the idea of marrying again. He feared that the struggle to regain his writing power might cause a "compensatory loss" in their relationship, and, conversely, that their love might hurt his writing. He was also aware that in Morath's frequent absences on assignment he wasn't coping very well. "I missed her sense of the hour's importance, the possibilities awaiting in the unfolding day. . . . I needed help in order to live," he said. On the other hand, "The despair I felt was impossible to face or flee, and my only certainty was the hunger for long stretches of uninterrupted time to find my feet as a writer again. No partner ought to be asked to contribute to silence." Nonetheless, Morath, whose nickname for Miller was "Abba" (or "Father"), continued to dole out maternal solicitude, wanting, she said, "to make your difficult life more easy": "There is pride in me, Abba, that

I could offer you all this and there is pride in the hope that it might make you trust that our relationship could be not selfish but a ground to grow toward our aim, in whose moral superiority I continue to believe."

"I guess a third marriage takes some thinking," Miller said. "I did a lot of thinking." Much of that thinking went into *After the Fall*, where Miller's alter ego, Quentin, a guilt-raddled, twice-divorced lawyer persecuted by his memories and his doubts, admits, "I'm a little afraid . . . of who and what I'm bringing to her. . . . And the doubt ties my tongue when I think of promising anything again." When Miller looked in the mirror, he saw a bad marital bet. He had two failed marriages. He was egotistical and self-involved. His previous wives had come to dislike his work, and anyone taking him on would require "a strength, a forbearance, even a disinterestedness worthy of a goddess," he wrote to Morath. He continued to straddle the fence. "I live on the edge of some ultimate abyss," he wrote, unable to trust her assurances of love or his own desires. However, in the ways of the heart, Morath was much more experienced and clear-eyed. She knew herself, which Miller did not. ("I'm a stranger to my life," Quentin admits in the play.) "Waiting is only a solution for the falling away of things," Morath wrote to her skittish suitor. "Time will not solve feelings—a certain amount of it will clarify but beyond that . . . a decision will have to be made."

Three months later, on February 17, 1962, Morath, now pregnant, married Miller in a small Connecticut ceremony that nonetheless received global coverage. "I guess we finally decided we had fallen in love and might as well," she said. "I was not banking on this marriage being for ever." Miller remembered one morning, about a year after they were married—by which time she had become "the great mother, the mistress of a very busy house"—Morath suddenly exclaiming, "My God, we've been married all year!" By the time Miller was working on the final drafts of *After the Fall*, they were living with their baby daughter, Rebecca, in a sixth-floor suite at the louche Chelsea Hotel, a sort of dilapidated hostel for artists on West 23rd Street, in Manhattan. "It was not part of America, had no vacuum cleaners, no rules, no taste, no shame," Miller wrote of the hotel, which was their New York home until 1967.

"This is a happy play, the happiest I have ever written," Miller told the assembled cast at Lincoln Center on the first day of rehearsals for *After the Fall*. The play inaugurated the long-awaited Lincoln Center Repertory Theatre, whose ambition to be America's national theater had reunited Elia Kazan, who was co-artistic director of the new enterprise, and Miller. "There continued to be an unspoken tension between Art Miller and me, but also a little of the affection that had once been there," Kazan wrote. "The problem was that the discord between us was unarticulated, we were both determined to get along for the sake of the Repertory Theatre." Kazan went on, "We were together on a raft in the middle of the ocean, and there was nothing for us to do but to paddle: to save my life, I had to save his."

As the play begins, its narrator and central character, Quentin, estranged from his life, is looking for a reason to go on. Set entirely within the mind of the desperate and desolate Quentin, the play is as flooded with memory as Quentin is with the anxiety of shame over his lack of feeling for others ("I don't seem to know how to grieve"), his loss of identity ("I felt I was merely in the service of my own success"), his inauthenticity ("I don't know if I have lived in good faith"), his gullibility ("God, when I think of what I believed, I want to hide!"), and his murderousness ("I am full of hatred. . . . I hate the world!"). With the stone tower of a concentration camp throwing its dark shadow over the play's proceedings, Miller was trying to trap the impulse in himself and in society that kills the heart and seeks the destruction of others; he was trying to follow the advice that Quentin gives to his suicidal wife, Maggie: "Do the hardest thing of all—see your own hatred, and live!"

In a way, playwrights don't know what they've written until their characters, those ghosts of the unconscious, are embodied in three dimensions. Certainly Miller didn't. Looking at Quentin early in rehearsals, he gave Kazan a note about the role: "His innocence. Puzzling things out. Awkward. Childlike. All in all a bit of a shnook." The play, Miller later explained, is a trial— "the trial of a man, by his own conscience, his own values, his own deeds." It is also an indictment of Miller's delusions in his romance with Monroe. Quentin, who has his mother's words echoing in his head—"Be a light, a light in the world!"—cannot resist Maggie's vision of him as her savior. By idealizing the humiliated, unmoored Maggie—"that wishing girl, that victory in lace"—he preserves the illusion of her goodness, and she does the same for him. ("She . . . *gave* me something! She . . . let me change her!" Quentin says.)

What begins as a dream of mutual redemption ends in a mutual hell. Quentin is trapped by Maggie's neediness, Maggie by Quentin's festering contempt. Her disenchanted cruelty is matched by his equally punishing disaffection. "The question is no longer whether you'll survive, but also whether I will," Quentin tells her. "Because I'm backed up to the edge of the cliff, and I haven't one inch left behind me." Exhaustion has eroded his empathy; distrust has replaced her desire. The play follows the outline of Miller and Monroe's estrangement, even to the point of using the words from his diary that drove the first stake into their marriage only months after they'd exchanged vows: "The only one I will ever love is my daughter." Those words are thrown in Quentin's face as he is trying to wrestle Maggie's pills from her. "I am not the Savior and I am not the help. . . . You are not going to kill me, Maggie, and that's all this is for!" he says, adding, as he squeezes her wrists, "Drop them, you bitch! You won't kill me."

For Quentin—and for Miller it seems—the dark truth is that on some level he wanted Monroe's death. "I heard. Those deep, unnatural breaths like the footfalls of my coming peace," Quentin says of the sound of Maggie struggling to breathe after overdosing on barbiturates, "and knew—I wanted them. How is that possible? I loved that girl." At the finale, as the apparitions of his past are illuminated around him, Quentin acknowledges the vindictive triumph of his own survival. "I loved them all, all!" he says. "And gave them willingly to failure and to death that I might live, as they gave me and gave each other, with a word, a look, a trick, a truth, a lie—and all in love." In a sense, *After the Fall* allows Miller to arraign himself in his own court—"humiliated defendants. As all of us are," he wrote. It presents the case for both views of the catastrophe and finds him guilty, only to let him off for good behavior. "The wish to kill is never killed, but with some gift of courage one may look into its face, when it appears, and with a stroke of love—as to an idiot in the house—forgive it, again and again . . . forever?"

At the finale, in a sort of conga line of culpability, Quentin ascends the stairs "with his life following him," the stage directions read (a conclusion that Kazan found "insufferably self-favoring and noble"). He moves toward Holga, who awaits him with outstretched arms. "He is struggling against that homelessness, that alienation whose victory is assured at the beginning," Miller explained in a letter to Kazan. "It is the struggle itself which is his home, which inadvertently, unconsciously, he has erected, and which at the end of the play he will enter as into his own house."

The excitement around *After the Fall*'s opening was huge: "one of the most potentially significant events in the history of American theater," the *New York Times* called it. The ANTA Washington Square Theatre, Lincoln Center's temporary downtown home on West 4th Street, which had 1,158 seats, sold nearly

8o percent of the tickets for the six-month run before previews even started—three-quarters of a million dollars' worth. Miller was on the cover of *Newsweek; Life* gave the play a six-page spread; and the *Saturday Evening Post* published a special edition containing the complete script. The play, the last that Kazan would ever direct, was an indubitable commercial success, but although it was generally well received by the daily reviewers, it was mugged by the highbrow critics, whose vitriol stained its legend. "The bright boys from every side rushed to [Monroe's] defense," Kazan said.

Robert Brustein, writing in the *New Republic*, called it "a spiritual striptease . . . a three-and-a-half-hour breach of taste, a confessional autobiography of embarrassing explicitness." Miller, he went on, "has created a shameless piece of tabloid gossip, an act of exhibitionism which makes us all voyeurs." Other cognoscenti piled on: Susan Sontag ("wanting in intelligence and moral honesty"; *Partisan Review*); Kenneth Tynan ("A tinted blow-up of Mr Miller himself. . . . He has neither turned himself into a symbol nor trusted himself as a fact"; *London Observer*); Richard Gillman ("not even a modicum of drama"; *New York Herald Tribune*); Philip Rahv ("a disaster, a piece so pretentious and defensive, that virtually nothing good can be said about it"; *New York Review of Books*). Miller, who had refused to name names to HUAC, now stood accused of informing on Monroe.

Two weeks after the opening, he answered his critics in *Life*, in an article titled "With Respect for Her Agony—but with Love." The characters in *After the Fall*, he wrote, "were drawn, not reported." He added, "The play is neither an apology nor the arraignment of others; quite simply, overtly and clearly, it is a commitment to one's own actions. . . . What Quentin tries desperately to do is to open Maggie's eyes to her own complicity in her self-destruction." In the play and in his subsequent defense, Miller remained blameless in his own eyes. Lillian

Hellman, who had mocked his earlier claim that he'd been "to hell and back" when he wrote *The Crucible*, now went one step farther and parodied him in print: "Lillian Hellman Wants a Little Respect for Her Agony: An Eminent Playwright Hallucinates After a Fall Brought on by a Current Dramatic Hit."

Miller felt that the critics were reviewing him, not the play; and to some extent he was right. (Decades later, once the memory of both Miller and Monroe had dimmed in the collective unconscious, the play's eloquence could be more easily recognized and admired.) But in that turbulent first response, Miller saw the writing on the fourth wall. "I clearly have a lonely row to hoe from here on in," he wrote to Kazan a couple of weeks after the opening. "And can only hope that some people still exist who for one reason or another are interested in what I see." He went on, "The play, without planning it so, has at least turned me from the shelter of political and moral orthodoxy. Literally, now, I see no place on Broadway for myself whatsoever."

The unmooring pall of the Kennedy assassination had hung over the rehearsals of *After the Fall*, sounding the republic's retreat from normality. In the following years, the deracinating ructions of unrest at home and abroad in Vietnam left the American public numbed and outraged, polarized by fear and fury. "We are on the verge of Armageddon and await an apocalypse," Harold Clurman observed in 1967. The American theater, with its eclectic European influences, registered these paroxysms—whether through the grimace of laughter that refused suffering (Joe Orton, Charles Ludlum's Ridiculous Theater), violent physical transformations (Jerzy Grotowski), startling enactments of rebirth (Sam Shepard, the Living Theatre, the Open Theatre), or Absurdist nightmares (Beckett, Ionesco, Pinter). "Don't trust anyone over thirty"—a motto first voiced in 1964—was the new mantra. The times were combative, the mood polemical, the aesthetic presentational. America seemed to have lost both its through line and its claim to righteousness.

In this tempest-tossed climate, the narrative conventions of the traditional play no longer mirrored real life—the collapse being played out on the streets and on television screens. Miller admitted that "a strange futility had crept into the very idea of writing a play." Given the public's distaste for reality and its distrust of language, penetration, onstage, was replaced by presentation. In a culture that encouraged people to "turn on, tune in, drop out," Miller wrote, "the very notion of thinking, conceptualizing, theorizing—the mind itself—went up the flue."

Miller and Tennessee Williams, the other postwar Broadway grandee, were caught in the riptide of the national trauma. Miller's moralizing and Williams's solipsism no longer sat well with the paying customers; the playwrights found themselves at once dismissed *and* despised. "If only he could give piety a rest," the cultural critic James Wolcott said later. "Arthur Miller's sermonettes come straight from the gassy void." (In England only a few years earlier, a similar paradigm shift, brought on by the emergence of the welfare state and the demand for working-class heroes, had abruptly deposed Noël Coward and Terence Rattigan from their West End preeminence.) "Who is touched and by what is the big question these days," Williams wrote to his publisher around this time. Sensing audiences' growing lack of interest in his florid literary style, Williams tested their appetite for the grotesque, with *The Gnädiges Fräulein* (1964), a surreal Ionesco-inspired clown play, which "fit people and societies going a bit mad," he said.

Miller, a liberal humanist, was philosophically and emotionally unable to make that kind of stylistic accommodation to the zeitgeist. "Reason itself had become un-aesthetic, something art must at any cost avoid," he said. Miller got the picture; he just didn't want to paint it. To him, the Absurdist dramatists celebrated "the impotence of human hopes" and "the futility of action," in plays that "indicated rather than felt emotion." "I wanted to convey the emotions as I felt them," he said. "The real job for me was not parody at all. It was to try to create empathy in the theatre and not the kind of distancing, achieved through comic and grotesque means." He added, "I felt there was enough dissociation in life, without me adding to it in the theater." In his essay "Realism," he asked, "Can't it be art if it moves people? If the pun can be pardoned, man lives not by head alone."

As Miller saw it, the New Wave's theatrical minimalism and cynicism had made contemporary drama "narrower in terms of story, characterisation, and the traditions of story-telling." Absurdist plays were ahistorical; they dramatized the context of no context. Plays seemed to exist "entirely in the now." This had a subliminal appeal to a society that was increasingly polarized by the Vietnam War, at once uninterested and unable to see its roots in history. "The very idea of an operating continuity between past and present in any human behavior was démodé and close to a laughably old-fashioned irrelevancy," according to Miller. "It was as though the culture had decreed amnesia as the ultimate mark of reality. As the corpses piled up, it became cruelly impolite if not unpatriotic to suggest the obvious, that we were fighting the past."

The battle of contending historical narratives—the blood under the American bridge—was what Miller transposed into *The Price* (1968). Although the play makes no mention of Vietnam, Miller noted, "It speaks to a spirit of unearthing the real that seemed to have very nearly gone from our lives." Stepping back into the theatrical arena four years after the debacle of *After the Fall*, Miller fought his aesthetic corner hard. "I suppose I've become paranoid but I do think a certain school of critics truly hate me," he wrote to Kenneth Rowe in 1968. Nonetheless, *The Price* presented his critics with a well-made play that drew on his own emotional life, to which he added a new ingredient: a strong dose of humor. Laughter was the sugar to swat the fly of Broadway success, and Miller needed a hit.

Gregory Solomon, the ninety-year-old antiques dealer who arrives at a soon-to-be-demolished townhouse to offer to buy the furniture that once decorated its ten fancy rooms, is, "in brief, a phenomenon," as Miller's first stage direction says, by way of introduction. Part tummler, part tradesman, and all Yiddish shtick—"Water I don't need. A little blood I could use," he says as he enters—Solomon is Miller's first fully fledged comic character. "Jews been acrobats since the beginning of the world. I was a horse them days: drink, women, anything—on the go, on the go, nothing ever stopped me. Only life," he says.

Solomon is at once a catalyst and a referee in the negotiation between the two Franz brothers: the dutiful Victor, a policeman whose disgruntled wife tells him, "I want money," and the ambitious Walter, a surgeon who is more successful at making money than at making a life. As the characters haggle over the price of the family heirlooms—a harp, a dining-room table, a chiffonier—their pasts and their present collide. Their disagreement plays out behind a "monstrously crowded and dense" pile of old "Germanic furniture"—the detritus of Victor and Walter's childhood—whose value is questionable and which neither sibling wants. ("Nobody wants that kind of furniture because it implies a past and it implies that a past can't be broken," Miller explained.) As Solomon says to Victor, "What is the key word today? Disposable." He goes on, "Years ago a person, he was unhappy, didn't know what to do with himself— he'd go to church, start a revolution—*something*. Today, you're unhappy? Can't figure it out? What is the salvation? Go shopping. . . . With this kind of furniture the shopping is over, finished. . . . So you got a problem." As it turns out, the brothers' problems aren't only commercial. The ever-present mound of furniture makes the haunting visual point that the brothers' parents are within them even as they reject them.

Miller began *The Price*—then titled "Third Play"—when he was still working on *After the Fall*; it emerged from the same self-questioning emotional turmoil of marital collapse, and in the same confessional spirit. Miller's best material had to be experienced; as Kazan observed, "he reported on his inner condition." *The Price* zeroed in on his defining sibling rivalry. As a boy Miller had looked up to Kermit, who was swift of foot and mind; as an adult, Miller outpaced him. He was haunted by what he called Kermit's "pathological honesty" and his modest circumstances. "Kermit had the good and questionable luck of the first born; as such he was expected to carry the family's flag and far more was expected of him than of me," Miller said at his brother's memorial. "He could not desert his father whose desperate struggle to hold onto his business he saw as heroic, something even colored with romance." Miller added, "When Kermit glimpsed an ideal he was helpless to shut his eyes."

Miller's own idealism was gleaned from his brother's model. A terrible student and a late bloomer, he had acquired even his literary ambition at Kermit's knee. "Kermit had a pleasing cursive handwriting and a knack for a kind of elevated formal Victorian language and all he lacked was a space in the tiny house to call his own—a space where he could be himself but without turning his back on those he helplessly loved," Miller said. These included Miller himself, whom Kermit defended against their father's full-court press to join his business. *No Villain*, Miller's first play, for which he used "members of my family as models," tells the story of a strike in a garment factory that sets a younger son against his overbearing father and dramatizes Kermit's support of Arthur's newfound calling. ("Writing and cloaks don't mix. . . . He'll never get in that business if I can help it," Ben, the older brother, a self-sacrificing college drop-out, says.)

In reality, Arthur and Kermit had worked out a compromise to accommodate their father, Isidore. Kermit's son Ross Miller explained, "The plan was for my father to continue at N.Y.U. and Arthur to take a leave and work for Izzy." But by the time Kermit drove to Ann Arbor to visit his brother at the end of his first semester at the University of Michigan, Miller had "fallen in love with the place" and with the idea of himself as a playwright. Miller reneged on their deal. "The result of all this was that my father spent another five years in harness. Arthur never tried to intervene," Ross said. The incident was a watershed that echoes in *The Price*'s argument about choice and destiny: Victor has dedicated his life to saving his father; Walter has dedicated his life to saving himself. "You had a responsibility here and you walked on it," Victor reproaches his brother. "I wanted the freedom to do my work," Walter says. For Miller, as for his theatrical simulacrum, opportunity knocked; for Victor and for Kermit, it didn't. *The Price* is a dissection of Miller's survivor's guilt.

The Miller brothers' history forms the scaffolding of the play. When the curtain rises, Victor is waiting for his brother, who is not just absent but frustratingly incommunicado. By the end of act 1, when Walter finally shows up—"I came by to say hello, that's all," he says—Victor has almost sealed the modest deal and has some of Solomon's money already in hand. It's been sixteen years since the brothers' last meeting. But time is not the only measure of the distance between them. Walter is sophisticated, rich, and acclaimed; Victor is a police sergeant in Far Rockaway—"Siberia" he calls it—who apparently has neither the ambition nor the education to get a better job if he takes early retirement. His disappointed wife, Esther, who drinks, expresses the family resentment toward the "selfish bastard" Walter that the resigned Victor can never vocalize. Victor wants to share the money with Walter, whereas Esther wants him to keep it all, not just out of need but out of justice. "There's such a thing as a moral debt Vic, you made his whole career possible. What law said that only he could study medicine. . . . You were even the better student. That's a real debt."

The men parse their past and their chosen paths. At first, both put a heroic spin on their divergent trajectories. Victor depicts his life as a legend of selflessness, and himself as a kind of moral martyr, devoted to his Depression-ravaged father. ("Who the hell was supposed to keep him alive, Walter?") In response to their father's unfathomable collapse, Walter, by contrast, sought the armor of omnipotence: he fanatically pursued greatness and built a career so renowned that he could not be "degraded and thrown down" the way his father was ("There's so much to know and so little time. Until you've eliminated everything extraneous . . . including people."). Walter's endeavor, which he presents as a "quest," has come at the cost of a breakdown and the loss of his family.

So it was with Miller himself. In 1959, when Miller first agreed to attend Ross's bar mitzvah and then canceled, Kermit, furious, called him out for his insensitivity. Miller sent a letter explaining his behavior as the price paid for his literary accomplishment. Miller's justifications and his condescension almost exactly echo Walter's rationalizations to Victor:

> Since the beginning my work has enforced on me a regime and a viewpoint which are the price of a way of life that is in many ways unnatural and perhaps incomprehensible to others. I work all the time, at my desk or away; I am not inventing stories and entertainments, but making a record of my own struggle to find reality, the reality which convention covers and almost everything conspires to conceal. So that if I seem blinded at times it is not that I do not see or feel but that at any one time there is but one thing to do, one quest to pursue and all else, at such times, is and must be distant.

Which is far different than insensitivity. It entails a price, a loss, a sacrifice which I cannot regret without regretting my work itself. I have never had many friends for this reason, even when friendship is very pleasurable to me. This does not mean that I care little for others, but that most of my life is and has always been solitary, as it seems it must be. So that, for one thing, you ought not to make excuses for me, but say quite frankly that with any less "selfishness" there would be fewer results. So that when others find a lack of social response in me they ought, at the same time, to ask themselves if perhaps Arthur has other things he must do . . . not "more important things," necessarily, but things which inevitably accompany the work he has bound himself to perform.

Condescension, in *The Price*, is what tips the brothers' wary reunion back into acrimony. Walter knows exactly how to handle Solomon's low-ball offer, but he has to be strategic with his brother and "modify what he believes is his overpowering force," the stage direction reads. He suggests a slick tax maneuver. If Walter takes ownership of all the furniture and donates it to charity, then he can get a sizable tax write-off, which they'll split, much more than Solomon's offer. This seems to be an act of surprising goodwill. "I can't bear it that he's *decent*," Victor says, as Walter exits to negotiate in private with Solomon. He returns with the news that the antiques dealer's estimate is twenty-five thousand dollars. Walter offers to pass the entire amount to his down-at-the-heels brother. "Vic, you earned it. It's yours," Walter says. But Walter's munificence—he later offers to get Victor a job at one of his hospitals—is a gesture of reconciliation that casts him as a hero and diminishes Victor. "I've been walking a beat for twenty-eight years, I'm not qualified for anything technical," Victor says.

Walter wants to exorcise his guilt; Vic wants reparation for his brother's indifference down the decades. "We don't understand each other, do we? . . . Come on, we'll all be dead soon,"

Walter says, setting the stage for the brothers to dissect their shared history—an exercise in selective memory that turns out to be as much about the caprice of psychology as it is about destiny. At issue are the five hundred dollars that Walter refused to give his brother to allow him to continue his education and the measly monthly payment he made toward the family upkeep during the Depression, which is still vivid in Victor's story. "We *were* eating garbage here," he says, recalling the punishing sight of jobless men sprawled in Bryant Park "like a big open-air flop-house. And not bums."

"My five hundred dollars was not what kept you from your degree! You could have left Pop and gone right on—he was perfectly fit," Walter counters, adding, "He exploited you!" Walter then drops a bombshell: their father had four thousand dollars salted away. Walter knew about the money because their father had asked him to invest it. "I told him at the time, if he would send you through I'd contribute properly," he says, rationalizing not having told his brother about the nest egg. "I'm damned if I'd sacrifice when he was holding out on you. You can understand that, can't you," he asks the flabbergasted Victor.

Miller's family story—the transactional business of Augusta's arranged marriage, her vomiting at the news of her husband's bankruptcy, her blighted artistic ambitions, and Isidore's hidden cash—comes together in the mythology of this fictional family. In the brothers' vivid back-and-forth, each man's memory is modified, but neither seems capable of entirely abandoning his self-image or his grudge. "You could see in front of your face that he had some money. You knew it then, and you certainly know it now," Walter says, challenging the dutiful Victor, who needs to believe in his father's love. "How could he be holding out on me when he loved me?" Victor says. Idealization requires denial, and Walter flushes Victor's self-deception into the open. Victor admits that he knew his father had something and that he challenged him with the fact. In response, his father laughed. "To tell you the truth I don't think a week has gone by that I haven't seen that laugh. Like it was some kind of a wild joke," he says. Victor's performance of fealty has been a masochistic masquerade, designed to allow him to hold on to the notion of family cohesion. "I can't explain it; I wanted to . . . stop it from falling apart," Victor says. "What was unbearable is not that it all fell apart, it was that there was never anything here," Walter replies, adding, "There was no love in this house. There was no loyalty. There was nothing here but a straight financial arrangement. That's what was unbearable. And you proceeded to wipe out what you saw."

"The characters were not based on Kermit and me, we were far different from these two, but the magnetic underlying situation was deep in my bones," Miller wrote disingenuously in *Timebends*. (On the issue of autobiographical elements in his plays, Miller always boxed clever.) "There's no one character who's actually me, that I'm sure of," he said, adding, "You can't write convincingly about a character unless you identify with them." In the case of *The Price*, Miller's claim certainly was not credible to his brother or his sister, Joan Copeland. "The tension between these characters was so honest and so true and so Arthur and Kermit," Copeland said.

"Kermit was not a cop; Arthur was not a world-renowned doctor; I didn't go to M.I.T.; but the play does reveal accurately his attitude toward his older brother," Ross Miller maintained. "Arthur craved fame and celebrity and got it. My father, who didn't give a shit about fame, got a good woman and a smart kid. But at what price?" He continued, "The real price my father paid for doing 'the right thing'—he enlisted as a private and was discharged as a captain—was the collateral damage he suffered in combat. My father never said anything about Arthur dodging the draft with an old 'football injury'; but after the war my father could never take Arthur's moralizing and pontificating seriously. The price Arthur paid was the loss of his brother's respect." (According to Ross, Kermit's autographed copy of *Timebends* remained unread on his bookshelf.) Although in later years, Kermit moved closer to Miller's home in Roxbury, they saw each other infrequently. When Kermit died, on his brother's birthday (October 17) in 2003, Miller hadn't seen him for "maybe a year," Ross said. According to Ross, who had to inform people of his father's death, "My mother said, 'Well, don't call Arthur. He's shown no interest.'"

The Price broods fiercely over aspects of Miller's guilt-ridden past, including, in a coded way, the birth in 1967 of his son Daniel, a child with Down Syndrome who was never taken home but, following the medical advice of the day, put into a special-care facility. "I was very confused as to why he didn't come home," Rebecca Miller told her father's biographer, Christopher Bigsby, adding, "My mum saw him the most. My mum carried the burden of the whole thing. . . . No one ever told me why they did what they did. I think it has to do with not being able to deal with it, to look things in the face."

Although years later Morath was forthright to Bigsby about their anguishing choice—"It would have ruined our entire life"—Miller publicly drew a curtain over Daniel's existence. He acknowledged Daniel in his will, but he does not mention him in *Timebends;* this abandoned child was at once a secret and a dereliction that did not jibe with Miller's public image, his "resistance to our soul's sloth," as Harold Clurman called it. In *The Price*, the charge of moral inertia sends Walter into a defensive tailspin. Of his brother's pragmatic decision to cut himself off from family responsibility, Victor says, "I wish I'd done the same thing. But, to come through all those years knowing what you knew and saying nothing." The accusation of betrayal cuts Walter to his core. "Does that mean I stole your life?" Walter cries out. "You made those choices, Victor! And that's what you have to face!"

The brothers lock horns. If their lives represent "two seemingly divergent paths out of the same trap," as Walter says in an emollient moment, the brothers have also acquired the same habit of denial. Victor, who has finally come clean about his own self-deception, challenges his brother to face the vindictive triumph behind the equipoise of his success: "You end up with respect, the career, the money, and the best thing of all . . . that you're one hell of a guy and never harmed anybody in your life!" Victor says. Here, in an inspired rhetorical volte-face, Walter tries to turn the tables by projecting his unacceptable feelings onto his brother. "And you? You never had hatred of me? Never a wish to see me destroyed?" he rants. "To destroy me, to destroy me with this saintly self-sacrifice, this mockery of sacrifice? . . . To prove with your failure what a treacherous son of a bitch I am—to hang yourself in my doorway."

In the middle of his paranoid rage, Walter turns to Esther. "He's sacrificing his life to vengeance," he tells her. "Nothing was sacrificed," she replies. Her simple statement turns the brothers' battle into a stalemate. Esther, who earlier seemed to side with Walter and threatened to leave Victor if he didn't take the inflated "legal" offer, signals a reunion with her husband: she accepts him, their life, his deal. "Leave him, Walter, please," she says, a command that seems to emanate from the authority of a solid marriage that has produced well-adjusted children—a legacy that Walter cannot claim. Walter and his version of events are silenced. "Humiliated by her," according to the stage direction, he storms out, throwing a ballgown of his mother's that he had earlier wanted to salvage from the sale in his brother's face. Now there is nothing to salvage. Walter's parting shot is "You will never, never again make me ashamed!" But he *is* ashamed. As he exits, he fixes his brother with a glance: "The flick of a humiliated smile passes across Walter's face. He wants to disappear into air," the stage direction reads. It's an admission in theater that Miller could never make in life.

"Out of experience came his good work, conceived in ambivalence and his own confusion and resolved in pity and a recognition of terror," Kazan said of Miller's plays, of which *The Price* was the last major one. The brothers battle to a stand-off, but it's left to Solomon, living up to his name's biblical associations, to pronounce a verdict. "Let him go," he tells Victor, who wants to run after his brother. Solomon, like the other characters, is no stranger to loss, but unlike them he is clear-eyed and refuses melancholy. "I had a wife . . . well, what's the difference," he says at the opening of the play. And, as he finalizes the bargain with Victor at the end, he recalls his daughter, who committed suicide nearly sixty years before. "Every night I lay down to sleep—she's sitting there. . . . But if it was a miracle and she came to life, what would I say to her?" he asks, counting out the money into Victor's palm. When Victor wishes him good luck with the inventory as he exits, Solomon sends him off with a stoic farewell: "Good luck you can never know till the last minute, my boy."

In the play's final image, Solomon sits centerstage amid the mountains of furniture, totting up the value of these family memories. He finds a Gallagher and Shean vaudeville record, which Victor had dusted off and briefly played on his first entrance; Solomon plays the record again. The sound slowly eases the gravity of the scene. Solomon smiles, chuckles, and remembers. He begins to laugh first at the record and, by degrees, at his past. The laughter builds until Solomon is sprawled in his chair with tears in his eyes, "howling helplessly into the air." The curtain comes down on this comic grimace—an image of both terror and elation—which brings felt emotion to the absurd.

By the time *The Price* opened, on February 7, 1968, the play had replaced two of its actors and its director, Ulu Grosbard, who fell out with the cast. Miller took over the direction in the final two weeks and "managed to give certain scenes a form and drive which, I guess, made the difference," he said. Although in his opinion the premiere of *The Price* "was far from being a really fine production," he confided to Kenneth Rowe, "for myself I like the play extremely. It is a solution to the theatre *as theatre*, rather than an off-shoot of the movies. Consequently, or partly as a consequence, the French and English reviews have been marvelous." The New York reviews were predictably mixed, but the audience voted with its feet. *The Price* ran for a healthy 429 performances.

By the time *The Price* received its second Broadway revival, in 1992, Miller had been kicked into the long grass. His stock had declined so precipitously that the *New York Times* covered the play not in a theater review but in its "Home" section. Miller wrote in protest to the *Times*'s executive editor, Max Frankel. His reply only added fuel to Miller's ire. "After all, a first-class revival of a play of mine in a Broadway theatre would seem of *some* public interest," Miller wrote to his agent, Sam Cohn. He went on, "But Frankel's letter tells me there was no mistake; that the *Times* does not believe that any such interest exists, or more precisely, ought to exist. 'We certainly don't intend to ignore it; we will review.' I admit I had to smile with wonder at this, it sounded so utterly Papal. Imagine, the newspaper of record will indeed review *The Price* on Broadway! What a sublime sense of responsibility toward the arts." Miller ended his letter with the plaintive aside of a forgotten man. "I have been writing plays in America since 1935."

Epilogue

> How many really good plays does a writer have
> in him? How many lives can he live?
>
> —Elia Kazan, *Kazan: A Life*

"I'M BECOMING INVISIBLE in my own land," Miller said in the late seventies. By the turn of the twenty-first century, in some American intellectual quarters he had vanished completely. "The former playwright" is how Christopher Hitchens name-checked him in his book *No One Left to Lie* (1999). But, in fact, until he died, in 2005, Miller never stopped writing for the theater. He continued to work his words the way he worked wood—slowly and always with an eye to balance and shape. "Balance is all," he said. To him, a piece of wood was like a blank page: it was "waiting for the human hand to turn it into something useful, or beautiful. It's exciting to think of it like that. It's like the beginning of the world before it was shaped."

Miller's work could always find a stage; it just couldn't always find an audience. *The Creation of the World and Other Business*, from 1972, ran for twenty performances; *The Archbishop's*

Ceiling (1977) was withdrawn after its Kennedy Center debut; *The American Clock* (1980) had twelve performances, *The Ride down Mt. Morgan* (1991) forty, and *Broken Glass* (1994) seventy-three. "I didn't speak with a contemporary accent," Miller explained. His well-crafted loquaciousness did not resonate with an uncertain, discombobulated society that had been turned upside down by violence and desperation—"the indigenous American berserk," as Philip Roth referred to life from the sixties on. Miller's style of playmaking was discounted, rather like the fine family furniture in *The Price*. "People don't like this stuff anymore," Solomon says of the heavy mahogany pieces. "This stuff is from another world."

If Miller seemed to have lost his inspiration, he never lost his renown as a public intellectual. He became the president of PEN International (1965–1969), a vocal opponent of the Vietnam War, a campaigner for Eugene McCarthy's presidential bid, and a Roxbury delegate to the 1968 Democratic National Convention in Chicago. He traveled with Inge Morath, writing essays to accompany her photographic studies of Russia ("In Russia"), China ("Chinese Encounters"), and, closer to home, their rural Connecticut landscape ("In the Country") and New York. He journeyed to Stockholm and Beijing to direct productions of *Death of a Salesman* and wrote a book about his Chinese adventure (*"Salesman" in Beijing*).

While his new plays were consistently panned—"There seems to be a delight on the part of the critics to see that nothing survives," he said—revivals of his classic plays earned him some good press and good paydays. The 1984 Broadway revival of *Death of a Salesman*, with Dustin Hoffman as Willy Loman, for instance, yielded Miller nearly a million dollars (about sixty-three thousand dollars a week). A subsequent CBS televised version of *Salesman* played to an audience of twenty-five million. Miller was perhaps the most lionized of outcasts. While he was in the wilderness, he received the Creative Arts Award from

Brandeis University (1970), the Kennedy Center Honor for Lifetime Achievement (1984), the National Book Awards' Medal for Distinguished Contribution to Literature (2001), and honorary degrees from Oxford (1995) and Harvard (1997). He was elected to the American Academy of Arts and Letters, and the Arthur Miller Institute for American Studies was established at Britain's University of East Anglia.

Although theater seemed a bad bet for Miller, he could still have a flutter in film. His name on a screenplay attracted outstanding actors to his projects—among them, Vanessa Redgrave, Daniel Day-Lewis, Nick Nolte, and Debra Winger—which also won awards. *Playing for Time* (1980), Miller's television adaptation of a memoir by Fania Fénelon, a cabaret singer and a member of the French Resistance who survived Auschwitz thanks to her musical gift, won him an Emmy. His screenplay for the 1996 movie adaptation of *The Crucible* was nominated for an Academy Award. But Miller's major literary achievement of the decade was *Timebends*, a prolix memoir which nonetheless took its place among the best books in its genre and bore important witness to his fruitful life.

Of Miller's late plays, *Broken Glass* stands out as his most provocative and prescient, the one that best exemplifies his aim "to make human relations felt between individuals and the larger structure of the world." The play's title is a reference to the anti-Semitic mayhem of Kristallnacht in 1938, but it is also an allusion to the unspoken tyrannies that Sylvia and Phillip Gellburg, the central figures of this short, discursive play, impose on each other. The focus of the drama is a Jewish housewife's mysterious hysterical paralysis, late in her long and stifling marriage to a prickly self-hating banker. Sylvia experiences a morbid identification with the victims of the Nazi round-up. She is over-involved with the Jewish community, whereas Phillip, who identifies with the goyim—he is the only Jew at the bank where he heads the mortgage department—is under-involved. At the core of their emotional stand-off is the issue of sexual impotence, a byproduct of fear.

The Gellburgs never examine their terror; they sidestep in silence the dangerous regions of rancor and regret. "I guess you just gradually give up and it closes over you like a grave," Sylvia says of their inert sex life. Phillip lets his work close over him. "I kept waiting for myself to change. Or you," he tells her in desperation. In the couple's emotional masquerade, Miller found a metaphor for the cycle of blame that has continued to contaminate and stalemate modern American life—a prolifer-ating tribalism that separates communities, at once a mask and an admission of fear. "The reigning philosophy is, 'You are on your own.' As Mrs. Thatcher said, there is no society," Miller said, adding, "The idea of being paralyzed in the face of over-whelming forces we do not understand is the mark of our time." *Broken Glass* is an anatomy of denial; it attempts to trap this private and public sense of retreat, to penetrate, as Miller said, "the secret places of the heart where ethnicity snuggles."

When Miller handed *Broken Glass* to John Tillinger, who directed its Broadway premiere, he told him that "it came from the dark side of myself." His portrait of paralysis spoke as much to the anguish of his stalled career as to the alienation of the Gellburgs, who were painted with the pigments of Miller's own grief: the masquerade of his parents' marriage, the secret abdi-cations and tyrannies of his own, even, obliquely, his existential quandary over Daniel's institutionalization. At one point late in the play, Margaret, the robust wife of Sylvia's doctor who is trying to relieve Sylvia of her guilt over Phillip's sudden heart attack, launches into a story about working in a pediatric ward and the almost immediately discernible personalities of new-borns. "Each one has twenty thousand years of the human race backed up behind him and you expect to change him," she says. "So what does that mean? How do you live?" Sylvia asks her.

MARGARET: You draw your cards face down, you turn them over and do your best with the hand you got. What else is there, my dear? What else can there be?

SYLVIA, *staring ahead:* . . . Wishing, I guess . . .

After a fraught rehearsal period and a botched Broadway production—miscast, undercooked, with a confused finale—*Broken Glass* closed quickly, and Miller came in for his all-too-familiar critical shellacking: "The world's most over-rated playwright" (John Simon, *New York*); "Just another spiral in a stumbling career" (Robert Brustein, *New Republic*). In London, however, Miller had never gone out of fashion. Disparaged at home, he and his plays remained big events abroad. "Just walking down the street with Arthur was like walking down the street with the Queen Mum," his sister Joan recalled. "People practically fell on their knees." The same awed enthusiasm greeted him inside British theaters. "Actors respond to Arthur Miller entering a rehearsal room as if Shakespeare had just walked in," said David Thacker, who directed the 1995 London production of *Broken Glass*, which featured a barnstorming performance by Antony Sher, a new five-page scene, and a modified ending, and won Miller the Olivier Award for Best New Play. At the opening-night curtain call, Inge Morath turned to Thacker. "You've made it possible for him to write another play now," she said. News of the play's accolades took a week to be noted in the *New York Times*, but the resurgence of Miller's reputation had begun.

Inge Morath died of lymphoma at the age of seventy-eight on January 30, 2002. "I'm still astonished by the happiness that was ours for forty years. And what happiness!" Miller wrote to her brother. With her Miller had managed that rare thing: a life of both creativity and contentment. (His will included instructions for burying him beside Morath, in a grave marked by a special black stone he had discovered in his field and which he had engraved with the name "Miller.") His forty acres, which the two had planted and patrolled through the decades, brought him solace. From his writing-room window, he reported in his memoir, sometimes he could see bears and coyotes make their way warily through the trees. "I am, I suppose, doing what they are doing, making myself possible." But after Inge, what was possible for him? "You know, when my wife died, I kind of cemented myself in a wall; you naturally assume you are supposed to be lonely to the end," a character in Miller's last play, *Finishing the Picture* (2005), says. But at a dinner party in 2002, Miller met Agnes Barley, a thirty-two-year-old abstract expressionist painter, who soon became his constant companion and his autumn romance. In December 2004, suffering from cancer and heart complications, Miller proposed to Barley, who was by then his caretaker. Although they never married, Miller left Barley his Manhattan apartment.

Arthur Miller left the world on February 10, 2005, fifty-six years to the day after *Death of a Salesman* opened on Broadway and Miller's plays became part of the American story.

———

Because many editions of Arthur Miller's plays are readily available, quotations from the plays are not cited here. Quotations in this volume are from the Library of America's three-volume *Arthur Miller: Collected Plays*, edited by Tony Kushner. Reviews of Miller plays are identified in text.

Abbreviations

AM	Arthur Miller, unpublished writings
AMKR	Arthur Miller–Kenneth Rowe Correspondence, Rare Book Collection, Harlan Hatcher Graduate Library, University of Michigan
AMNP	*Arthur Miller: New Perspectives*, ed. Robert A. Martin (Englewood Cliffs, N.J.: Prentice-Hall, 1982)
AMNY	Arthur Miller, "The Year It Came Apart," *New York*, December 30, 1974
AMSB	The Saul Bellow Papers, University of Chicago

AMW	*Arthur Miller: Writer,* directed by Rebecca Miller, HBO, 2017
ASTND	Tennessee Williams, *A Streetcar Named Desire,* introduction by Arthur Miller (New York: New Directions, 2004)
AUGM	Letters of Augusta Miller, HRC
BL	Barbara Leaming, *Marilyn Monroe* (London: Orion, 1999)
BOS	John Lahr, "Birth of a Salesman," *New Yorker,* December 25, 1995
CB1	Christopher Bigsby, *Arthur Miller: 1915–1962* (London: Weidenfeld and Nicholson, 2008)
CB2	Christopher Bigsby, *Arthur Miller: 1962–2005* (London: Weidenfeld and Nicholson, 2011)
CEAM	*The Collected Essays of Arthur Miller,* ed. Matthew C. Roudane (London: Bloomsbury Methuen Drama, 2015)
CUCOHC	Columbia University Center for Oral History Collection, Columbia University, New York
CWAM	*Conversations with Arthur Miller,* ed. Matthew C. Roudane (Jackson: University Press of Mississippi, 1987)
CWHC	*The Collected Works of Harold Clurman,* ed. Marjorie Loggia and Glenn Young (New York: Applause Theatre, 1994)
DOS	Arthur Miller, "Salesman at Fifty," in Miller, *Death of a Salesman* (Harmondsworth, UK: Penguin, 1999)
DS	Donald Spoto, *Marilyn Monroe: The Biography* (New York: Arrow Books, 1993)
EDC	Arthur Miller, *Echoes Down the Corridor: Collected Essays, 1944–2000* (New York: Viking, 2000)
ERM	E-mails from Ross Miller, John Lahr Archive, Howard Gotlieb Archival Research Center, Boston University. Reprinted by permission of Ross Miller.
F	Arthur Miller, *Focus* (New York: Penguin Classics, 2009)

GY	Arthur Miller, *The Golden Years* and *The Man Who Had All The Luck* (London: Methuen Drama, 1989)
HJQ	Arthur Miller, "His Jewish Question," *Vanity Fair,* October 24, 2009
HRC	Arthur Miller Collection, Harry Ransom Center, University of Texas at Austin
JG	James Goode, *The Story of The Misfits* (Indianapolis: Bobbs-Merrill, 1961)
JL	John Lahr, *Tennessee Williams: Mad Pilgrimage of the Flesh* (New York: Norton, 2014)
JM	Jeffrey Meyers, *The Genius and the Goddess: Arthur Miller and Marilyn Monroe* (New York: Arrow Books, 2009)
JR	Jacqueline Rose, *Women in Dark Times* (London: Bloomsbury, 2014)
JRL	John Lahr, *Joy Ride: Show People and Their Shows* (New York: Norton, 2015)
KAL	Elia Kazan, *Kazan: A Life* (1988; New York: Knopf, 1997)
KCHOH	Kennedy Center Honors Oral History Program, Interview of Arthur Miller by Mike Wallace, June 21, 1986
KOD	Elia Kazan, *Kazan on Directing* (New York: Knopf, 2009)
LG	Linda Gordon, *Inge Morath: An Illustrated Biography* (Munich: Prestel, 2018)
M	Norman Mailer, *Marilyn: A Biography* (London: Virgin Books, 2012)
MG	Martin Gottfried, *Arthur Miller: His Life and Work* (Cambridge, Mass.: Da Capo, 2003)
MM	Marilyn Monroe with Ben Hecht, *My Story* (Lanham, Md.: Taylor Trade, 2007)
MMC	Mary McCarthy, "Naming Names: The Arthur Miller Case," *Encounter,* May 1957
MWL	John Lahr, "Arthur Miller and the Making of Willy Loman," *New Yorker,* January 25, 1999

NR   Norman Rosten, *Marilyn: An Untold Story* (New York: Signet, 1973)

NYR   *New Yorker*

NYT   *New York Times*

RMNYT   Maureen Dowd, "Rebecca Miller: On the Mother of All Subjects: Her Father," *New York Times*, March 11, 2018

SA   Susan C. W. Abbotson, *Critical Companion to Arthur Miller: A Literary Reference to His Life and Work* (New York: Facts on File Books, 2007)

SLEK   *The Selected Letters of Elia Kazan*, ed. Albert J. Devlin with Marlene J. Devlin (New York: Knopf, 2014)

SN   Arthur Miller, *Situation Normal* (New York: Reynal & Hitchcock, 1944)

TB   Arthur Miller, *Timebends* (London: Methuen, 1999)

TEAM   *The Theatre Essays of Arthur Miller*, ed. Robert A. Martin (London: Methuen, 1978)

TYT   *Thirty Years of Treason: Excerpts from Hearings Before the House Committee on Un-American Activities 1938–1968*, ed. Eric Bentley (London: Thames & Hudson, 1972)

WOW   *Writers on Writing*, vol. 2: *More Collected Essays from "The New York Times"* (New York: Times Books, 2003)

WUCA   Elia Kazan Collection, Cinema Archives, Wesleyan University, Middletown, Connecticut

Chapter 1. Meeting Miller

This chapter has been adapted from my *New Yorker* profile "Arthur Miller and the Making of Willy Loman" (1999).

Shut the door . . . It was a purely instinctive act: MWL.

It's all right. I came back: MWL.

Imagine a salesman who can't get past Yonkers: MWL.

I started in the morning: MWL.

My eyes still burned: TB, 184.

He released it: KAL, 368.

Dream's quality: MWL.

He who understands everything about his subject: HRC, Death of a Salesman Notebook.

So he would kill himself: MWL.

Since the beginning of my writing life: MWL.

This play is written from the sidewalk: MWL.

Scene 1—Atop Empire State: HRC, Death of a Salesman Notebook.

In every scene remember: HRC, Death of a Salesman Notebook.

Have it happen that Willy's life: HRC, Death of a Salesman Notebook.

A salesman doesn't build anything: HRC, Death of a Salesman Notebook.

Roxbury—At night: HRC, Death of a Salesman Notebook.

The main house was occupied . . . In those days, I didn't think this hill was quite as steep: MWL.

It will last as long as it's painted: MWL.

I didn't know it was so tiny: MWL.

I did the concrete: MWL.

Selling was in the air: MWL.

My father had trouble staying awake: TB, 155.

I had never raised my voice: TB, 112.

That character's "dejected soul": BOS.

His emotions were displayed: BOS.

It was the same family: MWL.

People regarded him as a kind of strange: MWL.

Cute and ugly, a Pan risen out of the earth: TB, 122.

It was a house without irony: TB, 122.

That never stopped in his mind: TB, 122.

I always had to expect some kind of insinuation: TB, 124.

Buddy is doing very well: MWL.

Not the slightest interest . . . not sensuous enough: HRC, Mel Gussow interview.

I could now move into unknown territory: MWL.

The play had to move forward: DOS, xi.

Life is formless: HRC, Death of a Salesman Notebook.

There are no flashbacks: MWL.

The daylight continuity . . . In a dream you don't have transitional material: MWL.

Emergency speech . . . pretexts of "the natural": TB, 182.

What happens next: MWL.

He wanted a business for us: TB, 130.

This conventional, mundane wish: TB, 130.

What's he selling?: MWL.

Willy longs to take off, be great: HRC, Death of a Salesman Notebook.

The biggest boom in the history of the world: MWL.

The visible evidence: HRC, Death of a Salesman Notebook.

In a certain sense, Willy is all the voices: MWL.

Personal lyricism: Tennessee Williams, *Where I Live: Selected Essays* (New York: New Directions, 1978), 76.

What the name really meant to me: TB, 179.

He envies those who are blessed: MWL.

The whole idea of people failing: MWL.

Black addiction of the brain: Stephen Parker, *Bertolt Brecht: A Literary Life* (London: Methuen Drama, 2014), 179.

I don't care if you live or die: HRC, Death of a Salesman Notebook.

You lose your life to it: MWL.

Where's Willy in all this?: MWL.

It is the combination of guilt (of failure), hate, and love: HRC, Death of a Salesman Notebook.

It is necessary to (1) reveal: HRC, Death of a Salesman Notebook.

BIFF (to him): What the hell do you want from me?: HRC, Death of a Salesman Notebook.

He dies sending his son through the goalposts: MWL.

I want you all to know: HRC, Death of a Salesman Notebook.

The stage direction in the original manuscript . . . It was a play waiting for a directorial solution: KAL, 361.

To cut out Uncle Ben: MWL.

They had a list of about fifteen titles: MWL.

I'm not aware of any change: MWL.

The only theater available to a playwright in the late Forties: DOS.

That damned disturbing play: KAL, 356.
The curtain came down and nothing happened: MWL.

Chapter 2. Beginnings

Power seemed to have outgrown: Henry Adams, *The Education of Henry Adams* (Oxford: Oxford University Press, 2008), 415.
Sharp practices: TB, 19.
Had he taken the risk: TB, 20.
Bright idea of property: J. Hector St. John de Crèvecoeur, *Letters from an American Farmer* (Carlisle, Mass.: Applewood, 2007), 27.
While talking to them reasonably: TB, 5.
One of the largest such businesses: HRC, Arthur Miller to Maurice E. Sanders, Deputy Chief Probation Officer, June 10, 1957.
Our prosperity helped seal us: TB, 62.
A shwartz yu'r on alle goyim: CB1, 35.
Our family knew almost no gentiles . . . they were too busy trying to assimilate: TB, 62.
In my most private reveries: TB, 62.
I felt strangely at home with these New Englanders: TB, 43.
A scab on his head: TB, 9.
Never to see the inside of a school again: TB, 9.
There is a "Do you like me" in an orphan's eyes: TB, 9.
A baronial attitude: TB, 3.
Who were inclined to salute: TB, 24.
They were in there for hours: TB, 18.
She could read a novel: AMW.
She was pretentious: CB1, 63.
You are not to learn how to do this: CB1, 63.
She was a woman haunted by a world: TB, 17–18.
Was merciful, keeping him from worrying: TB, 19.
I couldn't help blushing for him: CB1, 50.
Vastly tall and competent: TB, 18.
The gazes of the help upon us: TB, 18.
What was the matter with me?: TB, 291.
What are you doing to me!: TB, 29.
Was passed over by education: KCHOH, 3.

Unencumbered by thought . . . too busy, in the street: KCHOH, 4.

When I first heard . . . Jews referred to as "the people of the Book": TB, 17.

My father's illiteracy: TB, 19.

Aren't there mothers: HRC, Arthur Miller Collection.

Our relationship was unfinished: TB, 594.

Probably the most autobiographical thing: KCHOH, 13.

I had, it seemed, always moved on two planes: TB, 146.

An unspoken conspiracy: TB, 11.

He loved Keats: CB1, 66.

Kermit was the man they relied on to carry on: CB1, 75.

I was caught between Joan: TB, 47.

A form of suicide designed to punish everybody: TB, 47.

My sallies into Harlem: TB, 63.

Had large breasts . . . Through French I learned: KCHOH, 4–5.

I hadn't realized that words were like that: KCHOH, 4.

What I hear means probably more to me than what I see: KCHOH, 5.

Once I listened to what I was singing: TB, 109.

Pull in your ears: TB, 12.

I write with my ears more than my brains: HRC, Interview with Mel Gussow.

Nothing was more enjoyable than mimicry: TB, 4.

Could always tell jokes: KCHOH, 5.

There was a mob of tap dancers: KCHOH, 6.

When it was over, out of the sound booth: KCHOH, 6–7.

I flew home on the subway: KCHOH, 7.

The first thing I had ever written was stolen: KCHOH, 7.

Miserable: CUCOHC, 917.

Although 97.5 percent of the American population owned no stock: David Kennedy, *Freedom from Fear: The American People in Depression and War* (New York: Oxford University Press, 1999), 41.

It was one of the most traumatic experiences of my life: CUCOHC, 916.

My father was the link: TB, 119.

Orgy of mad speculation . . . Great vaulting leaps: Kennedy, *Freedom from Fear,* 35.

The world-shaking discovery: KCHOH, 2.

People didn't know how to live without: CB1, 60.

The value system collapsed: HRC, Interview with Mel Gussow.

Inherited the views of those around me: HRC, Interview with Mel Gussow.

Never could bear the idea: HRC, "The Best Comedians," 31.

A move into the wilderness: KCHOH, 2.

The Wild West: CUCOHC, 915.

I couldn't have been happier: KCHOH, 3.

Even a fifty-dollar-a-month mortgage payment: TB, 108.

Grew more silent: HRC, Interview with Mel Gussow.

Deep down in the comradely world: CB1, 56.

Pipe down on the red flag raising: AUGM, Augusta Miller to Arthur Miller, March 1935.

Shuffling about in her carpet slippers: TB, 4.

She would put her head in the oven: CB1, 63.

God chosen: MG, 168.

My failures she simply swept aside: TB, 28.

I had a severe change of personality: KCHOH, 8.

I got there about seven o'clock to start studying: CUCOHC, 918.

I was so discouraged: CUCOHC, 918.

They were right: CB1, 68.

I suppose my first literary creation: CUCOHC, 919.

Remember the Goal: AUGM, Augusta Miller to Arthur Miller, October 5, 1934.

It was not so much death I feared as insignificance: TB, 69.

My home ceased to interest me: CB1, 98.

Chapter 3. Stirrings

College was, in one sense, very relaxed: CUCOHC, 918.

There was a kind of "time-out" . . . The pattern of society was destroyed: CUCOHC, 922.

I was thrown back on myself: CUCOHC, 917.

I had more to say: KCHOH, 10.

Make the most of your present opportunities: AUGM, Augusta Miller to Arthur Miller, October 5, 1934.

I was involved in the idea of how to become a writer: CB1, 97–98.

None of us was ever to be the same again: KAL, 116.

The Revolution's No. 1 Boy: John Lahr, "Stage Left: The Struggles of Clifford Odets," *New Yorker,* April 17, 2006.

The great creative engine of the moment: CUCOHC, 930.

A new phenomenon, a leftist challenge to the system: TB, 229.

Was branded by the beauty of the Group Theatre: CB1, 110.

Were of a different nature: CUCOHC, 931.

There was no politics in the American theatre until Odets: HRC, Interview with Mark Lamos, 20–21.

Michigan had one of the most politically active student bodies: CUCOHC, 919.

The place was full of speeches, meetings, and leaflets . . . the political facts of life: CEAM, 27.

I identified with the workers: TB, 265.

It was nearly incredible to me: TB, 265.

The fact that I came from bosses: CB1, 122.

Big again: CB1, 67.

I notice in the Student News something about expulsion: AUGM, Augusta Miller to Arthur Miller, March 31, 1935.

"Artovsky Millensky": CB1, 82.

We all see a great improvement in your English: AUGM, Augusta Miller to Arthur Miller, April 1, 1935.

Their Journalism School: AUGM, Augusta Miller to Arthur Miller, March 31, 1935.

I was lusting to put something down on a piece of paper . . . I had to tell my father something: KCHOH, 9.

Why it had to be a play: CB1, 92.

I knew when I started that I could write a play: CUCOHC, 920.

I had spilled out into that first play: CB1, 103.

Art was not a writer who made up stories: KAL, 368.

I had never known such exhilaration: CB1, 93.

It was very common in the Depression: KCHOH, 12.

I had my alarm clock: KCHOH, 13.

A playwright writes to hear it: CUCOHC, 934.

Close to despair that he might think nothing of it . . . uphill to the center of town: CB1, 93.

Condensation of language: TB, 226.

A horrible rendition: TB, 226.

When I saw the students laughing: MG, 28.

To say the unspeakable: CB1, 94.

Once I got the inkling that others were reached: CB1, 94.

I have never sweated an opening night: CEAM, 27.

Rushed outside to arouse relatives: TB, 224.

An artillery shell fired through the ranks of my opposing army: CB1, 99.

Psychic sun was on the rise: TB, 227.

Ten years!: TB, 226.

Hopeless: CB1, 108.

He was a great audience: CB1, 107.

A quiet refusal to encourage: MG, 33.

The last thing a dramatist should do: MG, 34.

It's hard to define what I took: CB1, 103.

Ibsen was the one modern playwright: CUCOHC, 931.

The basic structure of a play is the beginning of a conflict: Kenneth Rowe, "Shadows Cast Before," in *AMNP*, 13–14.

Professor Rowe, I've made a discovery: Rowe, "Shadows Cast Before," *AMNP*, 13.

Sitting straight, as usual, in the big Morris chair: Rowe, "Shadows Cast Before," *AMNP*, 13–14.

The general social problem: CB1, 108.

My plays were revolving around the question: CUCOHC, 923.

His fossilized individualism: CB1, 109.

A brooding young man: MG, 36.

I was one of the elite: CUCOHC, 923.

I became known in that little pond: MG, 36.

I wanted to get out of myself: TB, 93.

Turgid: SA, 135.

Monster . . . I laugh at the title: AMKR, Arthur Miller to Kenneth Rowe, November 10, 1938.

The scenario took me most of the time . . . By the time I was writing the third act: AMKR, Miller to Rowe, November 10, 1938.

I had the best time I ever had while writing . . . Finally they decided they didn't want to do another Jewish play: AMKR, Miller to Rowe, November 10, 1938.

Apparently the intense persecutions abroad have aroused: AMKR, Miller to Rowe, November 28, 1938.

Will I always have to write my plays over: AMKR, Miller to Rowe, October 6, 1939.

Great confidence in my ability: KCHOH, 65.

It was, of course, the mother, the first audience: TB, 327.

I have little money and many debts . . . I can see every square foot of Ann Arbor: AMKR, Miller to Rowe, November 10, 1938.

Chapter 4. The Greasy Pole

I was what you'd call a playwright without a theatre: CUCOHC, 923.

Show shop: Doris Alexander, *Eugene O'Neill's Creative Struggle: The Decisive Decades* (University Park: Penn State University Press, 1992), 127.

He had no relevancy at that time for what we were worried about: CUCOHC, 923.

Paid great attention: CUCOHC, 930.

The American theatre, excuse me, is vile: Clifford Odets, *The Time Is Ripe: The 1940 Journal of Clifford Odets* (New York: Grove, 1988), 31.

American theatre . . . five blocks long: CEAM, 47.

To burst the bounds of Broadway: EDC, 305.

I had no use for almost anything I could see: CUCOHC, 929.

Surreal Coney Island . . . a big calliope: CEAM, 49.

I had higher ambitions: CB1, 145.

The Federal Theatre Project introduced probably the only new form: CUCOHC, 926.

You could put forty-five people on stage: CUCOHC, 925.

Up to his neck in feverish anti-Fascism: CUCOHC, 925.

I was too appalled at the idea of not living: CB1, 125.

The forced return of clerical feudalism . . . The death of the mind: CB1, 125.

It was hard to sleep for weeks afterwards: GY, 10.

I recall feeling myself surrounded: GY, 10.

I can't imagine what I thought I was doing: GY, 7.

Montezuma, like the Democracies facing Hitler: GY, 10.

Weakened by self-doubt, he looks to Cortez: GY, 10.

I had never worked so long or so hard on anything: AMKR, Arthur
  Miller to Kenneth Rowe, May 14, 1940.

I looked around. I felt that even if the play were never produced: AMKR,
  Miller to Rowe, October 6, 1939.

Despite its ideological breadth: AMKR, Miller to Rowe, October 6,
  1939.

Next to nothing . . . why you wrote it in the first place: MG, 60.

Highly honored to play Montezuma: AMKR, Miller to Rowe, January 7, 1939.

Try to understand the audience: AMKR, Miller to Rowe, May 14,
  1940.

For a moment, I say all right, I'll comfort them: AMKR, Miller to
  Rowe, May 5, 1940.

Another hundred-odd pages: AMKR, Miller to Rowe, May 14, 1940.

I will never be able to write for our theatre: AMKR, Miller to Rowe,
  May 5, 1940.

Have I justified: AMKR, Miller to Rowe, May 14, 1940.

The bed is soft, the house warm: AMKR, Miller to Rowe, January 7,
  1940.

Kissed Ann Arbor goodbye . . . Of it all, a four minute radio sketch:
  AMKR, Miller to Rowe, May 14, 1940.

I expect to write contemporary people: AMKR, Miller to Rowe, May
  14, 1940.

Can a man give his twenties . . . I have always felt: AMKR, Miller to
  Rowe, May 14, 1940.

When he asked for a date: CB1, 143.

She was very smart and cool: CB1, 176.

People were either right or wrong: CB1, 142.

At the time I admired it: CB1, 142.

We were mysteries to each other: AMW.

Righteousness ticket: TB, 70.

Not so much under the wing of the church: TB, 72.

Left to myself I would not have gotten married: CB1, 171.

He needed somebody to adore him: RMNYT.

First audience: TB, 54.

I have never felt so solid: AMKR, Miller to Rowe, November 2, 1940.

Felt weird even to me: TB, 71.

I loved [Mary] more in the leaving: CB1, 179.

Art was not a writer who made up stories: KAL, 368.

There was almost no space for me between sexuality and art . . . My relationship to Mary and to all women was thin: TB, 145.

Swell here, alone with fine workshop: AMKR, Miller to Rowe, June 4, 1941.

High quality pulp: CUCOHC, 928.

I don't want to leave here: AMKR, Miller to Rowe, November 2, 1940.

I seemed to be part of nothing: CB1, 117.

Why are you a revolutionary: HRC, All My Sons Notebook.

A wish for community: MG, 72.

Wonderful racket: KCHOH, 18.

A kind of subsidy: CUCOHC, 929.

Ten to twelve thousand dollars: CUCOHC, 929.

I never had any illusions: KCHOH, 20.

They had orchestrations that thick: KCHOH, 19.

They would call me up and say: CB1, 204.

I began to feel that I could somehow make this happen: KCHOH, 17.

Less is better. Why?: CB1, 211.

We have had lots of readings of AM's TMWHATL: MG, 73.

I have been bested time and again by writers: MG, 75.

It is very hard to kill a good character: MG, 74.

The dedication of Arthur's army book: Ross Miller, "Relations" (unpublished manuscript).

I am the wandering disembodied spirit: SN, 16.

The question of the justice of fate: CB1, 237.

Why should such a successful young man: TB, 88.

Fear of a drift toward fascism: TB, 86.

Moved me inch by inch toward my first open awareness: Christopher Bigsby, *Arthur Miller: A Critical Study* (Cambridge: Cambridge University Press, 2005), 56.

Hellish cacophony, human screaming: CB1, 244.

Perhaps I was refracting my own feelings: TB, 90.

The overt story was only tangential: GY, 233.

Music played on the wrong instruments in a false note . . . It almost seemed a relief: CB1, 247.
I simply decided I would never write another play: MG, 83.

Chapter 5. Passion for Ignorance

So they didn't know you were a Jew: AUGM, Augusta Miller to Arthur Miller, October 5, 1934.
The Jews were the cause of every imaginable misfortune: HJQ.
A hard shell: HJQ.
Unlike most of the ads this one did not specify "Christian": HJQ.
In my two years on the job: HJQ.
As unshockable as I was at that time: HJQ.
Sense of emergency: HJQ.
Now the everyday slights and threats against me: HJQ.
The city was pulsing with hatred: WOW, 163.
I myself had been taken for all sorts of people: CUCOHC, 934.
The near absence among the men: F, 1.
They should be opposing it in every possible way: CB1, 250.
This was a fairly prosperous, middle-class group of people: WOW, 165.
Was like some shameful illness: CB1, 249.
The writing of Focus *was an attempt to break through that silence . . . Just putting down the words was a relief:* WOW, 165.
He backed away from the window . . . Her accent satisfied Mr. Newman: F, 9.
Secret game: F, 15.
He could not make out the man's eyes: F, 14–15.
Some day he must look into the various types: F, 15.
Probably he alone on this train knew: F, 15.
As though he had just seen a bloody fistfight: F, 13.
Clean out the neighborhood: F, 18.
The memory of sameness: F, 19.
It throws the whole office off: F, 14.
He was looking at: F, 31.
You know what they ought to do: F, 42.
Her malevolence was intimate: F, 40.
He sat there unable to speak: F, 40.

We don't feel you'll make a good impression: F, 47.

To lift the prejudice out of the skull: CUCOHC, 934.

No longer anonymous . . . the darting eyes: F, 202.

Often to destroy any impression of close-fistedness: F, 202.

He was not his face: F, 77.

Could it be . . . that his wife had always been right: F, 86.

As a Jewess she seemed dressed in cheap taste: F, 94.

The Jew is seen by the anti-Semitic mind: F, 5.

I tried [for a screen test] but I was a typist: F, 141.

It felt like he was talking to me: F, 104.

Nobody makes a Jew out of me and gets away with it . . . to go back to the old days: F, 147.

You're going to see fireworks: F, 145.

Sharp curiosity: F, 180.

It was as though all the tokens of the known world: F, 185.

A swift charge of lightning: F, 234.

There are the Finkelsteins on the corner: F, 234.

The protagonist's heroism has been clipped to his lapel: MG, 90.

It's like singing and you're deaf: CUCOHC, 934.

Offer the same kick: MG, 90.

No walls in the castle: CUCOHC, 934.

An excursion I was not at home in: CUCOHC, 933.

I wanted the audience never to think that this was written by anybody: CUCOHC, 932.

About which nobody could say to me: MG, 90.

Everything was up for grabs: JL, 64.

Wrong allies, wrong enemies, wrong outcome: David Caute, *The Great Fear: The Anti-Communist Purge Under Truman and Eisenhower* (London: Secker & Warburg, 1978), 41.

The nation was ready for witch hunts: David Halberstam, *The Fifties* (New York: Villard, 1993), 235.

Unhinged by fear: AMNY, 30.

The whole social dream of fraternity and justice: AMNY, 32.

The Big Conflict is between forces of Honor, of Responsibility: KOD, 31.

During the war I felt that the idea of social responsibility: HRC, Memo, "All My Sons," May 6, 1947 (handwritten).

Dramatic characters, and the drama itself can never hope: CB1, 267.

A smothered guilt for which he is trying to gain forgiveness: KOD, 33.

In a sudden fit of ennui: EDC, 2, 13.

Don't underestimate either her cunning, her strength: MG, 105.

Gussie never admitted anything unpleasant: ERM, August 21, 2018.

Like other plays being written then: KOD, 38.

If you think of Gussie as a gifted cover-up artist: ERM, May 9, 2018.

Recruited my father to take over Izzy's role: ERM, January 19, 2018.

Both brothers were lied to: ERM, May 9, 2018.

Carrying two heavy sample bags: ERM, January 19, 2018.

The fact that my father let me know about the betrayal: ERM, June 9, 2019.

I believe that my father found it impossible: ERM, August 21, 2018.

My father's nobility of character drove Arthur crazy: ERM, August 21, 2018.

Wants the father to help him fight the mother: KOD, 33.

I'm not holding the father himself solely responsible: CUCOHC, 935.

I have what you have not: Thomas Merton, *New Seeds of Contemplation* (New York: New Directions, 1949), 48.

Forced to be a hero: KOD, 37.

Final shot: TB, 244.

Every minute of it was going to work: KCHOH, 25.

I said, "I want my script back and all my other scripts": KCHOH, 25.

A fellow named Kazan: CUCOHC, 937.

Harold Clurman was, as far as I was concerned, God Almighty: KCHOH, 26.

Had a strength not found in the work of any dramatist: KAL, 319.

Art admired Harold but felt closer to me: KAL, 319.

I was really as green as I could be: CUCOHC, 937.

Quite marvellous: AMKR, Arthur Miller to Kenneth Rowe, undated 1947.

Any direction I've seen on Broadway: The Selected Letters of Tennessee Williams, vol. 2: *1945–1957,* ed. Albert J. Devlin, co-ed. Nancy M. Tischler (New York: New Directions, 2004), 97.

It was not an unimportant loss: KAL, 322.

His spine doesn't inspire any stage action: KOD, 34.

The war-profiteering aspect of All My Sons: *CWHC*, 109.
Without him, I'm not sure what would have happened: KCHOH, 27.
I sensed a warmth in the world that was not there before: MG, 111.
Seeing the audience held motionless in their seats: AMKR, Miller to
    Rowe, 1947 undated.
I was making money without working: CB1, 289. The hundred thou-
    sand dollars he would have earned in 1947 is the equivalent in
    today's money of $1.1 million.
Such guilt is a protective device: TB, 139.
A moral act of solidarity: MG, 109.
I didn't need to write another well-made play: MG, 109.
These people were totally depressed: CB1, 289.

Chapter 6. All the Wild Animals

Get the hell out of town: SLEK, 114.
I received five complete sets of Arthur Miller notices: JL, 173.
Planted the flag of beauty . . . granted a license to speak: ASTND, xii.
You have the dynamism: JL, 129.
After the performance he appeared: KAL, 361.
All My Sons *had hardly started its run:* CUCOHC, 940.
It didn't leave me time: CUCOHC, 943.
A kind of sonata: CUCOHC, 940.
Organized not around the theme: CUCOHC, 943.
It must have the vividness of an OPPRESSIVE NIGHTMARE: *KOD*, 74.
I couldn't find a way to include the dream: CUCOHC, 940.
A person comes to a point where he has to say: CUCOHC, 957.
Long delayed but always expected something: Tennessee Williams,
    The Glass Menagerie, in *Plays, 1937–1955* (New York: Library of
    America, 2000), 401.
Deferral and the refusal to think: Christopher Bollas, *Meaning and
    Melancholia: Life in the Age of Bewilderment* (Abingdon, UK:
    Routledge, 2018), 39.
There was too much crying going on: CUCOHC, 944.
Shroud of introspection: CUCOHC, 944.
Light on the condition of man: CUCOHC, 944.

I'd spent my life on the outside and now I was on the inside: CUCOHC, 943.

Medals! Ribbons! Christ sake: WUCA, Arthur Miller to Elia Kazan, April 27, 1949.

I tell ya, kid, Art pays: WUCA, Miller to Kazan, April 27, 1949.

The professional standing of a director: KAL, 319.

Kazan / Kazan / the miracle man: JL, 194.

Was that I might have something unique and personal: KAL, 319.

I immediately felt close to Art: KAL, 319.

We were soon exchanging every intimacy: KAL, 319.

Unsteady: KAL, 319.

During the production of All My Sons, *I thought him rigid:* KAL, 366.

We all puffed up: KAL, 366.

Touch of arrogance: TB, 193.

Acquired a new flash . . . a hint of something swashbuckling: KAL, 365.

There come moments: WUCA, Miller to Kazan, August 20, 1950.

He was at his best during this time: KAL, 365.

Sufficiently pontifical to be the first Jewish Pope: M, 191.

A new power, a power to make real everything: TB, 193.

I sensed in our silence some discomfort: TB, 194.

The last day of her innocence: HRC, "The Best Comedians," 37.

He would look up and wait for her word: HRC, "The Best Comedians," 37.

She would listen to anything: HRC, "The Best Comedians," 37.

A hand had been laid on him . . . God's chosen: MG, 168.

It made Art reckless: KAL, 367.

From the courtroom of his home: KAL, 366.

Art is acquiring all of your bad habits: KAL, 367.

At home all is well, unwell, by turns: WUCA, Miller to Kazan, August 20, 1950.

To reconstitute herself: KAL, 367.

He was longing for something nameless: KAL, 402.

A persistent dread: AMNY, 30.

Put himself to work: TB, 195.

A hand had been placed on him: HRC, "The Hook."

The strange, mysterious, dangerous thing: MG, 168.

I'm gonna live like a man: HRC, "The Hook."

I felt that Art had done a half-ass job: KAL, 402.

She hadn't even gone out with anyone since his death: DS, 30.

To set off the swiveling of her hips: TB, 303.

Flesh impact: BL, 140.

When we shook hands: TB, 303.

Just a freak: BL, 26.

I wouldn't say a word: KAL, 404.

All young actresses in that time and place were thought of as prey: KAL, 404.

The girl had little education and no knowledge . . . a stray cat: KAL, 407.

Starved for sexual release: KAL, 402.

We were essentially a threesome: KAL, 409.

I was still seeing her at night: KAL, 409.

Burn it . . . I'll go in with yiz: CB1, 391.

The all but announced themes of these evenings: TB, 301.

I was never alone with her for five minutes . . . She was unknown then: AM, Arthur Miller to his parents, May 9, 1956.

You couldn't help being touched: SLEK, 325.

He left while I was getting born: MM, 4.

You see I was brought up differently from the average American child: JR, 118.

My status as an orphan: MM, 30.

I can still remember how thrilled I was: MM, 12.

As I grew older I knew I was different: MM, 13.

Men do not see me: JR, 101.

A strange bird in the aviary: TB, 302.

Like the prow of a ship: BL, 9.

They'll eat her alive: CB1, 391.

The air around her was charged: DS, 204.

I gave her comfort: CB1, 390.

Like a cool drink when you've got a fever: CB1, 392.

Most people can admire their fathers: DS, 321.

For reasons which I have never understood: AM, Miller to his parents, May 9, 1956.

She deeply wanted reassurance: KAL, 407.

Life—I am both your directions: Fragments: Poems, Intimate Notes, Letters by Marilyn Monroe, ed. Stanley Buchthal and Bernard Comment (New York: Farrar, Straus and Giroux, 2010), 17.

How happy she was in his arms: KAL, 409.

The lovely light of lechery . . . I hadn't known he had it in him: JM, 7.

I knew I must flee or walk into a doom: TB, 307.

The sight of her was something like pain . . . until the solemnity of feeling: TB, 307.

I knew my innocence was technical merely: CB1, 397.

Spreading fear of uttering any opinion: TB, 310.

The last act, not the first: CUCOHC, 947.

The old political and moral reality had melted like a Dali Watch: Arthur Miller, "Why I Wrote 'The Crucible,'" *NYR,* October 21, 1996.

This unleashed a veritable holy terror: Miller, "Why I Wrote 'The Crucible.'"

Howling gale of the far right: Miller, "Why I Wrote 'The Crucible.'"

I knew for a fact that there were next to no Communists: TB, 308.

What was Art protecting?: KAL, 415.

There were nuns on their knees: CUCOHC, 945.

I was beginning to believe that a tremendous underground change: CUCOHC, 946.

IT'S INTERESTING: TB, 308.

Amazing kind of spaghetti was being cooked up here: CUCOHC, 949.

Treed: TB, 310.

Explained that Willy Loman was entirely atypical: TB, 315.

Why the hell did you make the picture: MG, 161.

Was like picking your teeth with a ball of cotton wool . . . I was sure that the whole thing would soon go away: Miller, "Why I Wrote 'The Crucible.'"

I began to despair of my own silence: "Miller Recounts McCarthy Era, Origins of 'The Crucible,'" *Harvard Crimson,* June 12, 1993, 3.

I tell you friend . . . They will hang us: MG, 161.

Couldn't behave as if my old "comrades" didn't exist: KAL, 449.

A kind of national parole board: Victor Navasky, *Naming Names* (New York: Viking, 1980), ix.

It was taken for granted—although Miller later denied it to HUAC: KAL, 449.

There was a certain gloomy logic in what he was saying: TB, 333.

You're not going to equate witches with this!: TB, 335.

Those witches did not exist: KAL, 449.

We weren't executed here . . . We died another way: CUCOHC, 951.

Brother-love . . . as painfully alive in me as it had ever been . . . the undeniable fact: TB, 335.

Dear Artie . . . S. Freud: CB1, 417.

Indeed, there are no witches: HRC, Arthur Miller to Molly Kazan, undated.

I seemed to have crossed some fundamental and incontrovertible line: KAL, 468.

On a great social griddle: John Lahr, "Method Man: Elia Kazan's Singular Career," *NYR*, December 5, 2019.

I take no attitude about it: JL, 253.

Don't worry about what I'll think: KAL, 461.

Gadg mourns your loss with unending sorrow: CB1, 420.

There was silence in the room: CB1, 429.

I would never really feel toward him quite what a friend should: KAL, 472.

Chapter 7. Collisions

Would really write about the outbreak in 1692: HRC, Arthur Miller, "Some Afterthoughts on the Crucible."

One of the strangest and most awful chapters in human history: Arthur Miller: Collected Plays, 1944–1962, ed. Tony Kushner (New York: Library of America, 2006), 345.

If I swore that you had sent out your "familiar spirit": Arthur Miller, "Why I Wrote 'The Crucible,'" *NYR*, October 21, 1996.

Salem became a sort of asylum: HRC, Miller, "Some Afterthoughts on the Crucible."

A lizardic dormancy: Arthur Miller, "Many Writers, Few Plays," *NYT*, August 12, 1952.

Cope with the evidence of their senses: CB1, 443.

One of the few dramas in history with a beginning, a middle, and an end: CB1, 443.

A drama cannot merely describe an emotion: TB, 331.

When irrational terror takes to itself the fiat of moral goodness: CB1, 456.

The old friend of a blacklisted person: Miller, "Why I Wrote 'The Crucible.'"

In primitive shorthand: Miller, "Why I Wrote 'The Crucible.'"

Both made offer to strike: Miller, "Why I Wrote 'The Crucible.'"

The thousand pieces I had come across: Miller, "Why I Wrote 'The Crucible.'"

My own marriage of twelve years: Miller, "Why I Wrote 'The Crucible.'"

I had to guess that Art was publicly apologizing: MG, 211.

I was trying to make my marriage work then: AM, Arthur Miller to his parents, May 9, 1956.

You get this absolutely crazy concentration on the work: CB1, 342.

He connected it with the cross: HRC, Mel Gussow interview.

I want to be cremated: MG, 213.

He had fought with practically everybody who was anybody: TB, 342.

Jed was a charming man: TB, 345.

Tremendous visceral force: MG, 214.

He couldn't read a newspaper without telling you it needed a rewrite: MG, 214.

What gives me a pain is this conception of Arthur as a big social thinker: MG, 217.

I knew we had cooled off a very hot play: TB, 246.

Dried up from the tryout ordeal: MG, 218.

It was the real high tide, and there I was spitting in the teeth of it: CUCOHC, 952, January 22, 1953.

What I had not quite bargained for was the hostility in the New York audience: TB, 347.

The audience clucked but they didn't applaud . . . They didn't want to have anything to do with me: CUCOHC, 952.

Before the curtain rose, the audience sat in such expectant silence: MG, 218.

The critics were insulated from it: CUCOHC, 952.

Several of my friends are witches: HRC, William Brower to Arthur Miller, March 7, 1953.

They hated it: CUCOHC, 953.

More than six million copies . . . I don't think there has been a week in the past forty-odd years: Miller, "Why I Wrote 'The Crucible.'"

If The Crucible *is still alive today:* Miller, "Why I Wrote 'The Crucible.'"

But it all seemed different: CUCOHC, 953.

It was not easy to go back to the desk again . . . I was growing more and more frighteningly isolated: TB, 350.

Just a story about a bad marriage: MG, 211.

Vindictive, punishing woman: AM, Arthur Miller to his parents, May 9, 1956.

Whenever I am quietly desperate: HRC, "The Best Comedians."

Other ways than writing to make a living: AM, Miller to his parents, May 9, 1956.

I write my life, as you know: AMKR, Arthur Miller to Kenneth Rowe, May 22, 1956.

Written out of desperation: AMKR, Miller to Rowe, May 22, 1956.

I was very resentful: CB1, 497.

She is trying to cripple me, as she has for years: AM, Miller to his parents, May 9, 1956.

Had taken on an immanence in my imagination: DS, 186.

If your wife had what I have under my dress: HRC, The Crucible Notebook.

Abigail has absolute conviction that John's love for his wife is a formality: MG, 223.

I'm going to marry Arthur Miller: DS, 294.

Try to cheer him up: KAL, 247.

I can't forget all the unhappiness: MM, 152.

To put it briefly, she had a quality no one else had: DS, 288.

He moves like a living statue: DS, 306.

He wanted me to be the beautiful ex-actress: DS, 246.

Hit Hollywood like an A-Bomb . . . no man can be a success in two national pastimes: JM, 76.

Refused to take one nickel from DiMaggio: AM, Miller to his parents, May 9, 1956.

I'm not interested in money: DS, 183.

I knew there was more I could do: DS, 255.

I want to be an artist not an erotic freak: CB1, 498.

I never had a chance to learn anything in Hollywood: DS, 330.

He just didn't have it: TB, 423.

She didn't know anything more about acting than a cleaning woman: JM, 120.

I still did not see her because I was going to hang on to the bitter end: AM, Miller to his parents, May 9, 1956.

I had lots to do: DS, 352.

A whirling light: TB, 359.

It was wonderful to be around her: DS, 351.

Chapter 8. Blonde Heaven

Living challenge . . . There must be a woman in the world: HRC, "The Best Comedians."

This tall and timid hero of middle-class life: M, 191.

"You aren't there": NR, 79.

She is enough new experience to last him a lifetime: M, 230.

I began to dream that with her: CB1, 507.

Idealized beyond all human weakness: CB1, 505.

So be my love as you surely are: RMNYT.

I was alternately soaring and anxious: CB1, 509.

A crazy friendship with sexual privileges: DS, 292.

Why would I do that? He's a married man: CB1, 518.

I have come alive at last: AM, Arthur Miller to his parents, May 9, 1956.

Equivalent to five new works by Williams: JM, 192.

A diamond mine for any playwright looking for a big play: M, 192.

Extreme cruelty, entirely mental in nature: BL, 224.

The hatred in her heart: AM, Miller to his parents, May 9, 1956.

While I want to marry her someday: AM, Miller to his parents, May 9, 1956.

A notorious and evil woman: AM, Miller to his parents, May 9, 1956.

That's a wife?: JM, 106.

Marilyn simply wasn't a wife: JM, 105.

Probe: TB, 325.

When I wrote the play I was moving through psychological country: MG, 260.

I was telling the world where I stood: KAL, 529.

It would have been nice if Art: JRL, 27.

What I think is interesting about A View *is that it develops a process:* HRC, Arthur Miller Collection, "Letter on Advertising."

There is no living soul nor tree nor shrub: AMKR, Arthur Miller to Kenneth Rowe, May 22, 1956.

I have a problem, however, of slightly unusual proportions: AMSB, Arthur Miller to Saul Bellow, March 15, 1956.

He talked non-stop about Marilyn: JM, 100.

Such was the hubris of the time: BL, 182.

Questionable political background: BL, 182.

I'm not calling him a Communist: HRC, *New-York Journal-American.*

She goes to meet him. He asks, "You are going to marry Mr. Miller?": AMSB, Miller to Bellow, June 2, 1956.

The next day the front page of the News: AMSB, Miller to Bellow, June 2, 1956.

The fact that America's best-known blonde: CB1, 518.

The House Committee on Un-American Activities: CB1, 519.

He's got to tell them to go fuck themselves: CB1, 526.

People feel that this subject has had it: MMC, 23.

The large number of reporters present: TB, 408.

How would you like to not have to go . . . I burst out laughing: TB, 406.

If Arthur Miller is now a disgraced person: CB1, 551.

The slightly amazing thing to me is that I never felt scared at all: AMSB, Miller to Bellow, July 8, 1956.

Mr. Miller was eager to talk about his present views: MMC, 24.

I am not here defending Communists: TYT, 806.

A man should have the right to write a poem: TYT, 807.

I take no more responsibility for who plays my plays: TYT, 817.

It was not necessary that Mr. Miller be an informer: MMC, 24.

The objective is double: TYT, 818–819.

He announced it before the whole world!: NR, 34.

*I want you to understand that I am not protecting the Communists . . .
I will be perfectly frank with you:* TYT, 820.

Any kind . . . Everything! . . . Haven't you seen him?: Norman Rosten,
Marilyn: A Very Personal Story (London: Millington, 1980), 27.

Despite June and Cupid: BL, 238.

The risk-taking conscience of his times: JM, 146.

Been to hell and back . . . Must have gone as a tourist: JM, 146.

It was an attempt on my part and on hers to transcend the barriers:
KCHOH, 51.

Oh, Papa, I can't do it: TB, 379.

She looked to me to keep everything happy: KCHOH, 45.

Art gave Marilyn a rose-tinted view of her future: KAL, 540.

She shattered a thousand years of British imperturbability: TB, 413.

More than seventy British bobbies: DS, 406.

There was little else in any newspaper the next day: TB, 412.

Arthur was going to make my life different: JM, 158.

Chapter 9. Love's Labour's

Each of us doing our own work side by side: TB, 386.

Terror beyond fear: JR, 127.

She had a bomb inside her: KAL, 405.

Art, by comparison, was an innocent: KAL, 667.

He saw me as so beautiful and innocent: CB1, 624.

Continuous time: AM, Arthur Miller to his parents, May 9, 1956.

She has a talent beyond most dreams: AM, Miller to his parents, May
9, 1956.

Went for the drug of reassurance: KAL, 540.

He, she said, is a great artist and she is just a beginner: AM, Miller to
his parents, May 9, 1956.

Arthur was plunged into a world of daily crises: MG, 302–303.

Her puddings of acting philosophy: TB, 421.

Poisonous and vacuous . . . nearly religious: DS, 410.

The beast: TB, 423.

She was on guard, suspicious, sullen, defensive: NR, 43.

He looked at me as if he had just smelled dead fish: JM, 163.

She doesn't really forget her lines: CB1, 588.

When the monster showed, Arthur couldn't believe it: CB1, 624.

She was like a smashed vase: TB, 422.

Bedevilled by feelings she could not name: JM, 163.

She had idealized Greene's ability to set up her financial life: TB, 422.

To me no film was worth this kind of destruction: TB, 435.

The little suicides each night: TB, 435.

Once she made a judgement in relation to people: NR, 44.

She was felled by my stubbornness: TB, 419.

It was something about how disappointed he was with me: CB1, 588.

England, I feared, had humbled both of us: TB, 436.

We were as we were before, but worse: TB, 435.

It would have been easier for me: CB1, 624.

I'd say out of five we had two good years: CB1, 643.

When she's high, a sweet chime of music surrounds her: NR, 45.

That's what I want most of all, the baby, I guess: MG, 313.

The kids were here until a month ago: MG, 314.

Her god, her guard, her attendant, and her flunky: M, 221.

Greatness of spirit . . . a crazy kind of nobility: TB, 458.

I have come out of the cold: JM, 158.

He stays as far away as he can: JM, 182.

Every morning he goes into that goddamn study: JM, 182.

In the third person: NR, 79.

I don't think I'm the woman for Arthur: JM, 183.

I have a feeling this boat is never *going to dock:* NR, 76.

With Arthur it all seemed sour: CB1, 609.

I discussed this project with my doctor and my psychiatrist: JM, 197.

I cannot let your vicious attack: CB1, 610.

The fact is that the company pampered her: CB1, 610.

Dislocation of people of my generation: DS, 480–481.

Too distant from me: JG, 75.

Respectful, ardent, humorous, and above all, kind: HRC, Arthur Miller to Billy Wilder, March 13, 1958.

I must perhaps dramatize her awareness of his distinctive *kindness . . . He conceives the mustang hunt to win her back:* HRC, Miller to Wilder, March 13, 1958.

There's no communication between us any more: CB1, 612.

I was sympathetic to Art, not her: KAL, 674.

He had kept her in New York until the last minute: BL, 363.

A representative of the movie industry: NR, 76.

How he saw me before we broke up: CB1, 624.

She is that girl . . . whose childhood has never ended, HRC, Arthur
 Miller to René Clement, December 11, 1957.

I want the speech rewritten: NR, 77.

She treated Miller very badly on the film: CB1, 623.

*She was incapable of rescuing herself or of being rescued . . . We got
 through it:* MG, 339.

He's a cold fish: JM, 238.

I spent four years doing nothing except The Misfits: CB1, 644.

I hoped that by living through this role: TB, 466.

He could have written me anything: CB1, 628.

Needed Arthur to love her in spite of all the shameful things: BL, 367.

They don't need me at all. Not to act—just for the money: CB1, 628.

I guess they thought I was too dumb to explain anything: DS, 482.

The ultimate motion picture: JG, 17.

I would be dead: JM, 240.

I hope and believe I'll have a play again soon: MG, 342.

Chapter 10. Darkness Visible

I can no longer take with ultimate seriousness: CUCOHC, 957.

The most personal statement that I've made: CB2, 38.

The play's auto-criticism exposes him to us: CWHC, 639.

Arthur was in bad shape: ERM, January 24, 2019.

Shy and strong at the same time: TB, 493.

He doesn't like being disturbed when he's working: LG, 114.

"Serious": LG, 115.

She brought me Europe: LG, 124.

Inge savored life: TB, 505.

A way of disarming men of power: TB, 568.

A traveller with a camera: LG, 158.

For Inge, to see a valise was to start packing: TB, 568.

European awareness: CB2, 18.

We all had one very strong thing in common: LG, 27.

Loved to work . . . infinitely dull . . . a waste": LG, 36.

Arthur was in despair: LG, 114.

Compensatory loss: LG, 116.

I missed her sense of the hour's importance . . . The despair I felt was impossible to face or flee: TB, 502.

To make your difficult life more easy: LG, 116.

There is pride in me: LG, 116.

I guess a third marriage takes some thinking: LG, 116.

A strength, a forbearance: LG, 116.

I live on the edge of some ultimate abyss: LG, 116.

Waiting is only a solution for the falling away of things: LG, 116.

I guess we finally decided we had fallen in love: CB2, 9.

The great mother . . . My God, we've been married all year!: CB2, 19.

It was not part of America, had no vacuum cleaners: AMW.

This is a happy play: CB2, 40.

There continued to be an unspoken tension between Art Miller and me: KAL, 629.

His innocence. Puzzling things out: MG, 365.

The trial of a man, by his own conscience: TEAM, 257.

Humiliated defendants: TB, 521.

Insufferably self-serving and noble: KAL, 630.

He is struggling against that homelessness: WUCA, Arthur Miller to Elia Kazan, September 1963.

The bright boys from every side: KAL, 290.

With Respect for Her Agony—but with Love: Life, February 7, 1964.

Lillian Hellman Wants a Little Respect: Show, May 4, 1964, 12.

I clearly have a lonely row to hoe: WUCA, Miller to Kazan, February 16, 1964.

We are on the verge of Armageddon: CWHC, 619.

A strange futility had crept into the very idea of writing a play: CB2, 160.

Turn on, tune in, drop out: CB2, 162.

If only he could give piety a rest: CB2, 369.

Who is touched and by what . . . fit people and societies going a bit mad: JL, 476.

Reason itself had become un-aesthetic: CB2, 156.

Impotence of human hopes . . . futility of action . . . indicated rather than felt: EDC, 310.

I wanted to convey the emotions as I felt them: EDC, 312.

Can't it be art if it moves people?: EDC, 312.

Narrower in terms of story . . . entirely in the now: KCHOH, 72.

The very idea of an operating continuity: CB2, 156.

It speaks to a spirit of unearthing the real: CB2, 156.

I suppose I've become paranoid: AMKR, Arthur Miller to Kenneth Rowe, February 20, 1968.

Nobody wants that kind of furniture because it implies a past: CWAM, 189.

He reported on his inner condition: KAL, 368.

Pathological honesty: TB, 12.

Kermit had the good and questionable luck of the first born: AM, Arthur Miller, Memorial speech, "My Brother Kerm."

Kermit had a pleasing cursive handwriting: AM, Miller, Memorial speech, "My Brother Kerm."

Members of my family as models: TB, 91.

The plan was for my father to continue at N.Y.U.: ERM, December 28, 2018.

Fallen in love with the place: EDC, 14.

The result of all this was that my father spent another five years in harness: ERM, December 28, 2018.

Since the beginning my work has enforced on me a regime: AM, Arthur Miller to Kermit Miller, March 24, 1959. Ross Miller mentioned one other time his father expressed his buried anger at Arthur: "The only other time I remember my father getting so angry was a Passover seder at my grandparents' house in Brooklyn. We had been delayed a little by heavy holiday traffic. The family had already started eating without waiting for my father who, as eldest son with a knowledge of Hebrew, had an important supporting role to play. He seemed especially incensed at my grandfather and Arthur. This was more than a breach in protocol. In retrospect I believe it was an eruption of anger long suppressed. The scene was never repeated" (ERM, January 20, 2020).

The characters were not based on Kermit and me: TB, 13.

There's no one character who's actually me: EDC, xiv.

The tension between these characters was so honest: CB2, 157.

Kermit was not a cop: ERM, January 19, 2018.

Maybe a year . . . My mother said: ERM, January 20, 2020.

I was very confused as to why he didn't come home: CB2, 135.

It would have ruined our entire life: CB2, 135.

Resistance to our soul's sloth: CWHC, 692.

Out of experience came his good work: KAL, 368.

Managed to give certain scenes a form and drive: AMKR, Miller to
	Rowe, February 20, 1968.

After all, a first-class revival of a play of mine in a Broadway theater:
	HRC, Arthur Miller to Sam Cohn, June 12, 1992.

Epilogue

I'm becoming invisible in my own land: MG, 412.

Balance is all . . . waiting for the human hand: HRC: Death of a
	Salesman Notebook.

I didn't speak with a contemporary accent: KCHOH, 65.

The American berserk: Philip Roth, *American Pastoral* (New York:
	Vintage, 1997), 86.

There seems to be a delight on the part of the critics: MG, 408.

To make human relations felt: SA, 88.

*The reigning philosophy is, "You are on your own" . . . The idea of being
	paralyzed in the face of overwhelming forces:* CB2, 437.

The secret places of the heart where ethnicity snuggles: CB2, 437.

It came from the dark side of myself: CB2, 427.

Just walking down the street with Arthur: MG, 426.

Actors respond to Arthur Miller entering a rehearsal room: CB2, 436.

You've made it possible for him to write another play now: MG, 441.

I'm still astonished by the happiness: CB2, 485.

I am, I suppose, doing what they are doing: TB, 599.

ACKNOWLEDGMENTS

By the time this book reaches its first reader, I will be eighty-one. I was just twenty when the notion of writing about theater in a different, more forensic way seized my imagination. Shakespeare was right: theatricals *are* "the abstract and brief chronicles of their times." As technicians of the spirit, actors and playwrights corrupt an audience with pleasure. Their big magic is to both banish Time *and* define it. From the outset, to interpret theatricals as metaphors of the moment, to honor their lives and their legacies, and to trace the synergy between their private and their public selves seemed to me a worthy undertaking.

My first subject was my father, Bert Lahr, a star turn for more than half a century, who had a closet full of press cuttings, notable mostly for their lack of insight into his personality or his craft. Down the decades, my profiles in the *New Yorker* have allowed me both unusual access and the space to follow my heart and my literary project. My ambition has been to capture what my subjects seek to *ex*-press and to leave a more accurate, nuanced story of their accompliments. To this end, in addition to the *New Yorker* profiles, which now number more than forty, I've written book-length studies of Noël Coward, Joe Orton, Barry Humphries (Dame Edna Everage), and Tennessee Williams.

I first encountered Arthur Miller in May 1980, at Mount Sinai Hospital, beside Harold Clurman's deathbed. Clurman, a renowned man of the American theater, as well as one of its most distinguished critics, was my mentor; he was also a significant figure in Miller's artistic life. Even in his last days—he died of cancer a few days later, at the age of seventy-eight—Clurman talked for victory, holding forth to the attentive coterie huddled around him, which included Miller's major producer Robert Whitehead and Whitehead's wife, the actress Zoe Caldwell. Nineteen years later, in 1999, I met Miller again in happier circumstances, this time at his spread in Roxbury, Connecticut, to write an article about the making of *Death of a Salesman* to mark the fiftieth anniversary of his epochal play. Miller liked the result; by way of thanks he sent me an inscribed copy of the anniversary edition, which now has pride of place in my library. "To John Lahr," he wrote, "who understands and who knows how to get it said." For Miller's sake and my own, I hope this volume gets it said.

Arthur Miller: American Witness is a short book which took a long time to write. Many people have been instrumental in realizing the endeavor. The Miller Estate has generously given me permission to quote from Miller's published and unpublished works. Rebecca Miller allowed access to the then-uncatalogued mounds of material at the Harry Ransom Center in Austin, Texas, which holds her father's voluminous archive. Steven Ennis, the director of the Center, and Eric Joseph Colleary, its curator of theater and dance, generously helped me to navigate the material. Sarah Chalfant of the Andrew Wylie Agency graciously held my hand through the prolonged mysteries of the permission process. A tip of the cloth cap also to Christopher Bigsby, Miller's most extensive biographer; Ileene Smith, the editorial director of Yale's Jewish Lives series; Heather Gold and Eva Skewes, of Yale University Press, who have overseen the book's production; Susan Laity for her generous, forensic fine tuning of the manuscript; Sarah Ruhl, for her enthusiastic reading of the manuscript; my kaffeeklatsch buddies David Aaronovitch and Stephen Grosz for their always stimulating insights and wise counsel; Ann Schneider, the supremo of photo researchers; John Glusman, the editor-in-chief of W. W. Norton, who cut me some contractual slack so that I could seize this opportunity; Ross Miller, the son of Miller's older brother Kermit and himself an author and university professor, who provided invaluable insight into the Miller family and its dynamics.

Every book is a collaboration. This one is dedicated to Georges Borchardt, whose idea it was. Georges and his wife, Anne Borchardt, have been my agents for nearly half a century. Their friendship and their faith in my writing have meant more to me than they can know. Deborah Treisman, my inspired *New Yorker* editor, has cast her expert eye over the manuscript and spruced it up. We call this mind-meld "a shampoo and blow dry," but it's no joke. A final high-five to my *New Yorker* comrade Ty Baldwin, who has transcribed every word of every profile interview since 1992, and who once again has been an invaluable sidekick on this literary excursion, wrangling information, footnotes, and the final draft.

And then there is my wife, Connie Booth: "The prune in my pudding / Pepper in my pie, / My package of peanuts / The moon in my sky."

INDEX

Bugsy Siegel: The Dark Side of the American Dream,
    by Michael Shnayerson
Solomon: The Lure of Wisdom, by Steven Weitzman
Steven Spielberg: A Life in Films, by Molly Haskell
Alfred Stieglitz: Taking Pictures, Making Painters, by Phyllis Rose
Barbra Streisand: Redefining Beauty, Femininity, and Power,
    by Neal Gabler
Leon Trotsky: A Revolutionary's Life, by Joshua Rubenstein
Warner Bros: The Making of an American Movie Studio,
    by David Thomson

FORTHCOMING TITLES INCLUDE:

Abraham, by Anthony Julius
Hannah Arendt, by Masha Gessen
Franz Boas, by Noga Arikha
Mel Brooks, by Jeremy Dauber
Alfred Dreyfus, by Maurice Samuels
Anne Frank, by Ruth Franklin
Betty Friedan, by Rachel Shteir
George Gershwin, by Gary Giddins
Allen Ginsberg, by Ed Hirsch
Herod, by Martin Goodman
Jesus, by Jack Miles
Josephus, by Daniel Boyarin
Louis Kahn, by Gini Alhadeff
Mordecai Kaplan, by Jenna Weissman Joselit
Carole King, by Jane Eisner
Fiorello La Guardia, by Brenda Wineapple
Mahler, by Leon Botstein
Norman Mailer, by David Bromwich
Maimonides, by Alberto Manguel